AF473770

Spelling Dystopia
スペリング・ディストピア

Nina Fischer
& Maroan el Sani

Christoph
Keller
Editions

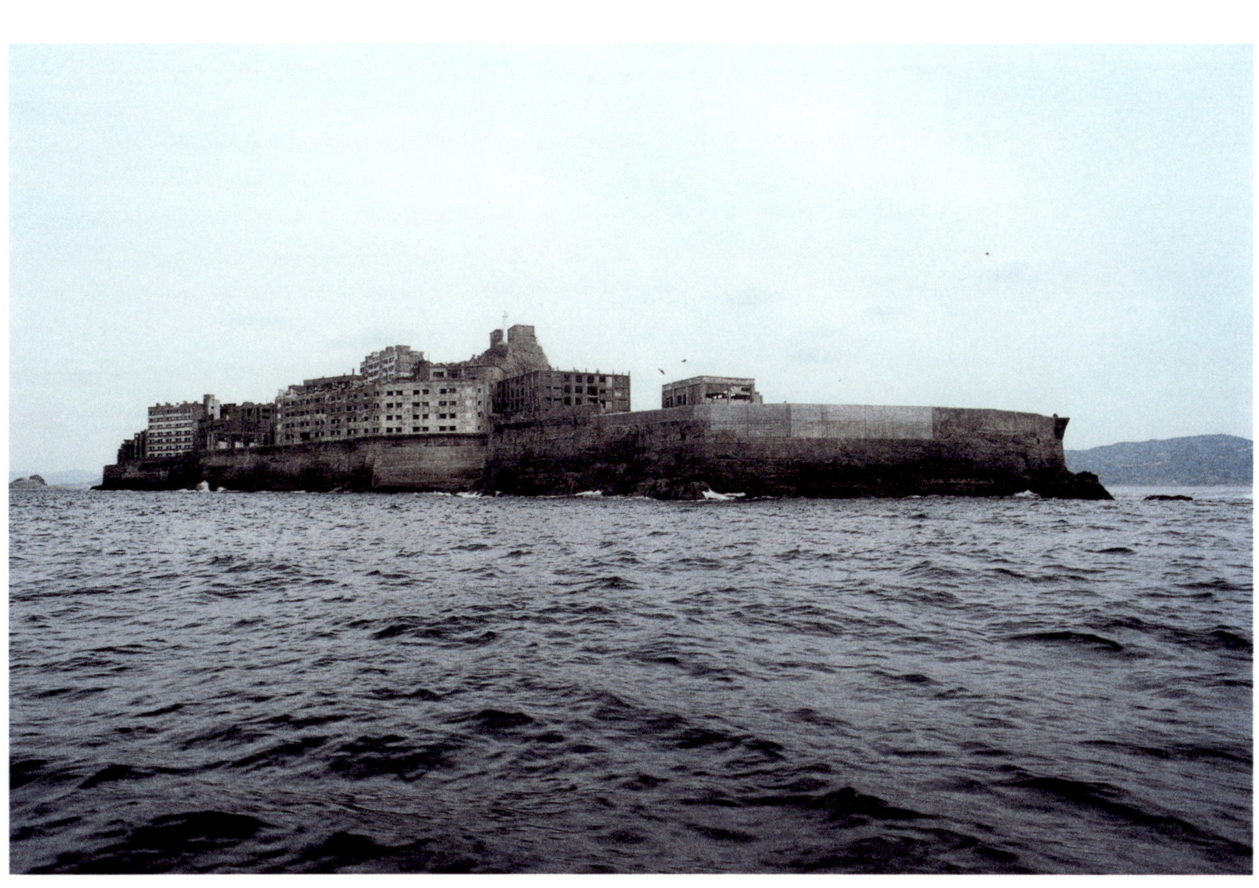

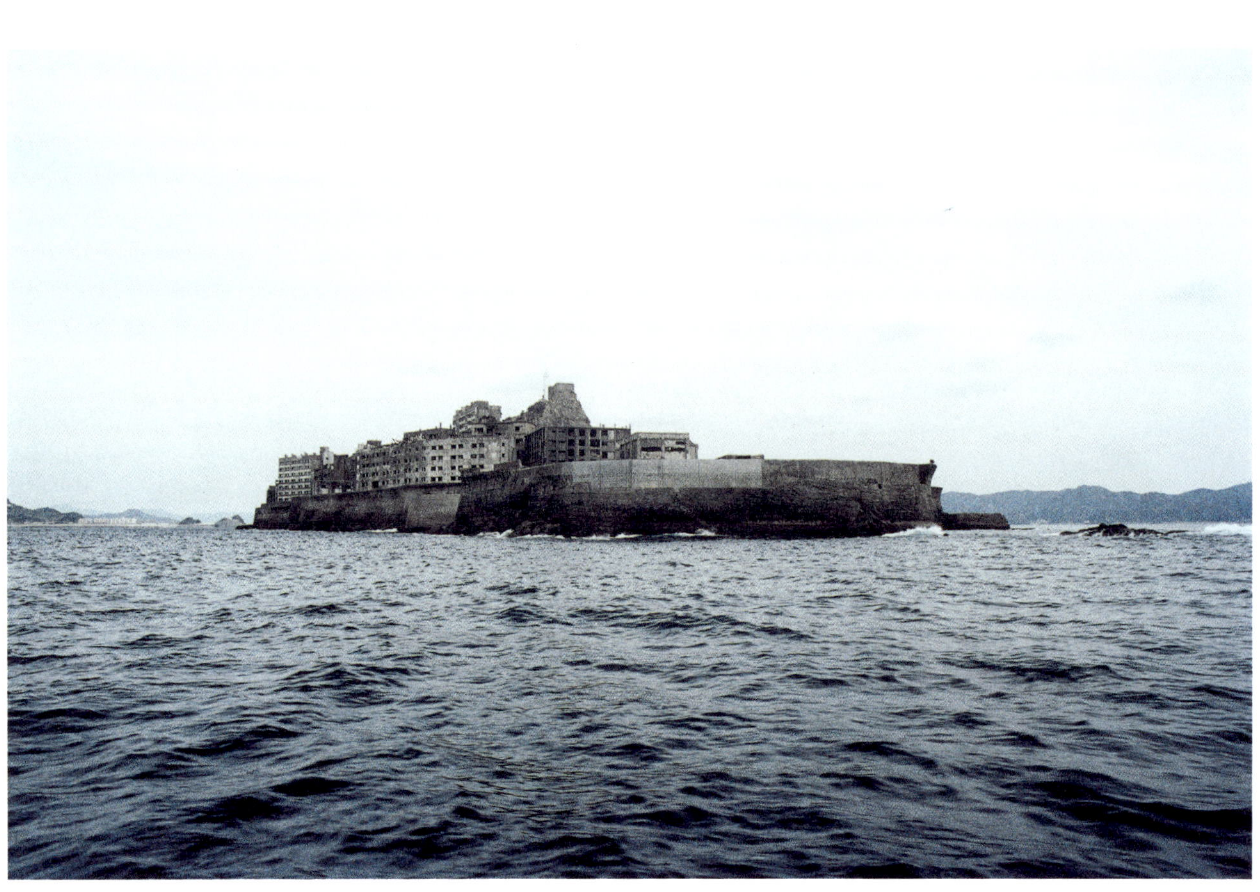

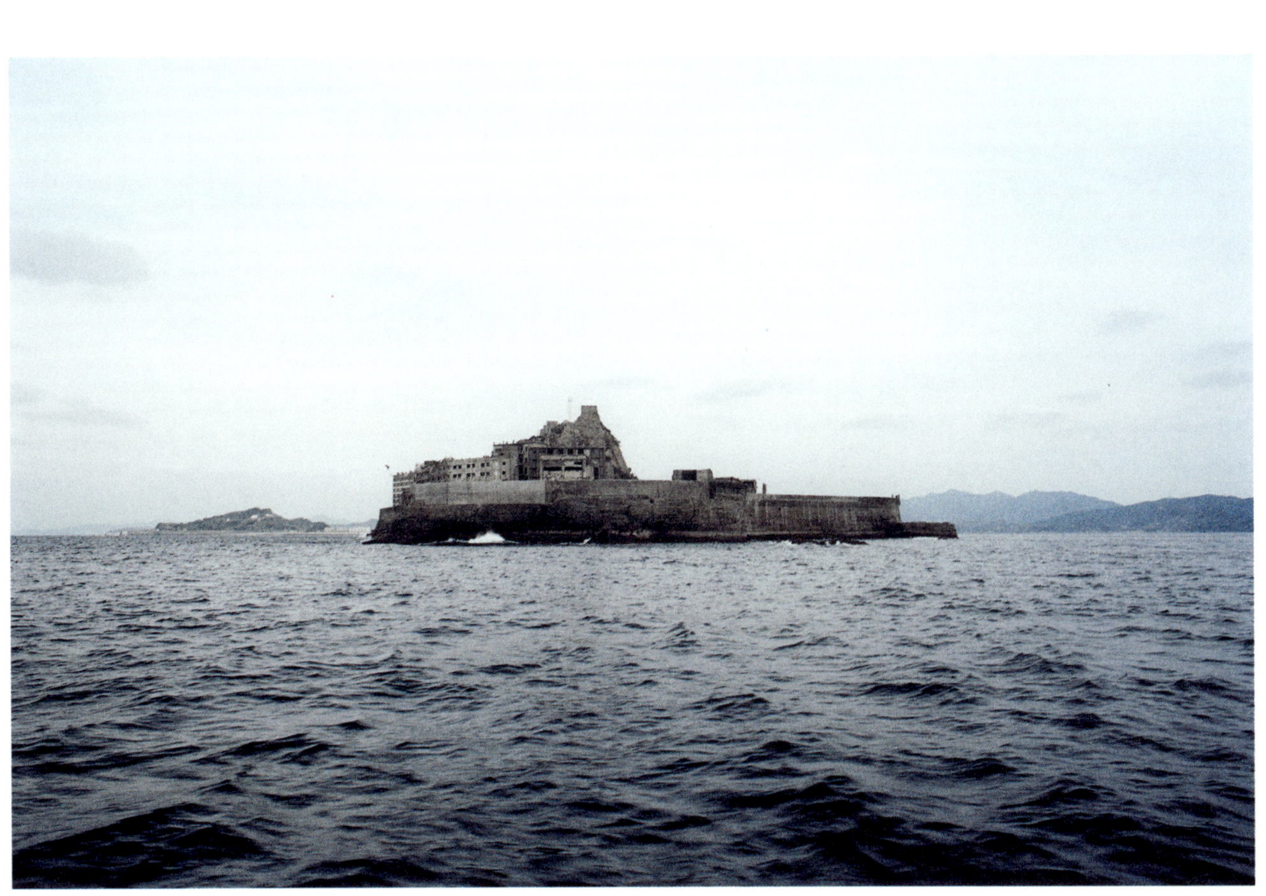

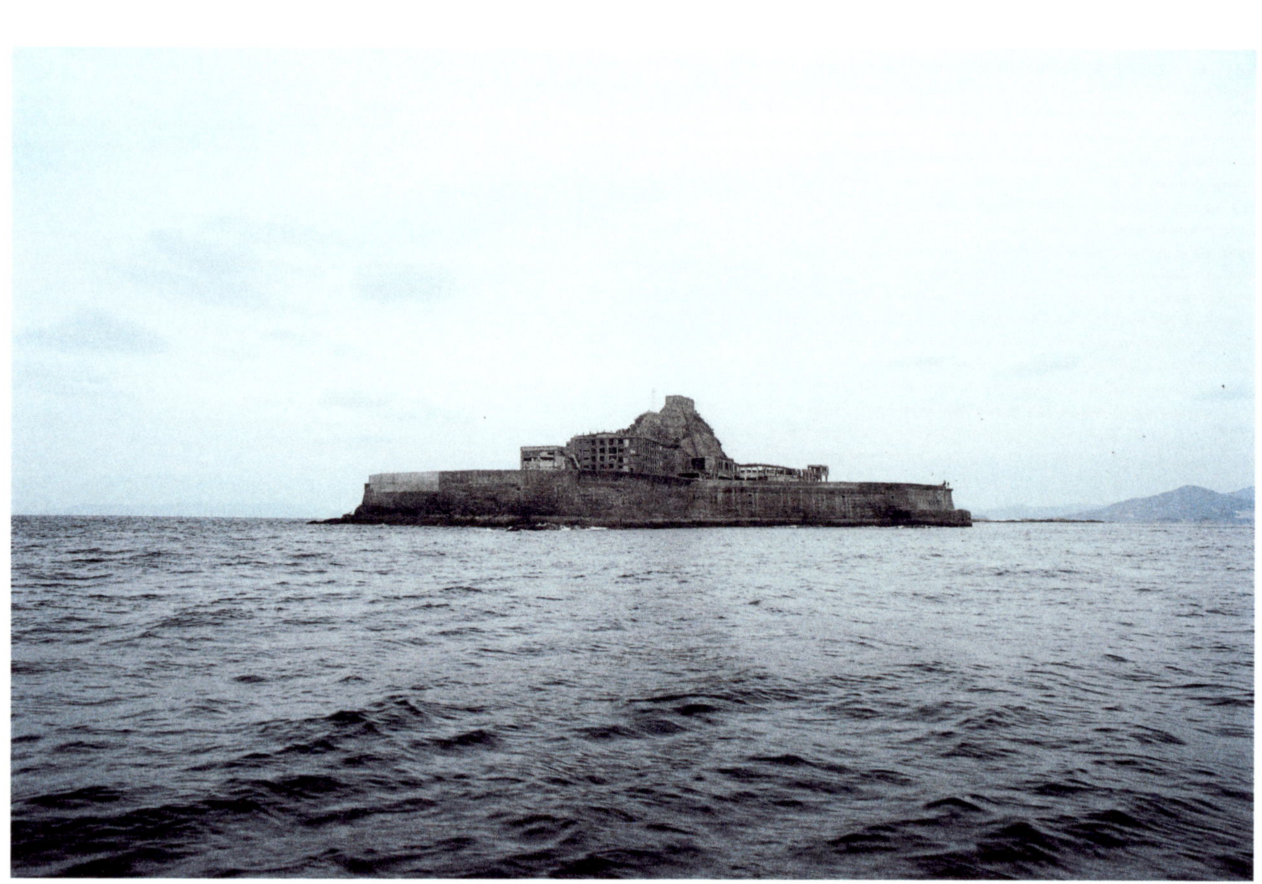

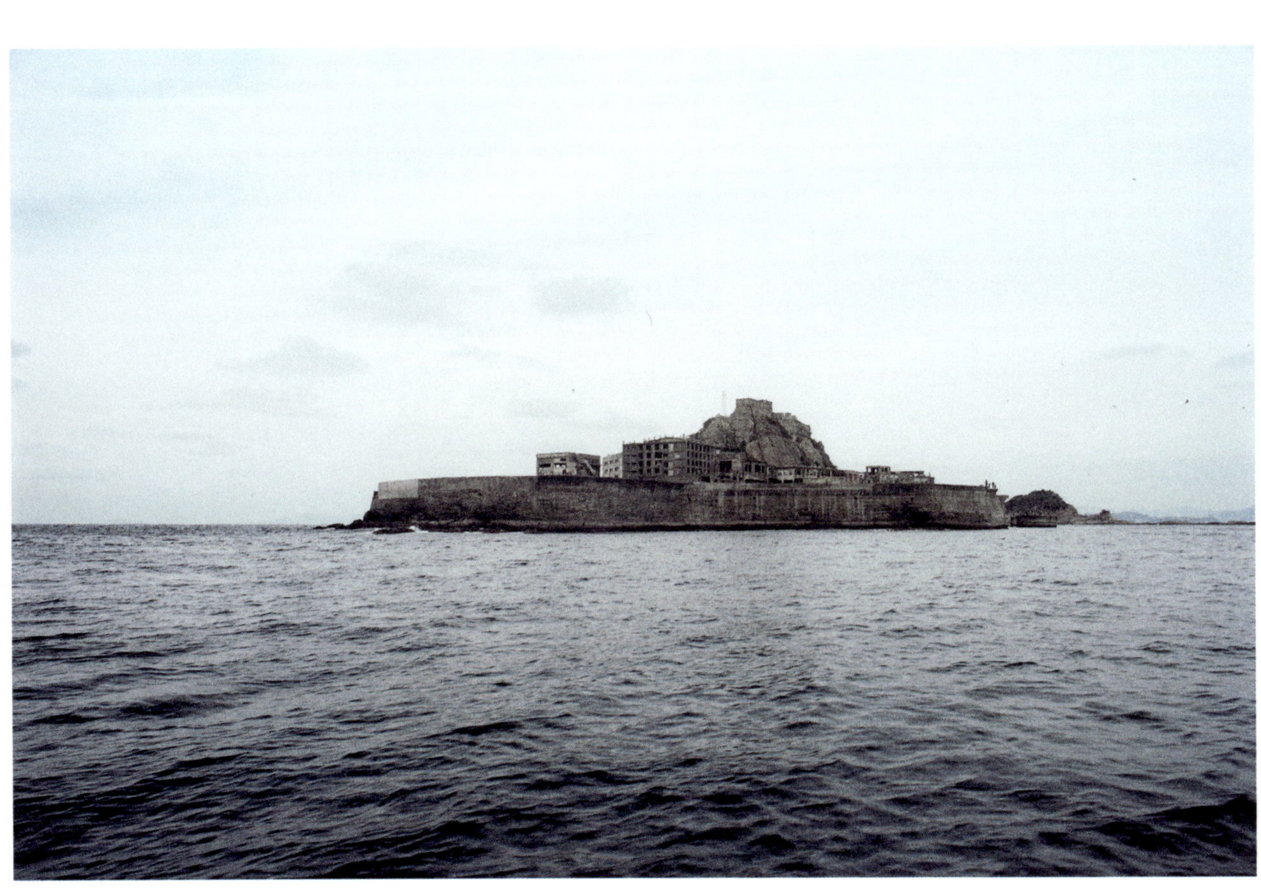

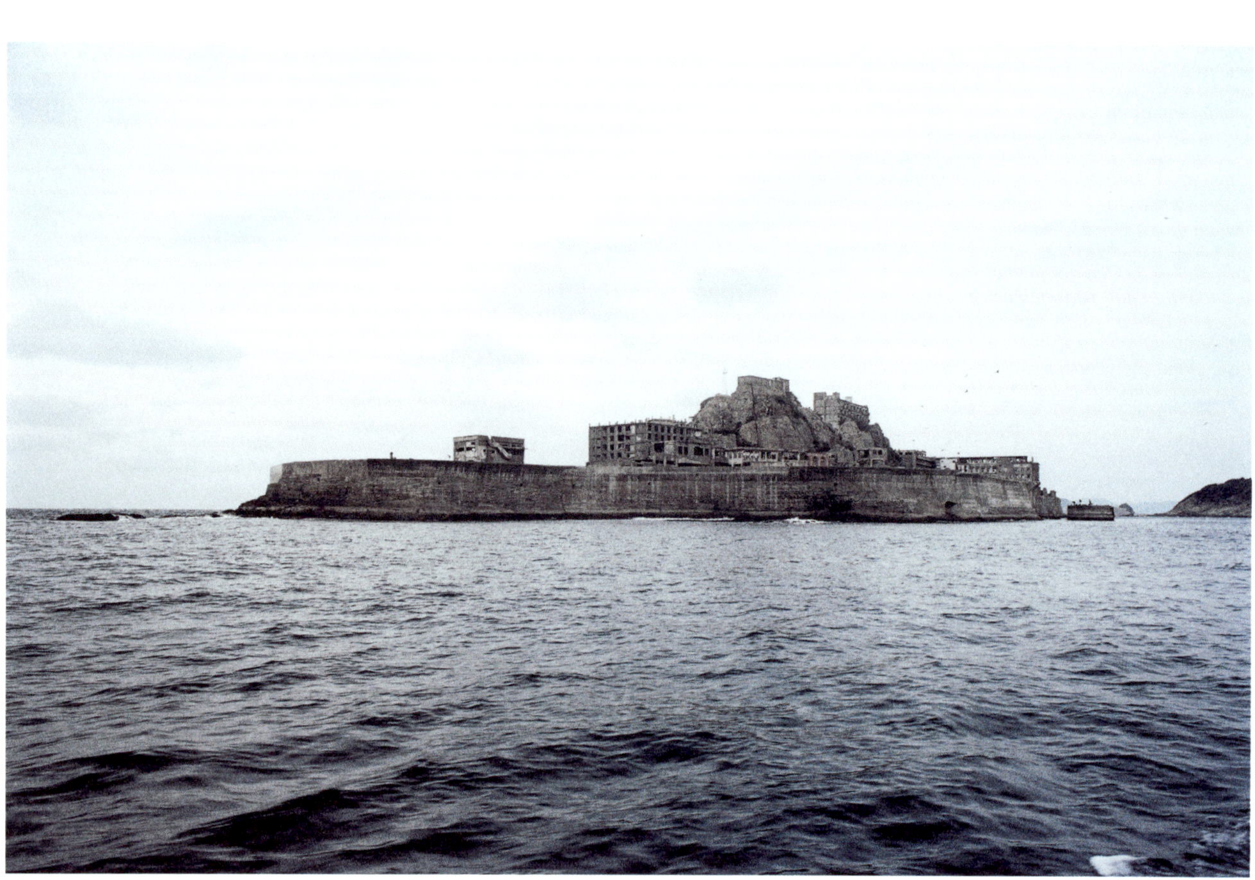

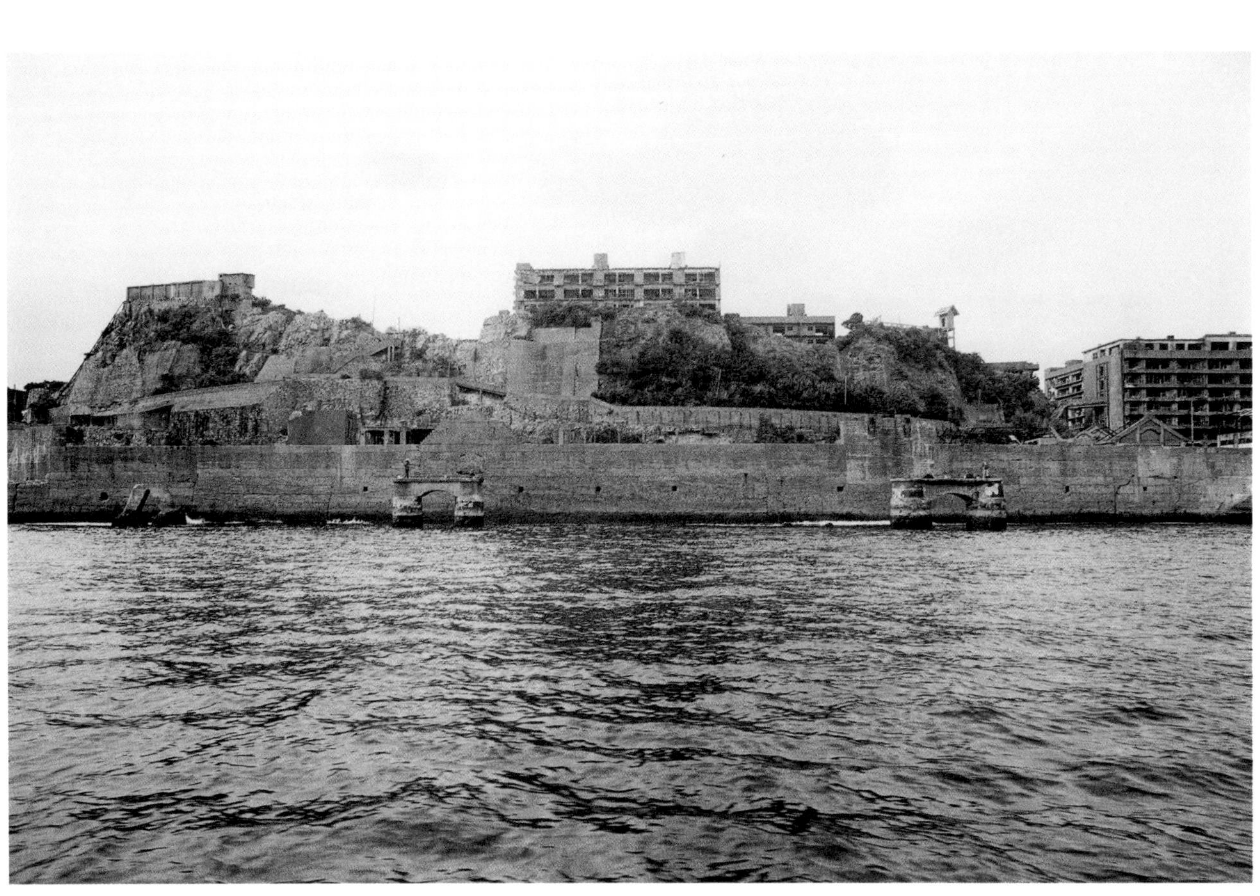

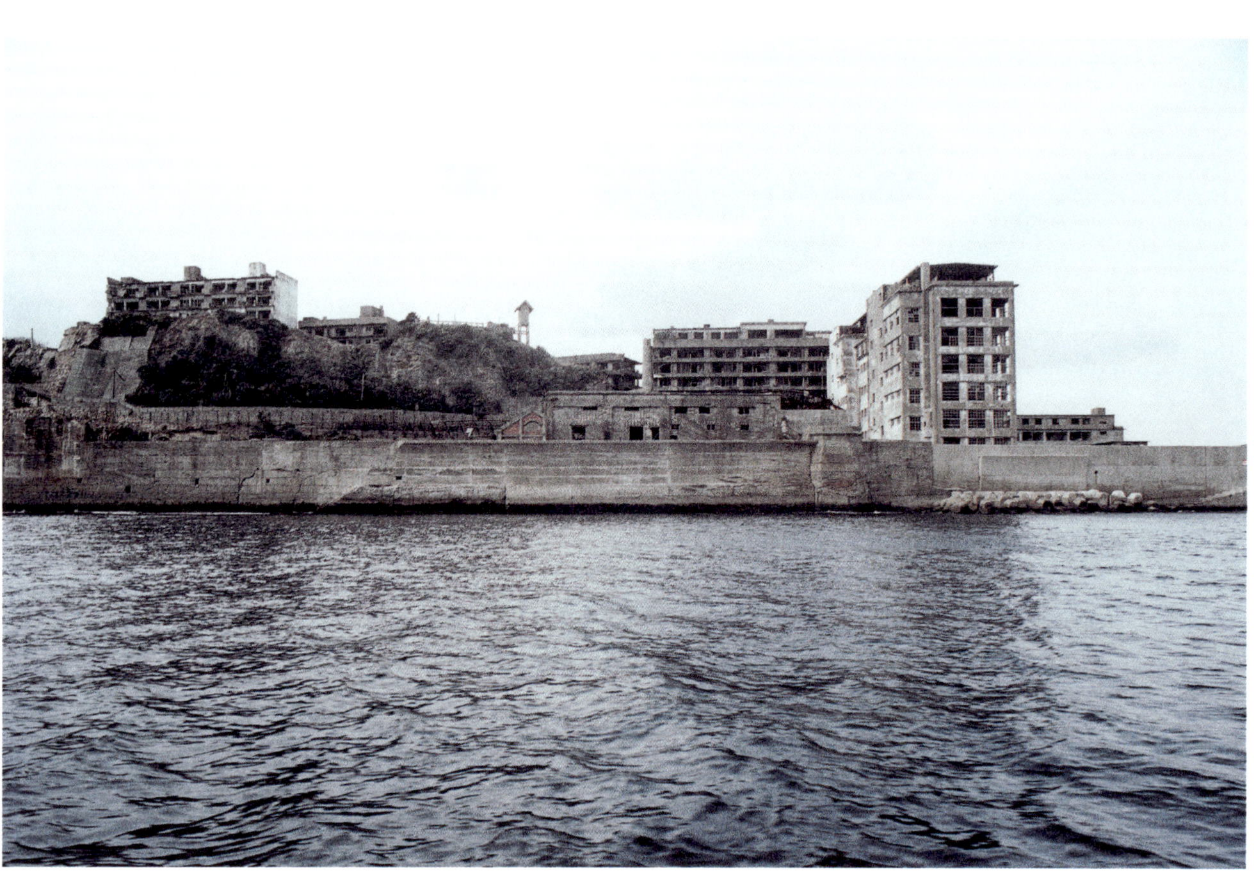

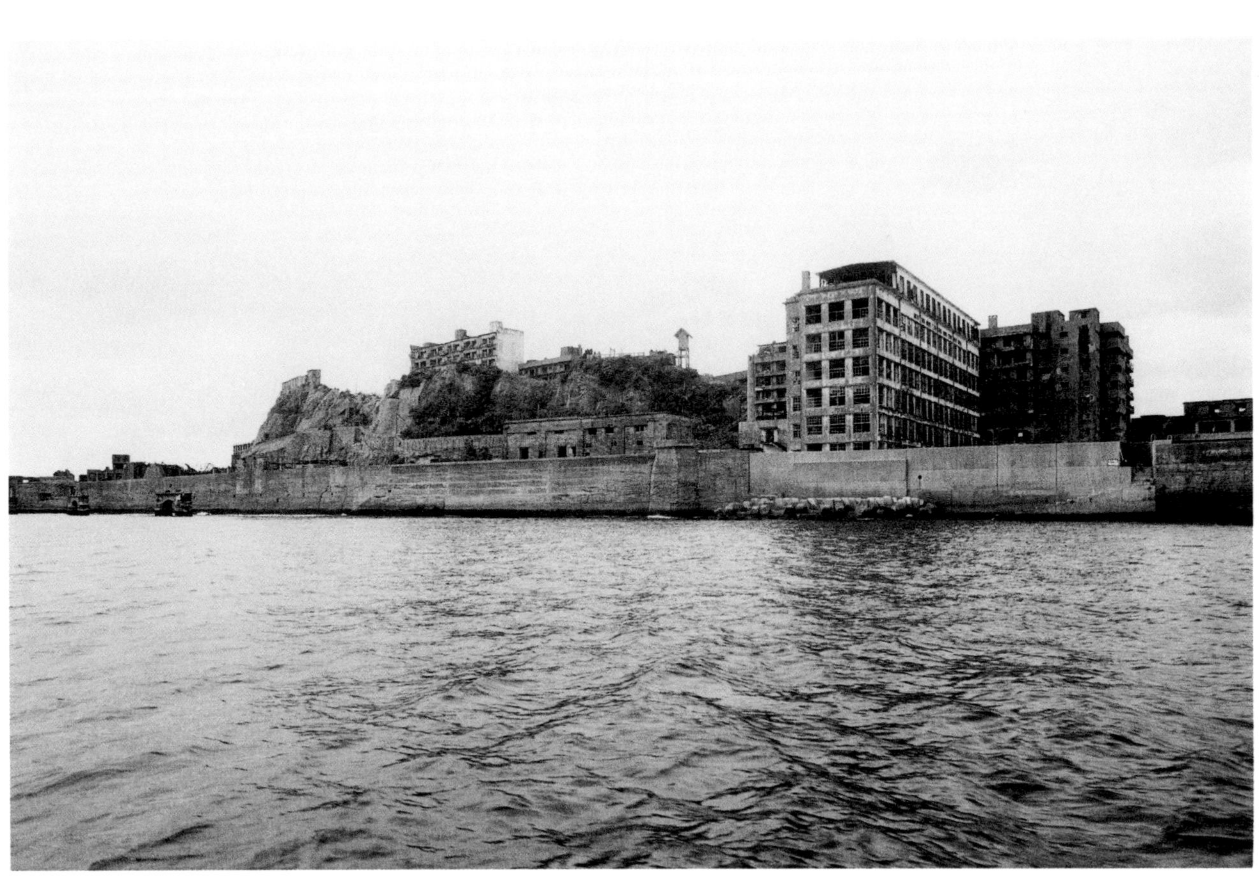

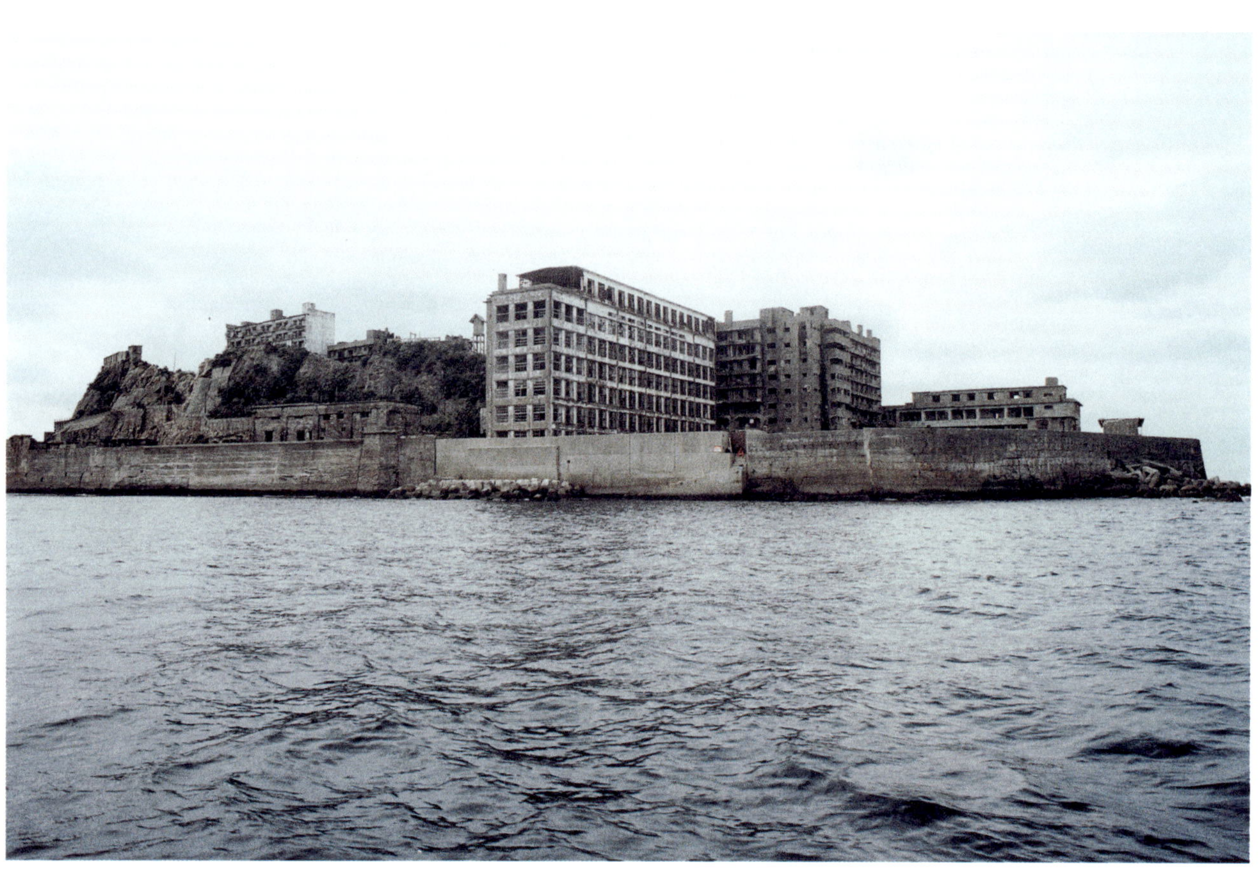

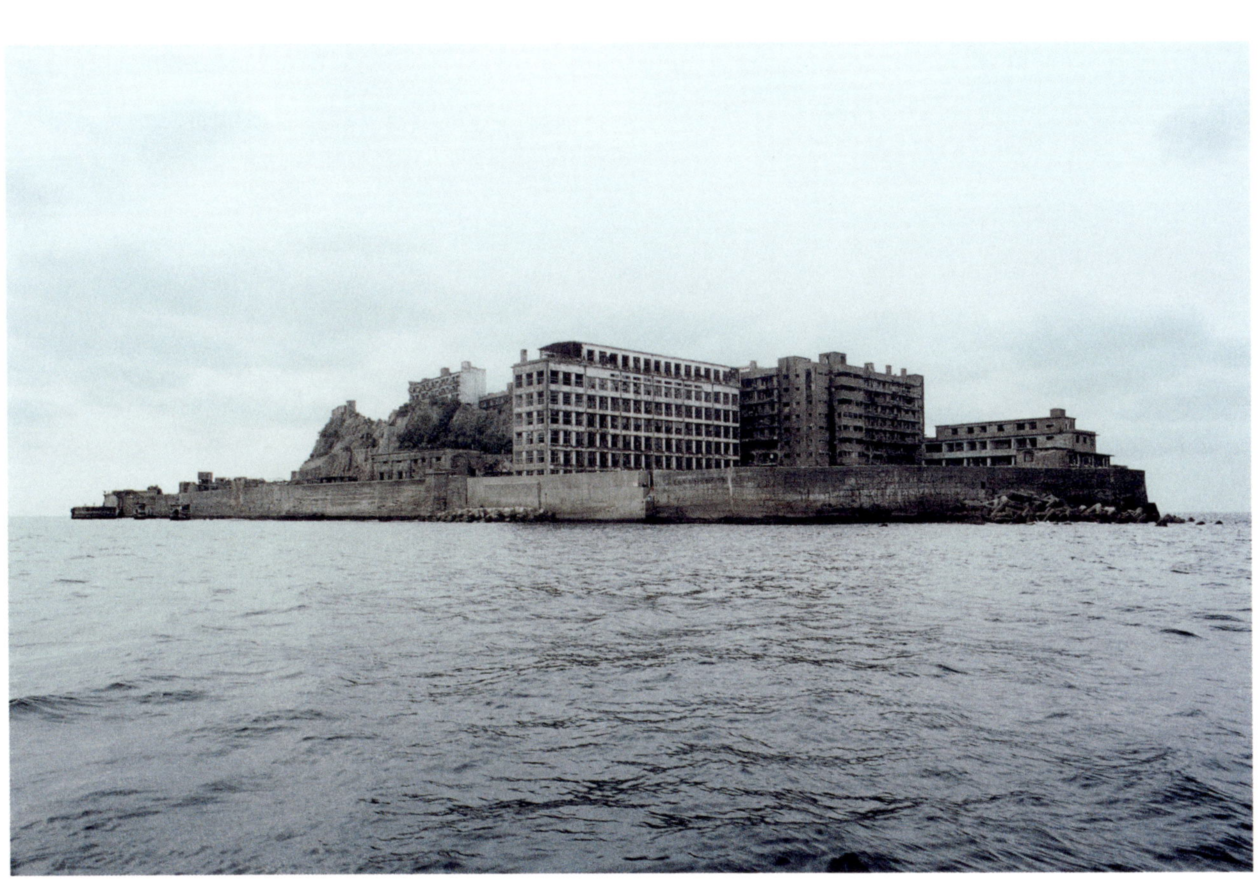

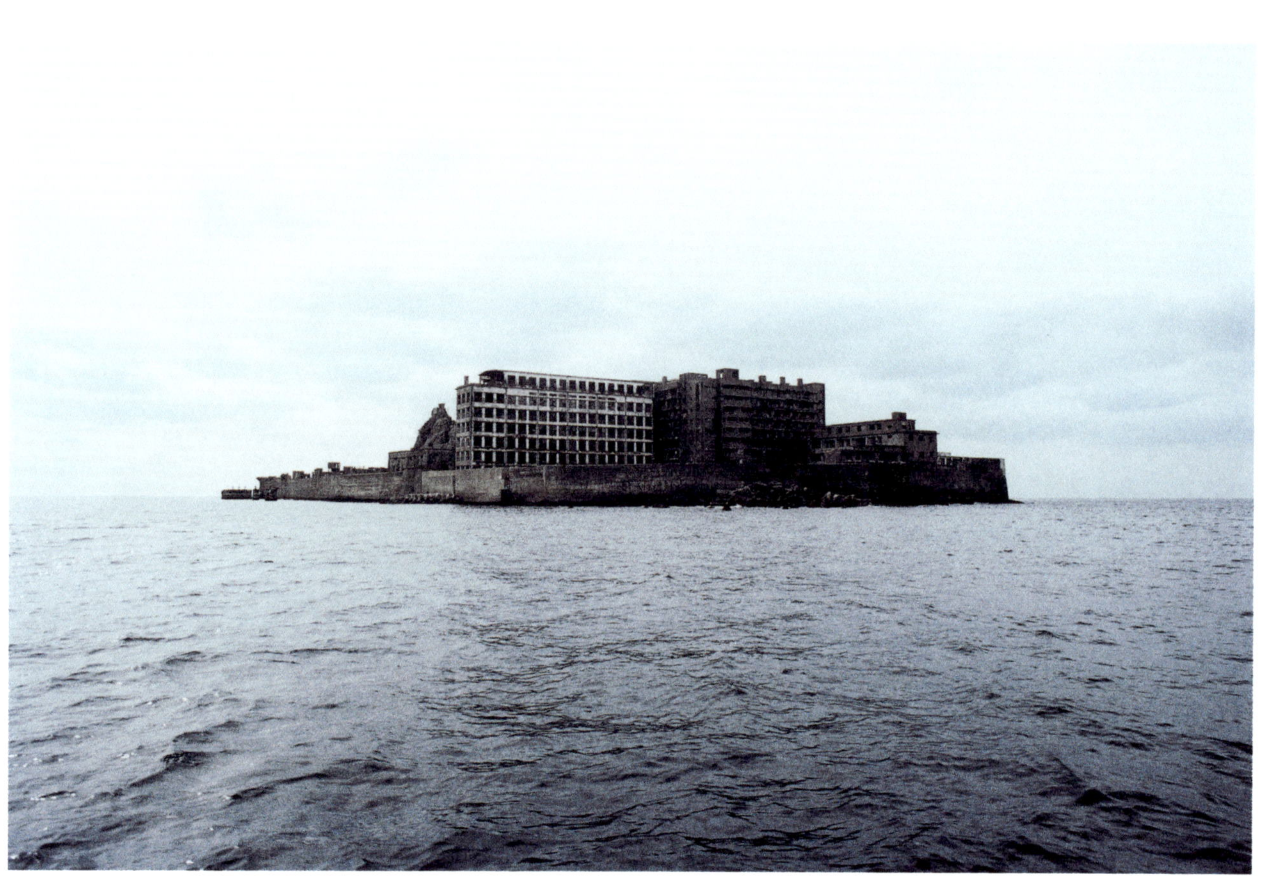

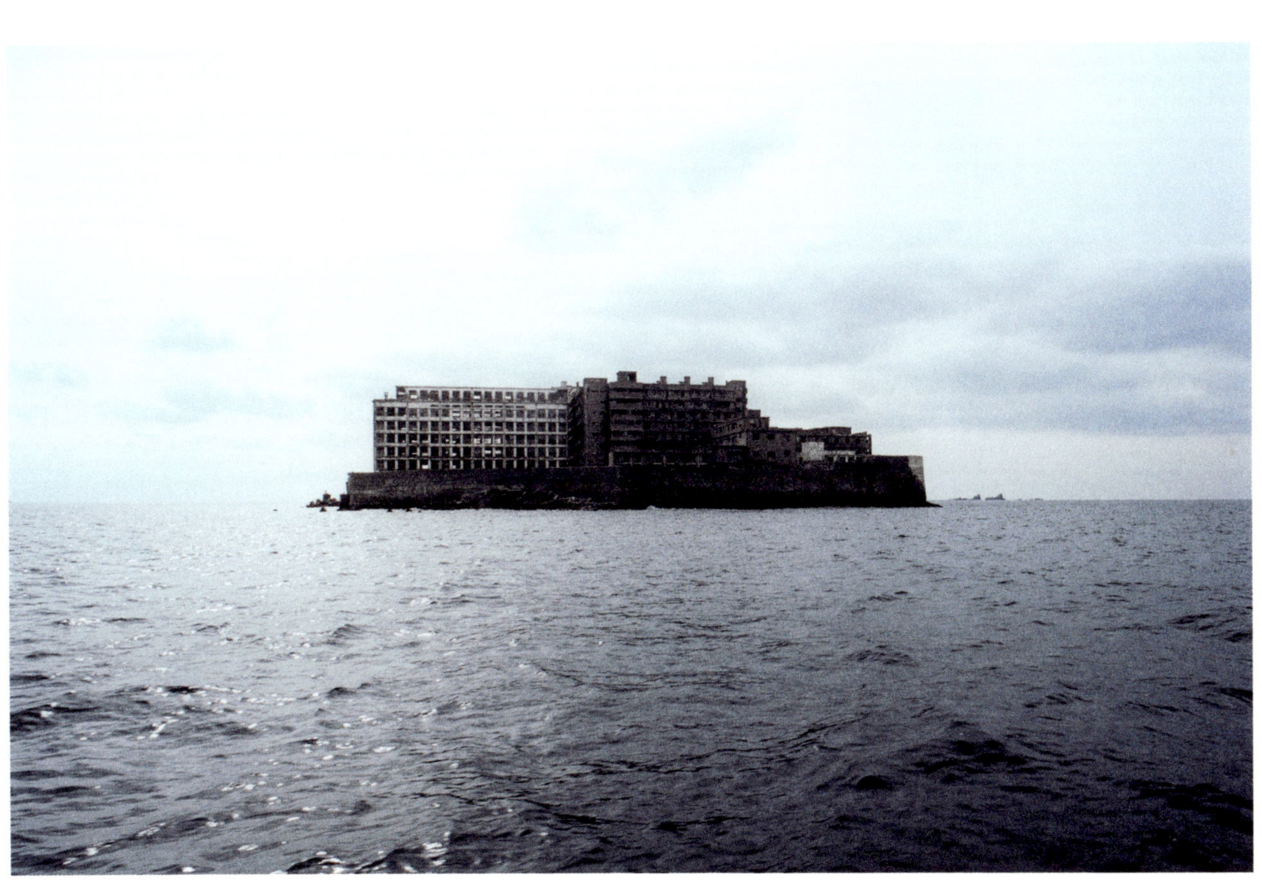

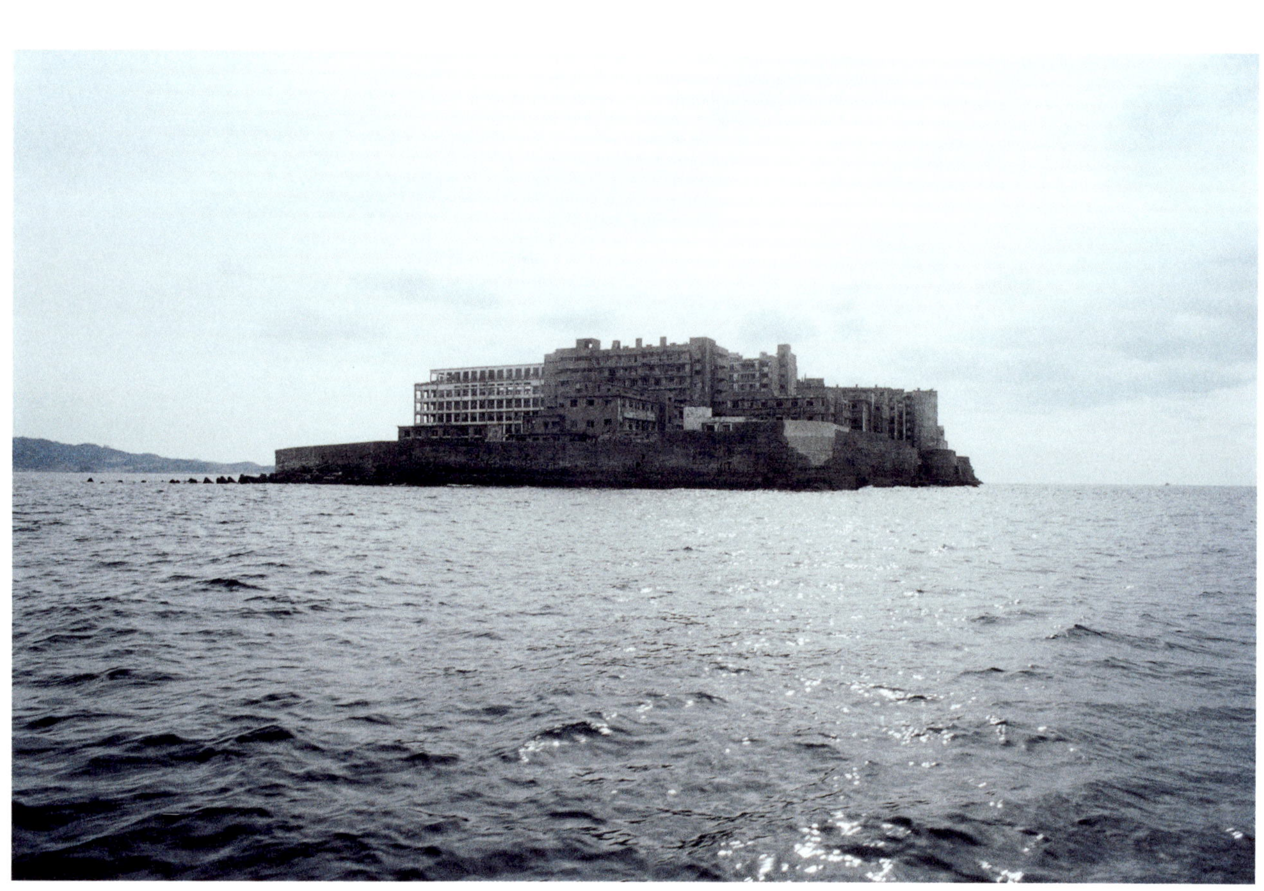

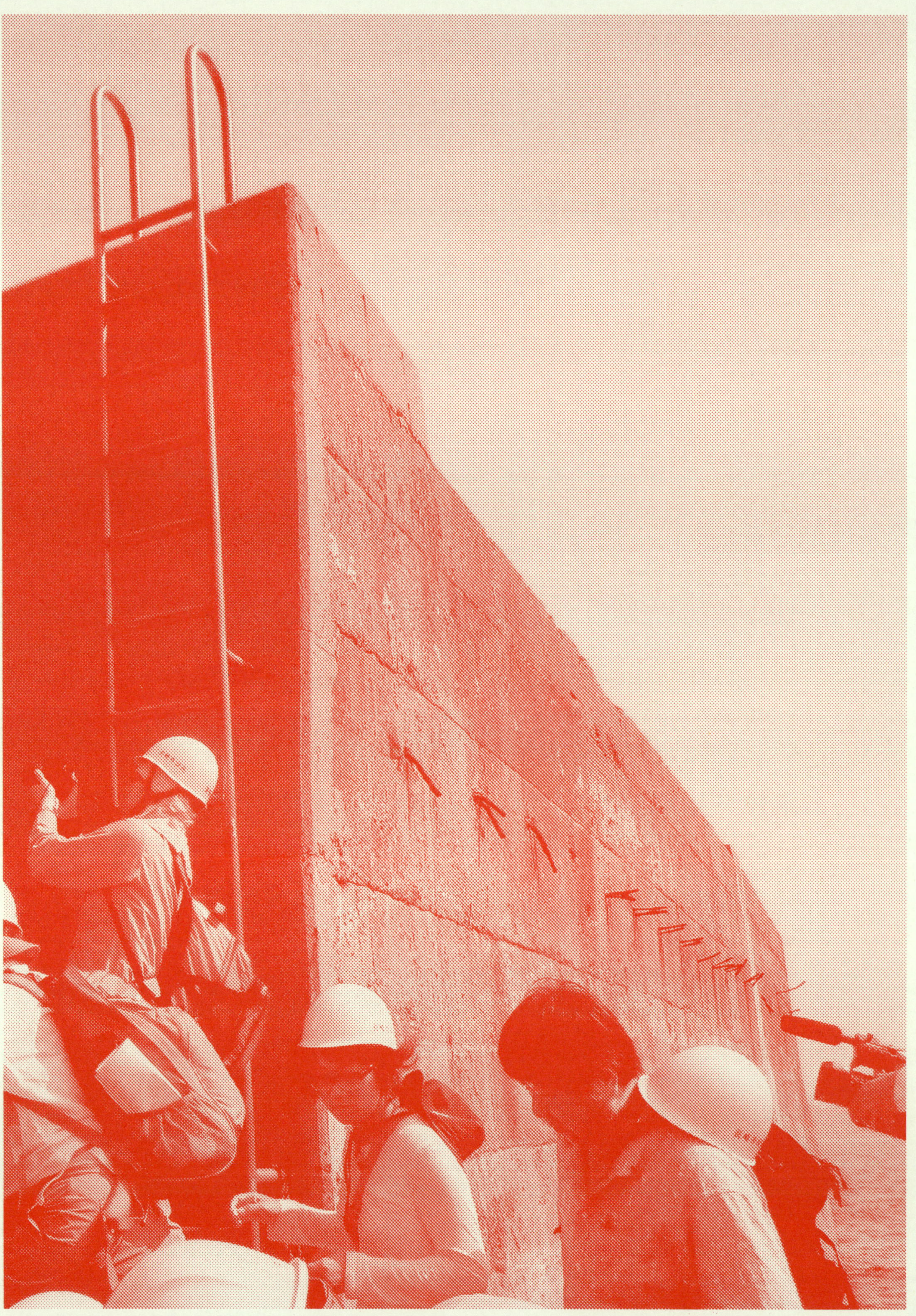

Fubuki Asahina, High School Student

朝比奈ふぶき、高校生

00:00:00 **One day, one whole class of a high school was rendered unconscious by gas during their school trip, kidnapped and taken to some island, and then these students were made to kill each other there.**

突然あるクラスが修学旅行に行く途中に、睡眠ガスで眠らさせられて、他の島に連れて行かれて、クラスメイト同士の殺し合いをさせられるお話なんですね。

00:00:20 **Each student was given a weapon, the boy was given a lid of a big pan and the girl was given a pair of binoculars; this whole thing was called "Battle Royale".**

それぞれ生徒には武器が与えられて、その男子生徒には鍋の蓋で女子生徒には双眼鏡だったんです。バトルロワイヤルっていうやつなんですけど、それを総称して。

00:01:10 **There were two people who had already been in this game before. One of them had some doubts about the game, and later saved the main characters.**

前にバトロワやった人とかが2人入ってて、そのうちの一人がこのゲーム自体に不満を持ってて、主人公達を助けてくれたりして。

00:01:40 **Though it could never happen to me, somehow it felt like it could happen to people around me, and I started to think that it would be scary if it happened.**

自分にとってはあり得ない世界なのに、そういうものを見ると身近な事に見えてきて、もしあったら怖いなと思ったり、そんな感じでした。

00:02:10 **The other one simply wanted to kill people. Students had different lives and dreams (in the film), and they were desperate to survive. Through that you start to see the human nature in the characters.**

もう一人のほうは単純に人を殺したいだけ、みたいな感じで。色々な生徒たちがそれぞれ何か違う生活とか夢があって、すごく生き残るために必死になっていて、人間性みたいなものがすごく見えた。

00:02:25 **Towards the end, many people died, but these two survived in the end. It wasn't a nice feeling to see people dying.**

最終的に段々人が死んでいってしまって、最終的にそのふたりは最後まで生き残るんです。普通に人が死んでゆくのが、あまり見てて気分のいいものではなかったです。

00:02:45 **And then there is the teacher, played by that famous director, Takeshi Kitano, him and the female student had a sort of relationship. He was originally a teacher before he disapeared, but then he was stabbed by this guy who fancied the girl. The knife used for the stabbing was held in her hand, and she had dreams about the teacher. There were a lot of things happening to the teacher and the girl.**

それを監督する先生がいまして、その人と女子生徒がちょっと関わりあって、その人が刺されてしまったんです。その女子生徒を好きだった人に。刺した時のナイフを女子生徒が持っていて、女子生徒はその先生との夢を見たりとか、その生徒と先生の間にも結構色々あったみたいで。

00:04:15 **The island was used to prevent the students from escaping, or to isolate them from the outside world. Maybe because it's easy to watch over them, I suppose?**
Because it is an island, it is free to use as you like, bombing it or burning it.
In that sense, it is a very useful island.

逃げ出さないようにというか、隔離するためのものでした。監視しやすいからですかね？やっぱり、孤立した島だから、すごく自由に使えますし。爆破したり、燃やしたり。そんな感じで、そういう意味では使い勝手の良さそうな島なのかな、そういうのには。

00:05:01 **The story before it became an inhabited island intrigues me. I hope it will become an island on which people live some day.**

軍艦島が無人島になる前の話とかすごい気になります。人がいる島になってほしいです。

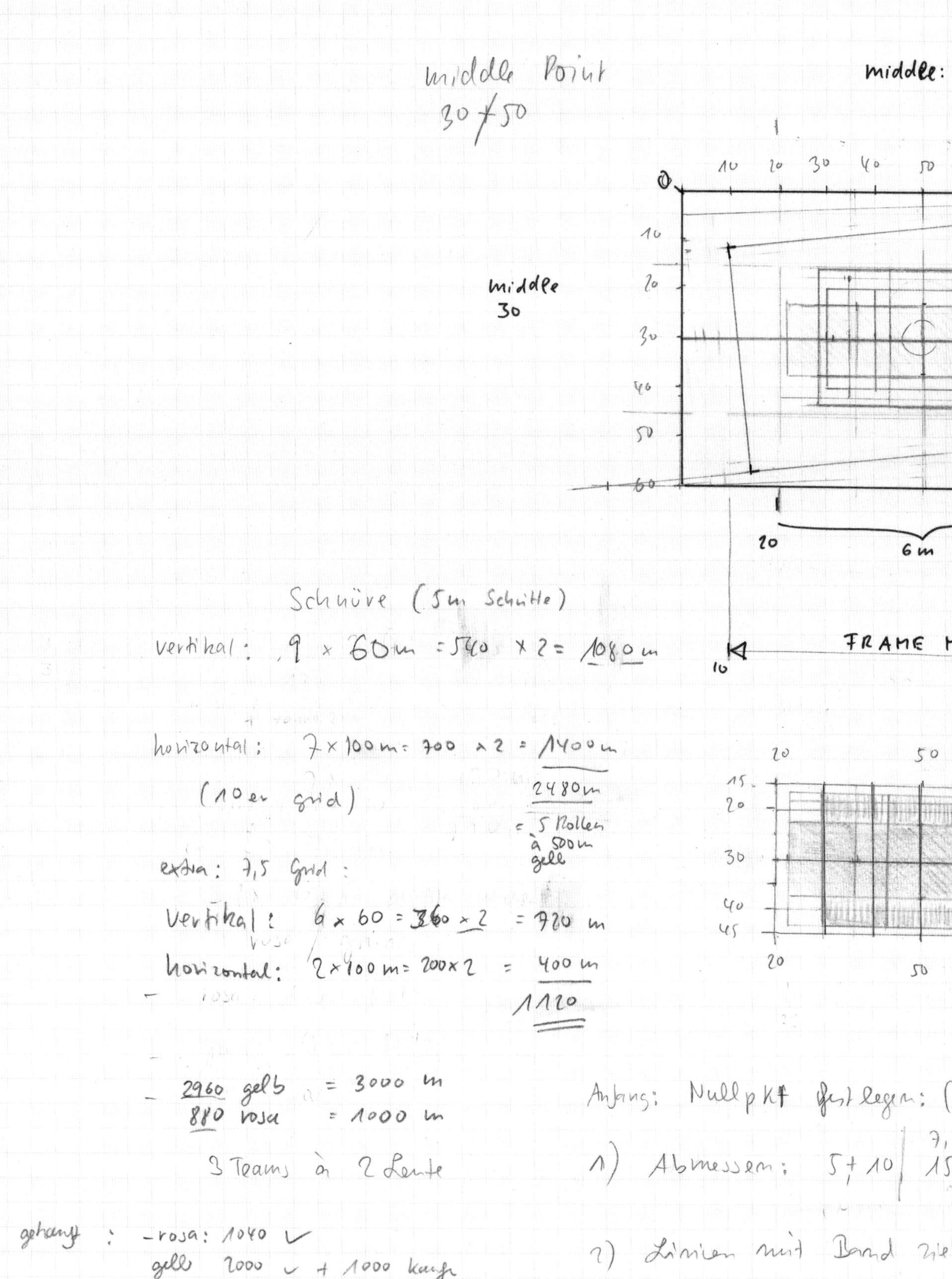

middle Point
30/50
middle:
10
20
30
40
50
0
10
20
30
40
50
60
middle
30
20
6m
Schnüre (5m Schnitte)
vertikal: 9 × 60m = 540 × 2 = 1080m
FRAME M
10
horizontal: 7 × 100m = 700 × 2 = 1400m
(10er grid)
2480m
= 5 Rollen à 500m gelb
20
50
15
20
30
40
45
20
50
extra: 7,5 Grid:
vertikal: 6 × 60 = 360 × 2 = 720 m
horizontal: 2 × 100 m = 200 × 2 = 400 m
1120
2960 gelb = 3000 m
880 rosa = 1000 m
3 Teams à 2 Leute
gekauft: rosa: 1040
gelb 2000 + 1000 kaufen
Anfang: Nullpkt festlegen: (
1) Abmessen: 5, 10 | 7,5 15.
2) Linien mit Band zieh
3) Katakana Hilfspun

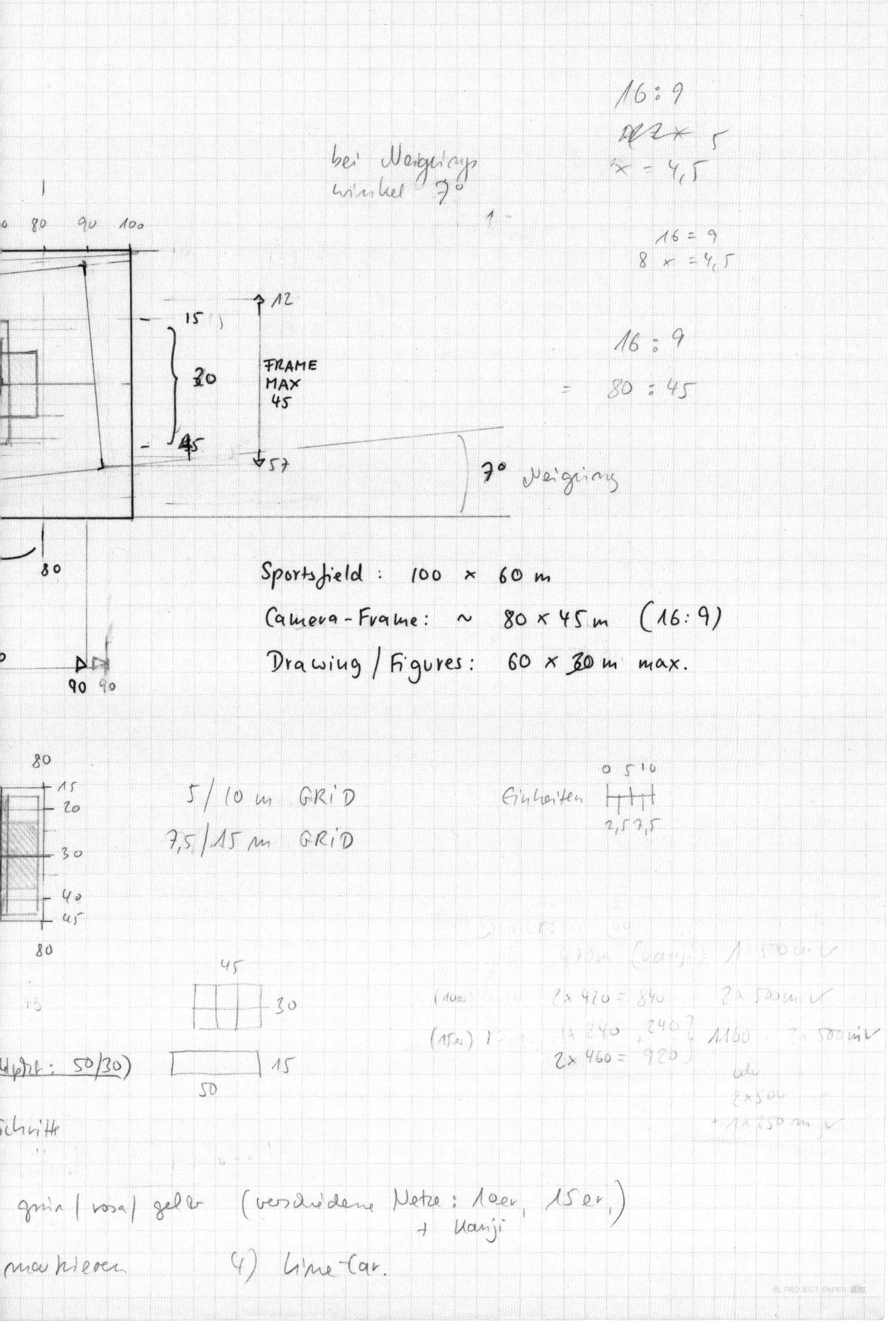

16 : 9
x = 4,5
bei Neigungs winkel 7°
80 90 100
16 = 9
8 x = 4,5
12
15
30
FRAME MAX 45
45
57
16 : 9
= 80 : 45
7° Neigung
80
Sportsfield : 100 × 60 m
Camera-Frame: ~ 80 × 45 m (16:9)
Drawing / Figures: 60 × 30 m max.
90 90
80
15
20
30
40
45
80
5/10 m GRID
7,5/15 m GRID
Einheiten
0 5 10
2,5 7,5
45
30
15
50
(100)
2 × 420 = 840
2 × 500 m
(15er)
1 × 240
240
1160
2 × 460 = 920
2 × 500 m
grün / rosa / gelb (verschiedene Netze: 10er, 15er, + Kanji)
markieren
4) Line-Car.

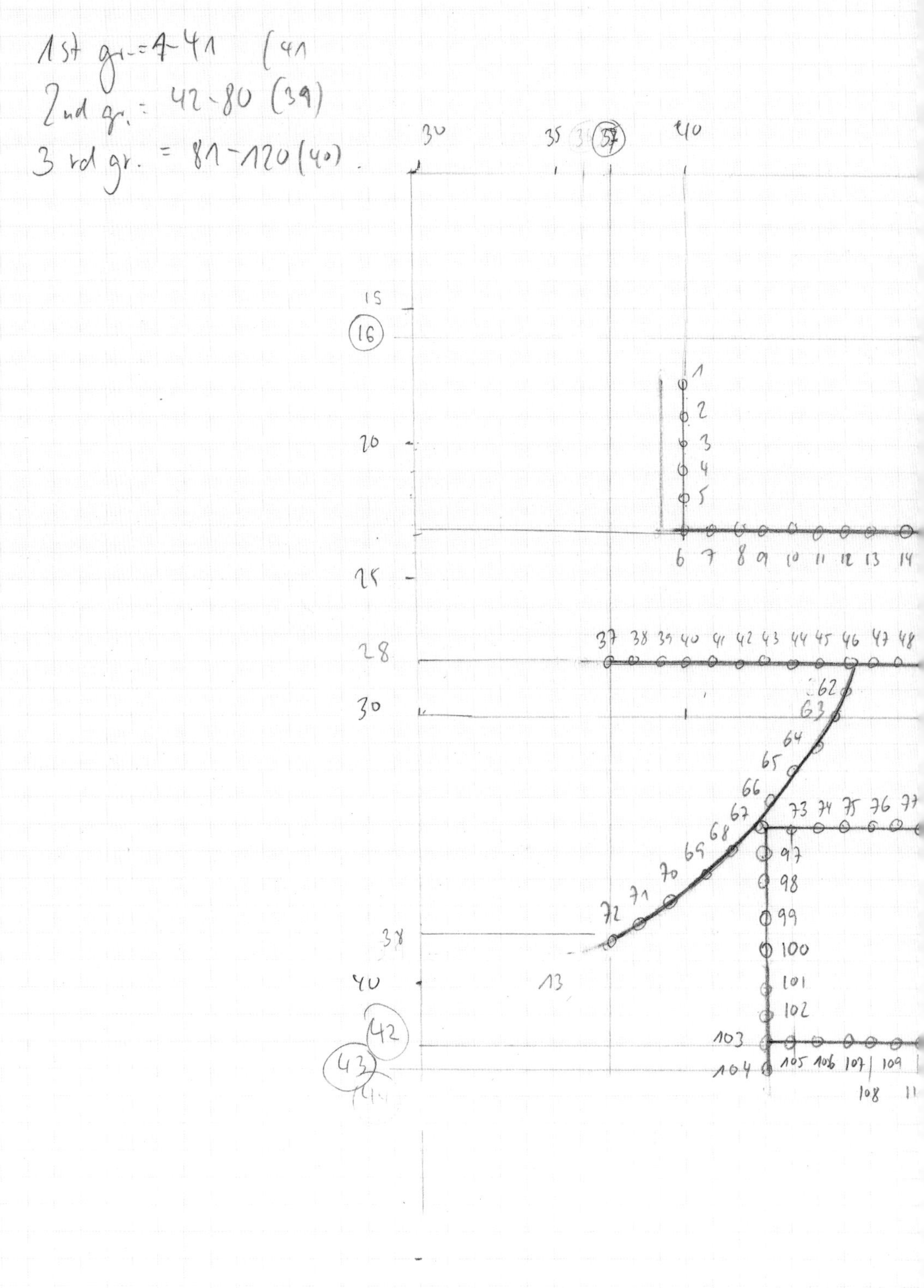
1st gr. = 1-41 (41
2nd gr. = 42-80 (39)
3rd gr. = 81-120 (40)

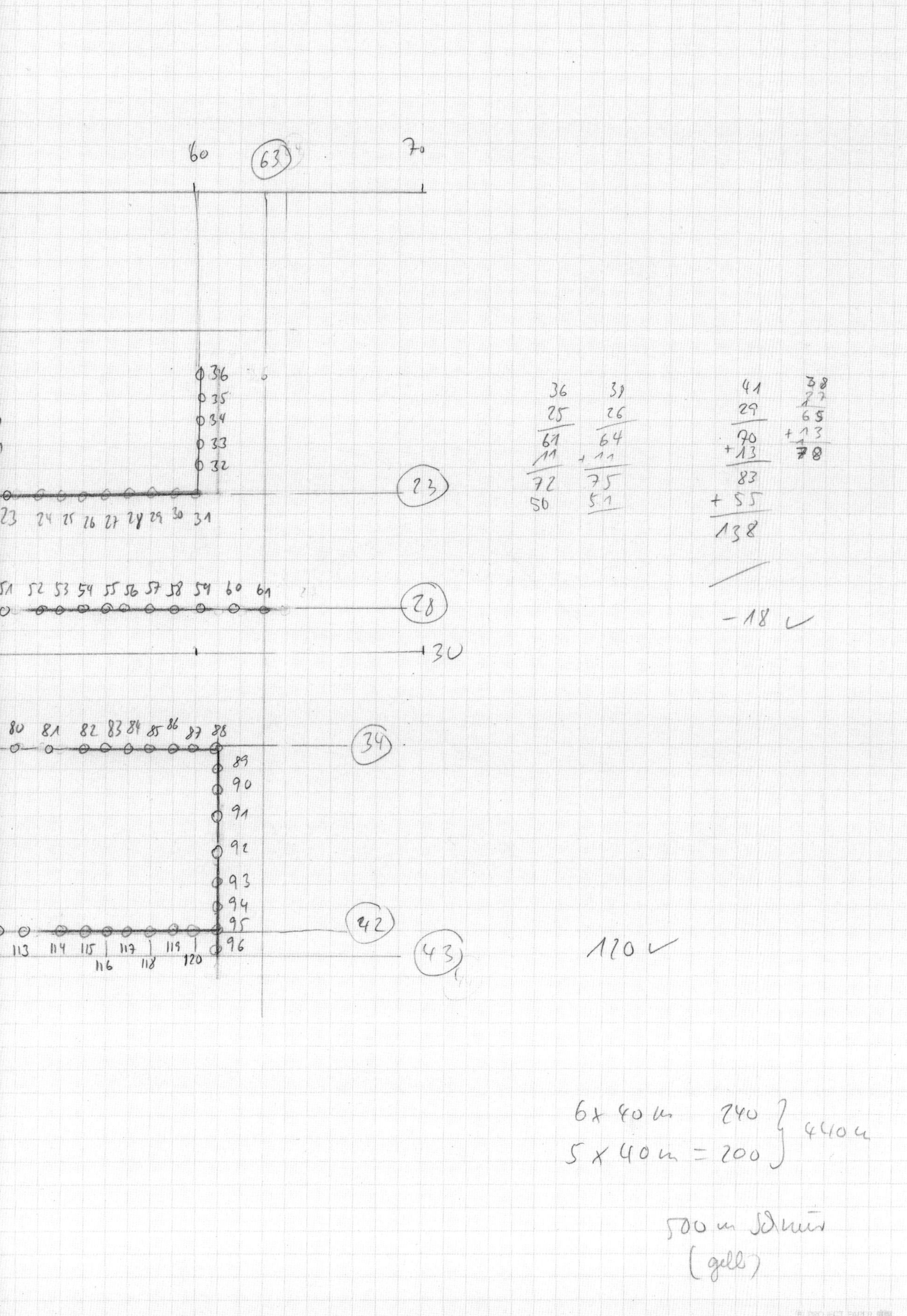

60
63
70
36 35 34 33 32
23 24 25 26 27 28 29 30 31
23
51 52 53 54 55 56 57 58 59 60 61
28
30
80 81 82 83 84 85 86 87 88
34
89 90 91 92 93 94 95 96
113 114 115 116 117 118 119 120
42
43
36
25
61
11
72
50
37
26
64
+ 11
75
51
41
29
70
+ 13
83
+ 55
138
– 18
38
27
65
+ 13
78
120
6 x 40 m 240
5 x 40 m = 200
440 m
500 m Schnur
(gelb)

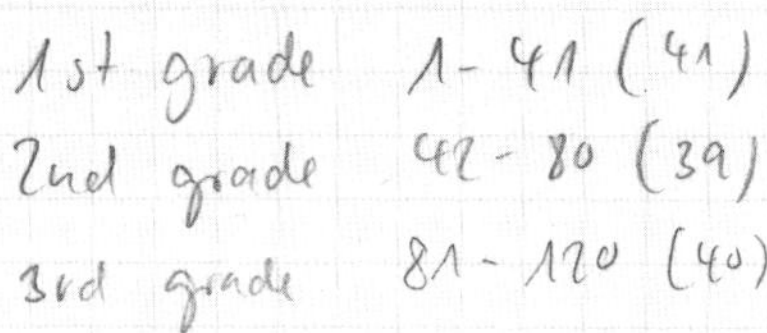
1st grade 1-41 (41)
2nd grade 42-80 (39)
3rd grade 81-120 (40)

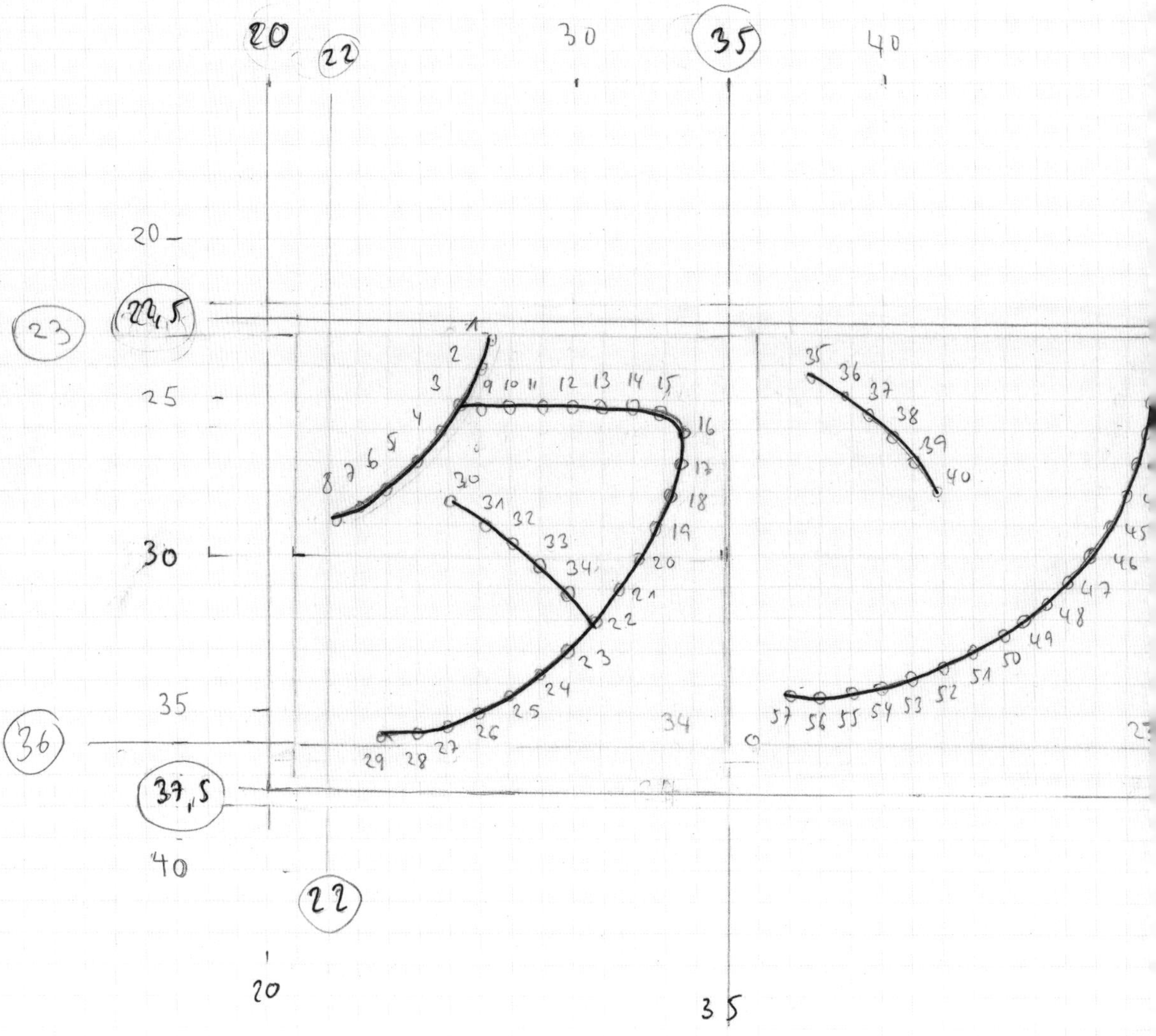

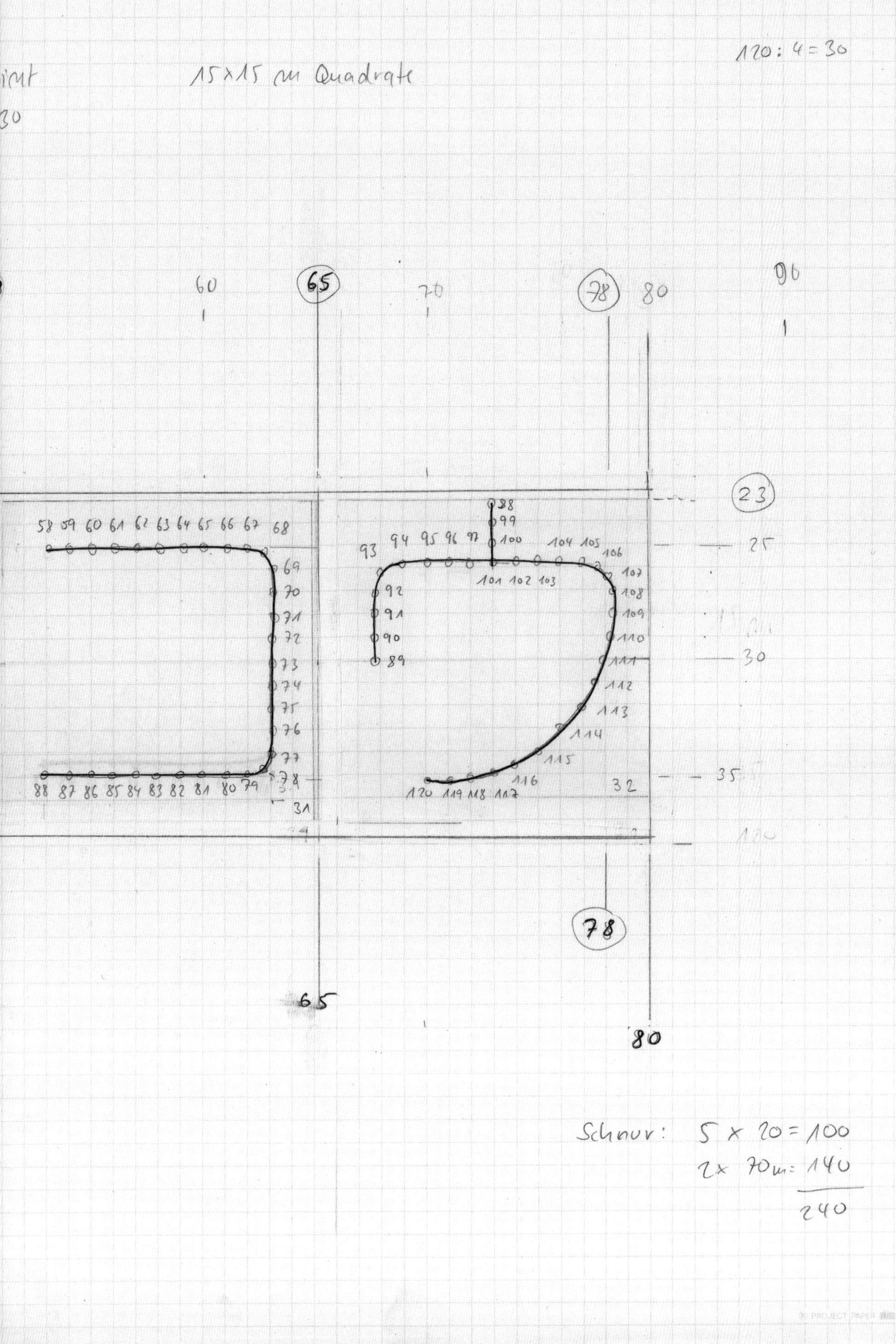

15×15 cm Quadrate
120 : 4 = 30
Schnur: 5 × 20 = 100
2× 70 cm = 140
240

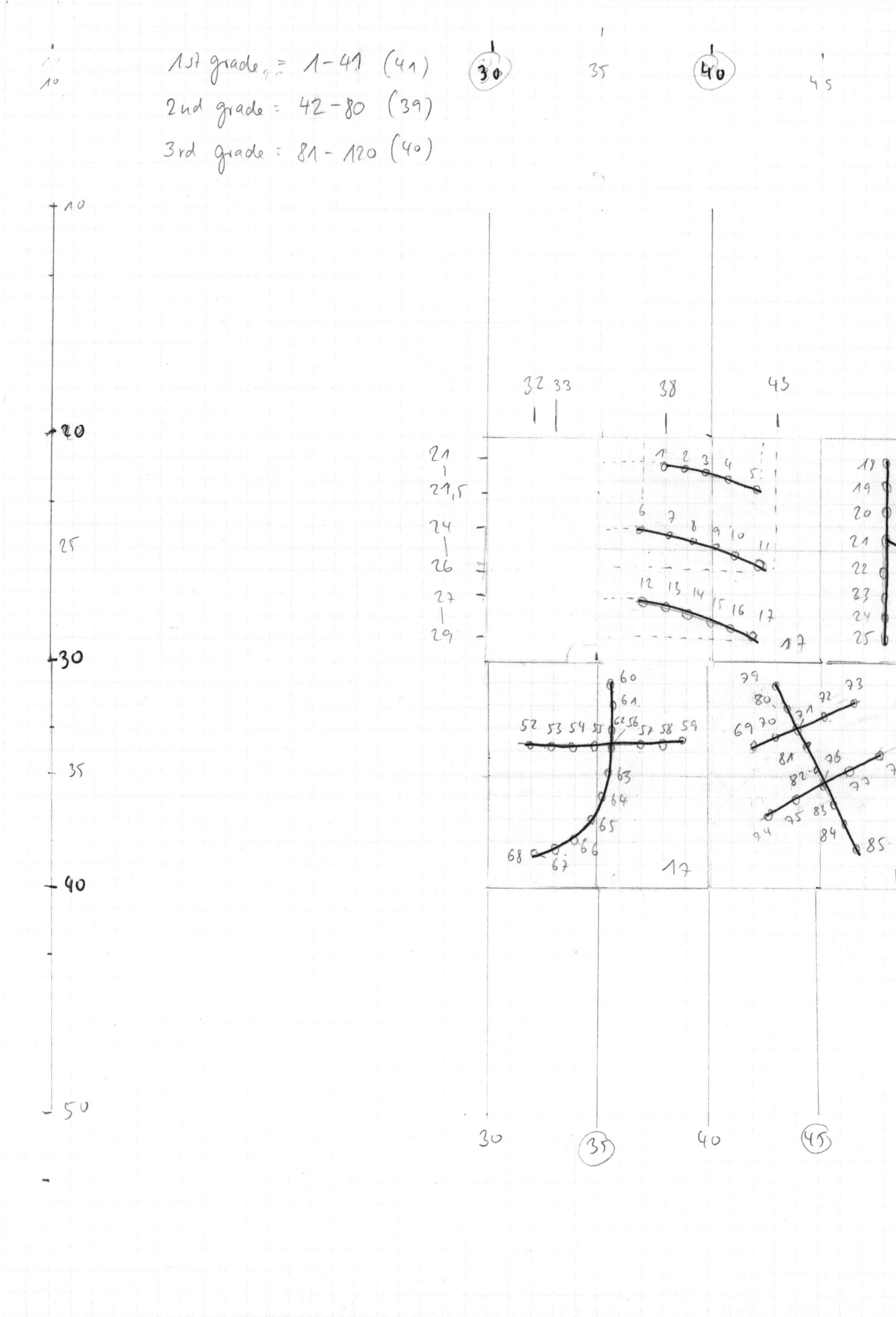

1st grade = 1-41 (41)
2nd grade = 42-80 (39)
3rd grade = 81-120 (40)

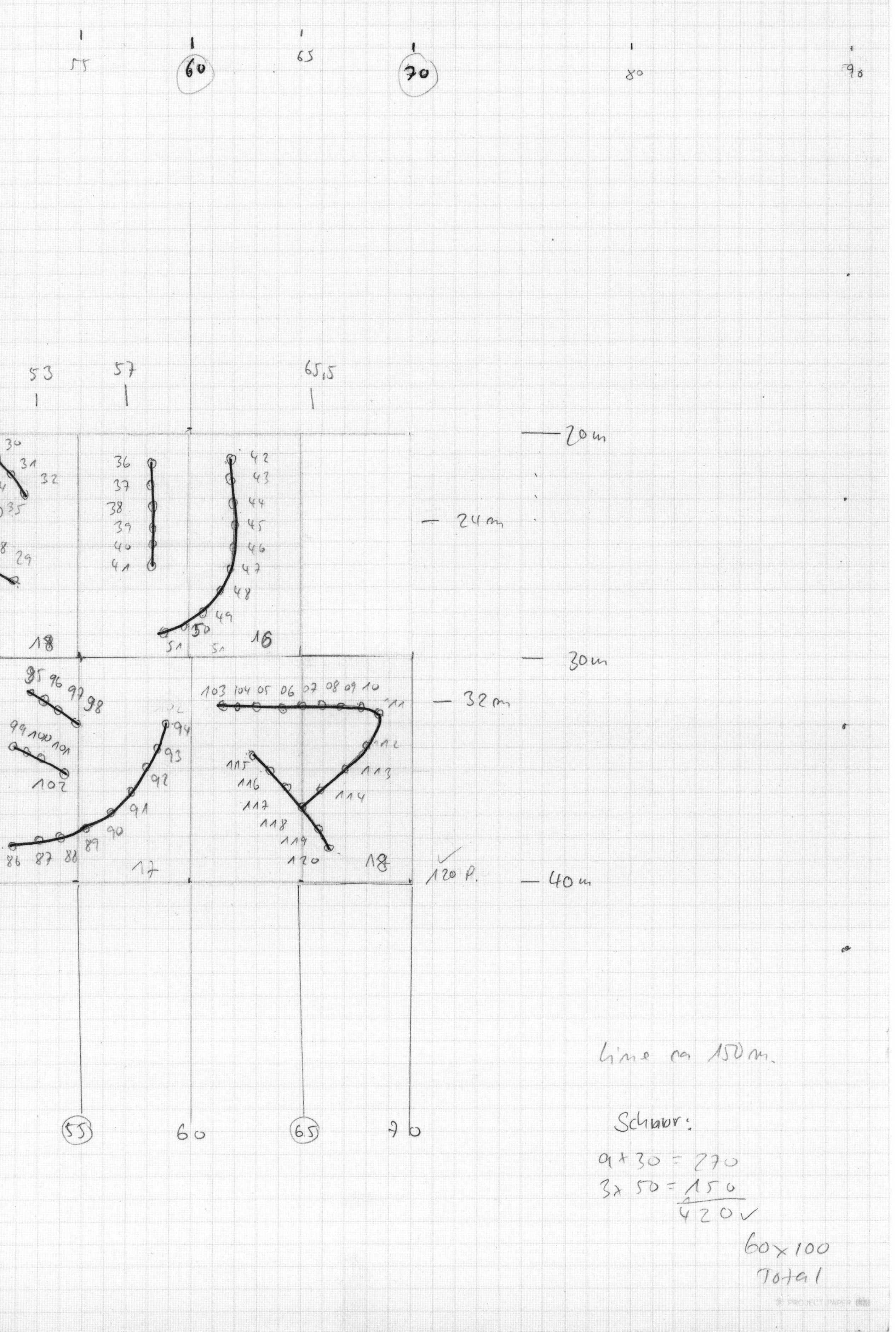

Line ca 150m.

Schnur:

9 x 30 = 270
3 x 50 = 150
420

60 x 100
Total

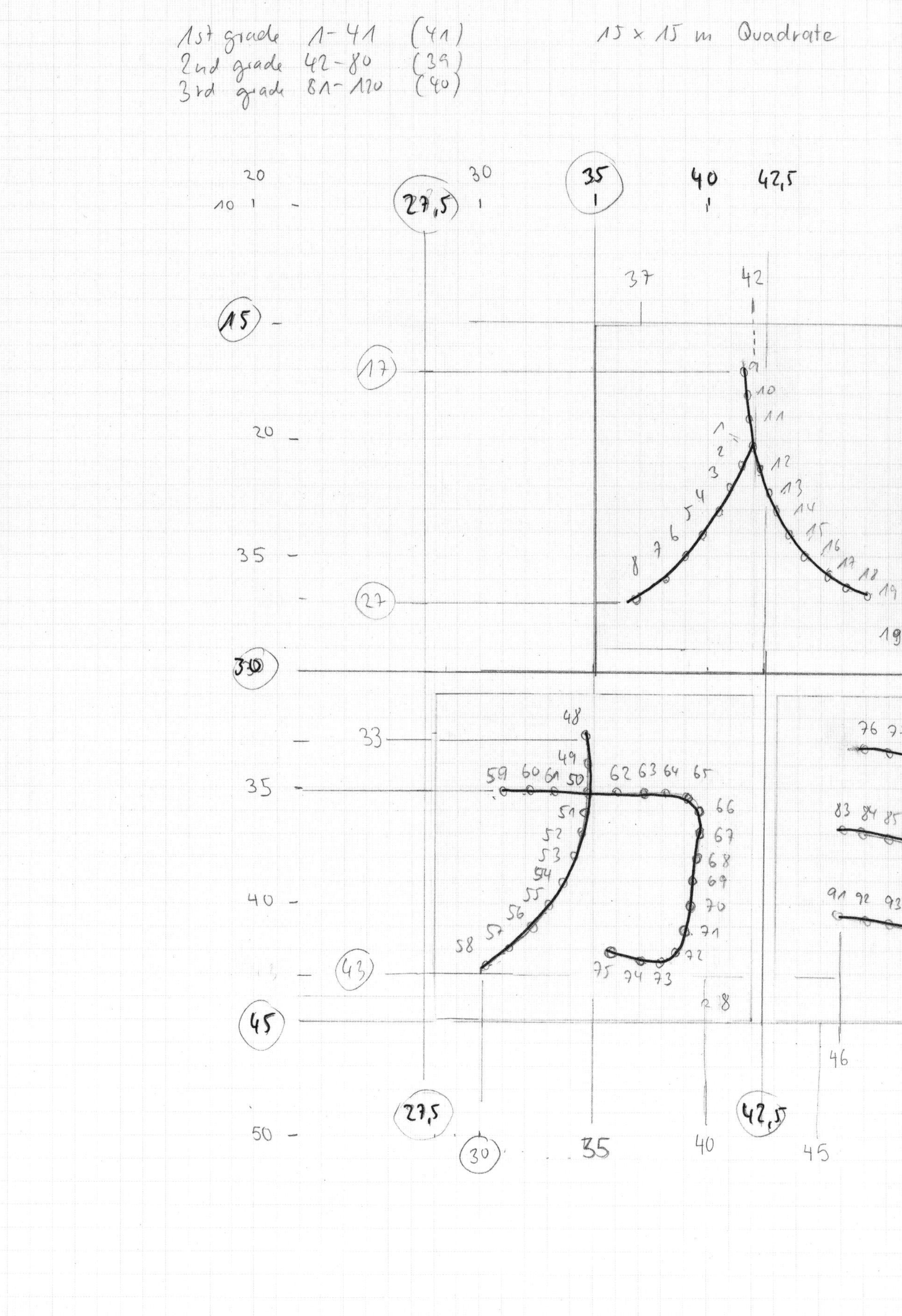

1st grade 1-41 (41)
2nd grade 42-80 (39)
3rd grade 81-120 (40)
15 × 15 m Quadrate

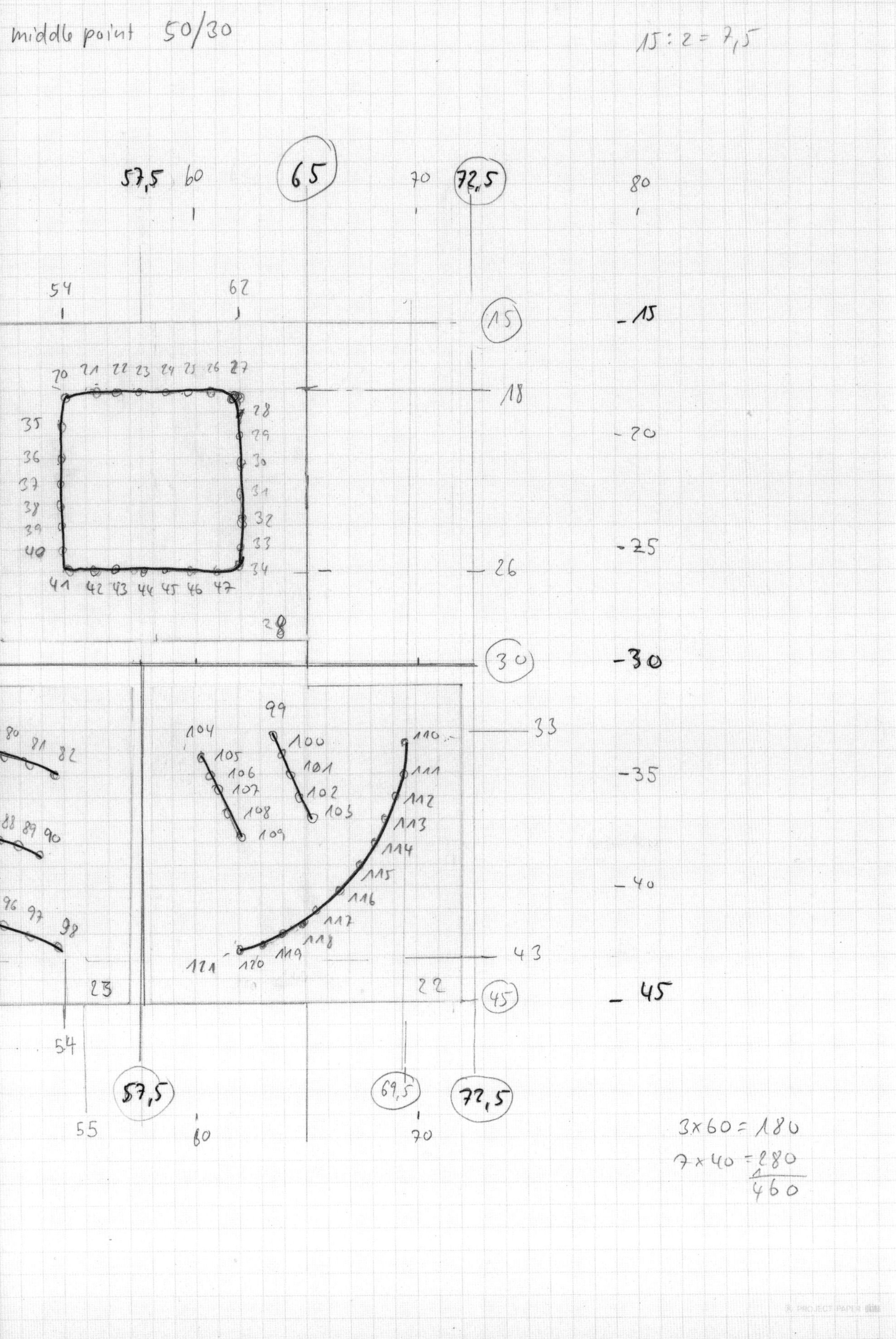

middle point 50/30
15 : 2 = 7,5
57,5
60
65
70
72,5
80
54
62
15
-15
18
-20
-25
26
-30
30
33
-35
-40
43
45
-45
54
57,5
55
60
69,5
72,5
70
3x60 = 180
7x40 = 280
460

1st = 1-41 (41)
2nd = 42-80 (39)
3rd = 81-120 (40)

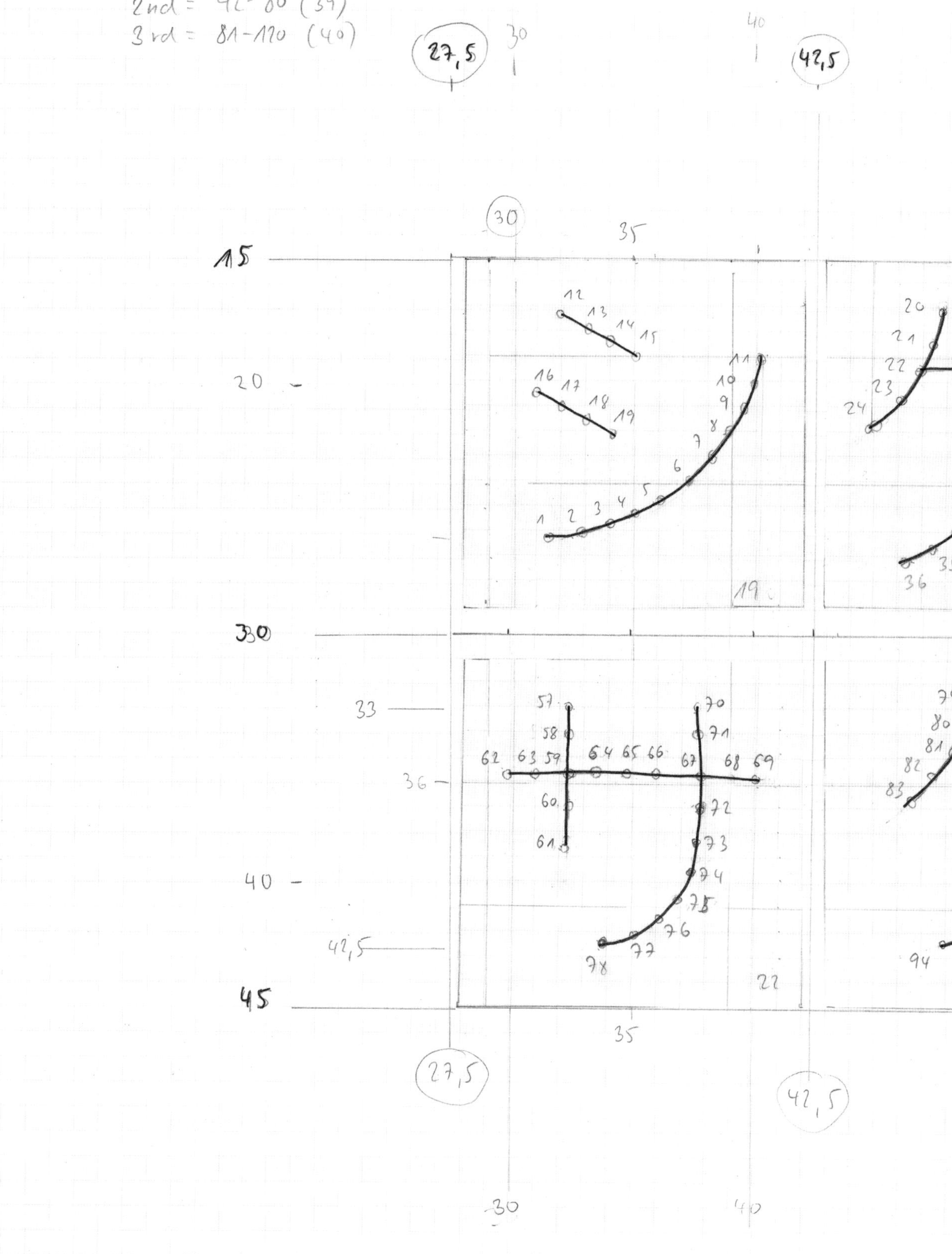

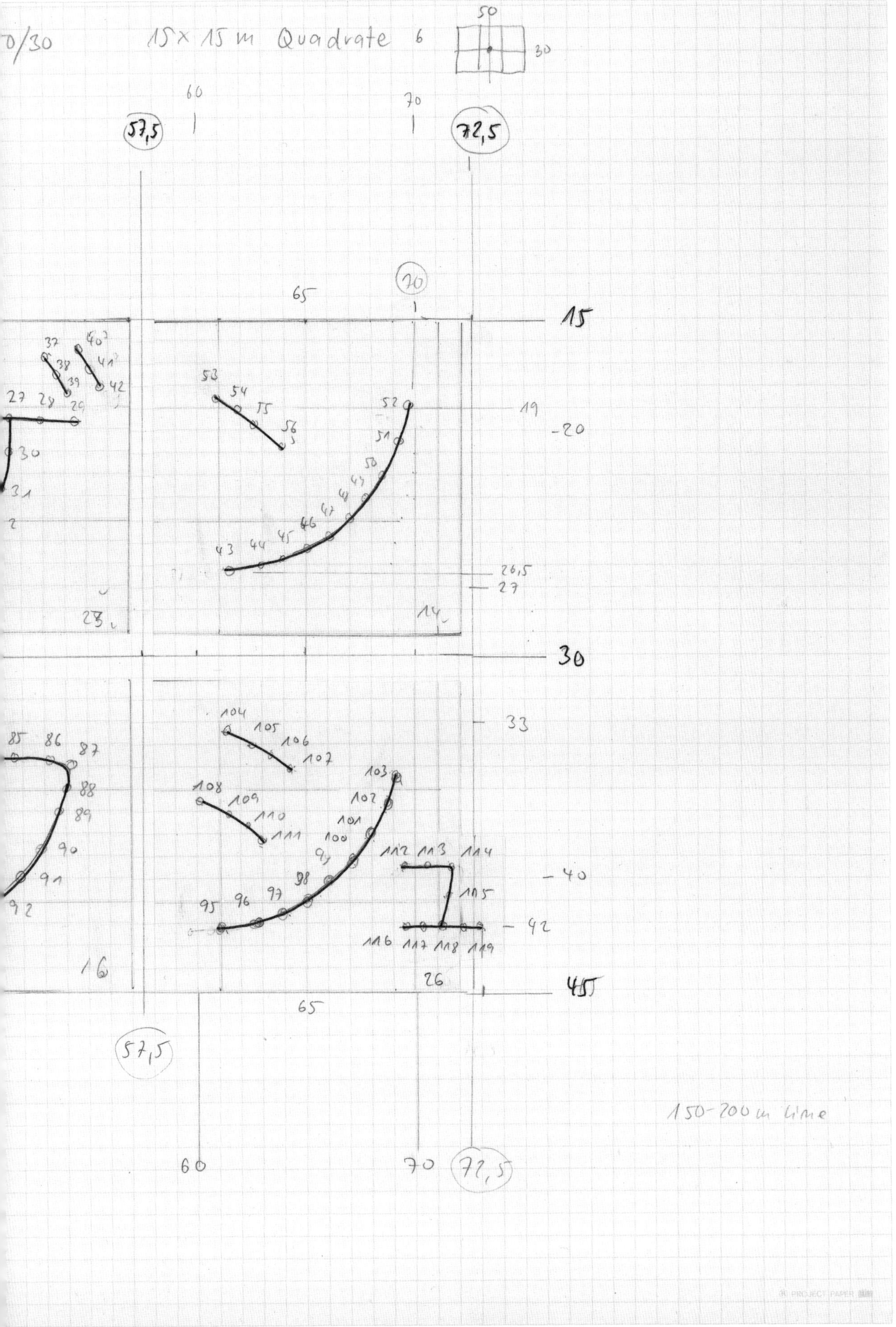
0/30
15 × 15 m Quadrate 6
50
30
60
70
57,5
72,5
70
65
15
19
20
26,5
27
28
14
30
33
40
42
16
26
45
65
57,5
60
70
72,5
150–200 m Linie

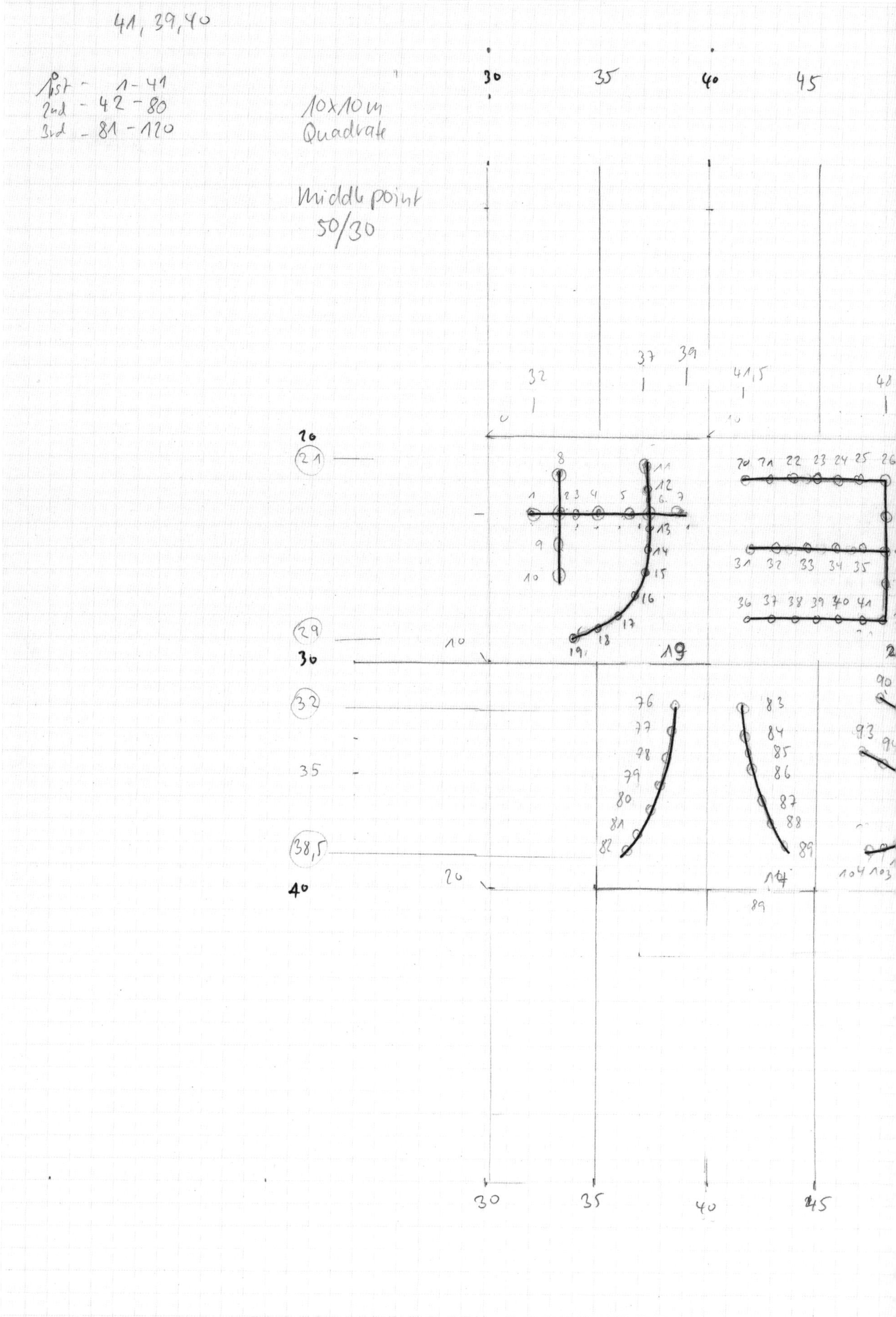

41, 39, 40
1st - 1-41
2nd - 42-80
3rd - 81-120
10x10 m
Quadrate
Middle point
50/30
30
35
40
45
20
21
29
30
32
35
38,5
40

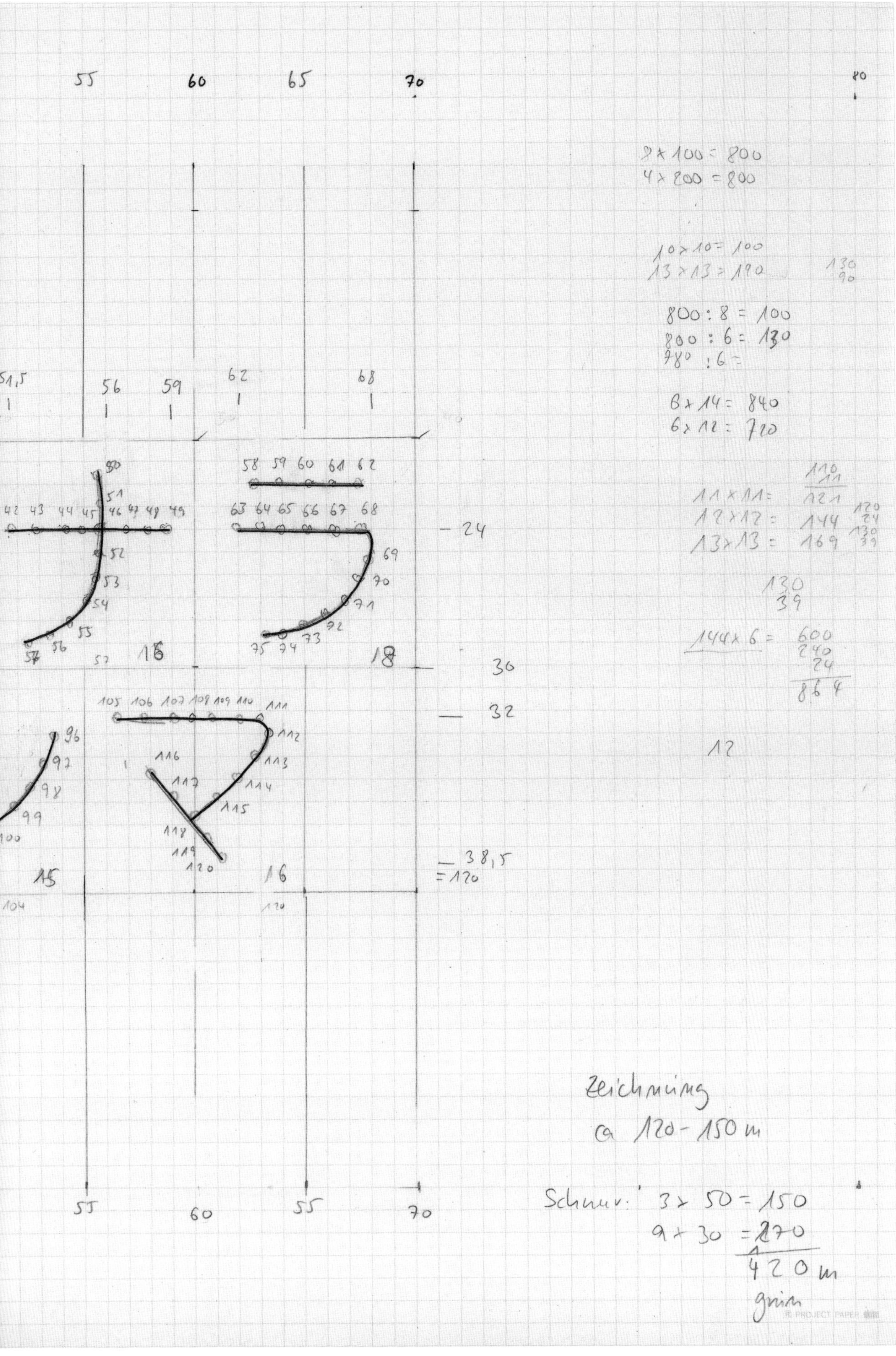

8 × 100 = 800
4 × 200 = 800
10 × 10 = 100
13 × 13 = 170
800 : 8 = 100
800 : 6 = 130
6 × 14 = 840
6 × 12 = 720
11 × 11 = 121
12 × 12 = 144
13 × 13 = 169
144 × 6 = 864
Zeichnung
ca 120-150 m
Schnur: 3 × 50 = 150
9 × 30 = 270
420 m
grün

Honami Ono, High School Student

小野ほなみ、高校生

00:05:43 The story, I think, is set in Japan in the future, society has gone mad. Children, without hesitation, beat people up or kick them and stuff at schools, so it became really out of control.

物語はたぶん未来の日本なんだと思うんですけど、世の中が荒れ狂ってて、子供たちとかも学校とかで普通に人を殴ったり蹴ったりとか教師刺したりとかして、教師も手に負えなくなっちゃってる世界だと思うんですよ、その日本は。

00:05:46 The government then tried to change this, and set such a law as Battle Royale Act where children kill each other.

その政府が子供たちを変えようと思ったのかわからないんですけど、その政策でバトルロワイヤル法っていう法律みたいなのを作って子供たちをいきなり殺し合いさせるみたいなことがありまして。

00:06:40 The school (which the main characters go to), was selected by some kind of lottery. During their school trip, they were taken to an uninhabited island, and there they were introduced to this Battle Royale Act, and were told to kill each other. The students have always been violent, but they said killing was another story, so there was antagonism. They were threatened that, if they went against teachers, the necklace that they were made to wear would explode.

その主人公達の学校がそのバトルロワイヤル法の抽選みたいなものに当たってしまって、その修学旅行の途中でいきなり無人島に行かされて、そこでいきなりバトルロワイヤル法の話をされて、殺し合いをしてくださいっていうことを告げられるんですよ。

00:06:55 At first nobody wanted to kill each other, but slowly they went insane, and started to kill their friends without hesitation. That was scary.

最初はみんなすごい殺し合いとか嫌がってたんですけど、どんどん気が狂って友達とかもだんだん簡単に殺してくようになっていくあたりがすごく怖かったです。

00:07:20 In terms of Gunkanjima, the story was based on the island. In the beginning when the students were first taken to the island, they tried to run off and they sheltered at a water paddle at an elementary school site, which really existed on the island.

あと、軍艦島で言えばたぶん舞台が軍艦島をモデルにしてる感じで。最初、主人公達がその島にいたときに逃げるとき軍艦島に実際にあった小学校の下の水たまりみたいなところに避難してるんですけど、その軍艦島の荒れた感じがバトルロワイヤルの深刻さとかをすごい表してる感じがしました。

00:09:10 It's scary that humans can turn into anything and could do anything, and I thought it might have something to do with Gunkanjima. During the war they couldn't afford to build concrete houses in Japan, but Gunkanjima's resources were so rich that they could. I find it absurd that people could just abandon everything since the industrial revolution, and I thought it synchronised with the way students were killing each other in the film.

戦争中も日本はコンクリートの建物を建ててなかったのに軍艦島だけは建てるぐらい繁盛してたみたいなのに、産業革命が起こってからいきなりその財産をいきなり捨てていく人間の行動とかが非常識。それがバトルロワイヤルの友達を殺し合うのとリンクしてるんじゃないかと思いました。

00:10:57 Also by making it a world heritage site, I hope that people will think about the island more and more, and that even a place as New York could be like another Gunkanjima in the future.

世界遺産みたいなのに登録して、登録できたら、世界中の人が軍艦島についていろいろ考えるようになって、アメリカのニューヨークとかもいつかああなっちゃうのかなと考えるキッカケになればいいんじゃないかと思います。

00:09:58 I read on the Internet that they were trying to save it as a world heritage site to show how such prosperity could lead to such tragedy, such human foolishness, like the Hiroshima Dome.

インターネットで調べて知ったんですけど、世界遺産に登録して、人間の行い、盛り上がったというか、今は繁栄しててもいつかこうなるみたいなそういう人間のおろかさみたいなものを伝える遺産、日本にある原爆ドームみたいな役割を果たしてくれるんじゃないかと思っています。

00:11:35 I am also interested in the state of the island before it perished and it would be interesting for kids in Japan to read about it or see it in mangas and so on.
I did some research about Gunkanjima for this occasion as I became interested in it, so I would also like to make something about the island.

軍艦島の滅びる前の街の様子とか、それもすごい気になる。漫画とかが出れば、今の日本の子どもも興味を持つんじゃないかと思います。わたしも今回軍艦島に興味を持ったんでいろいろ調べて、わたしの作品もそういう軍艦島の良さを持ったようなものをつくりたいなと思います。

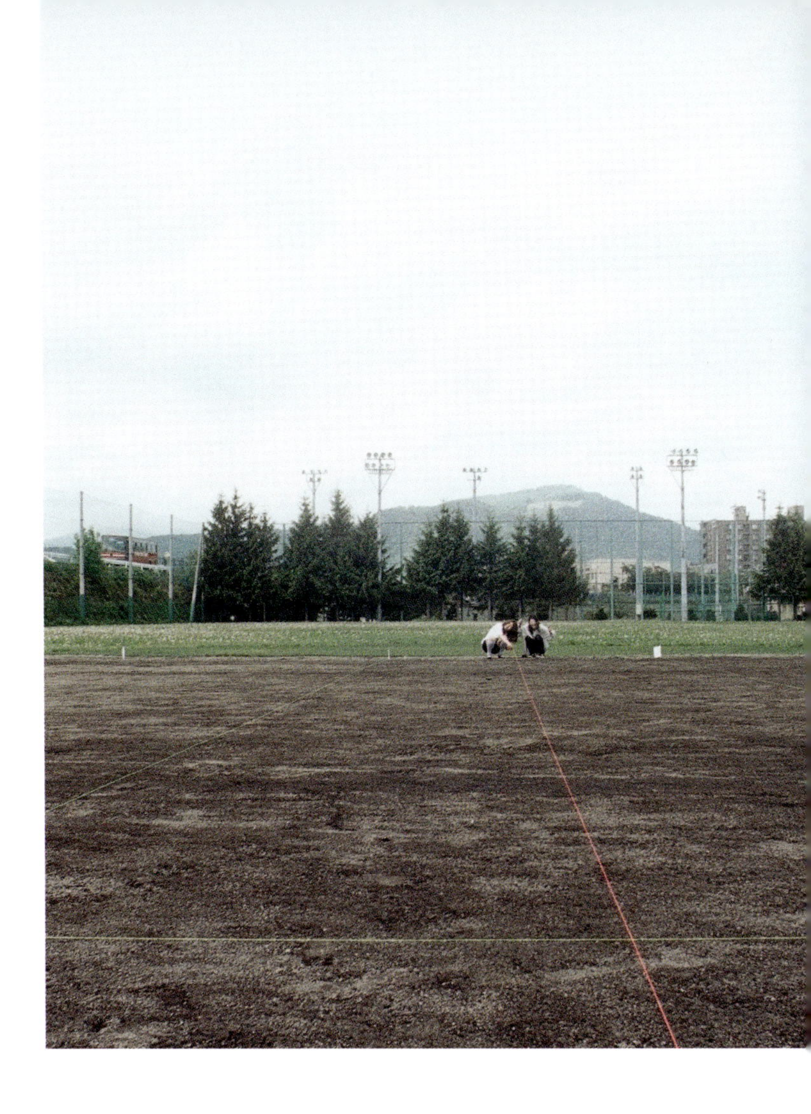

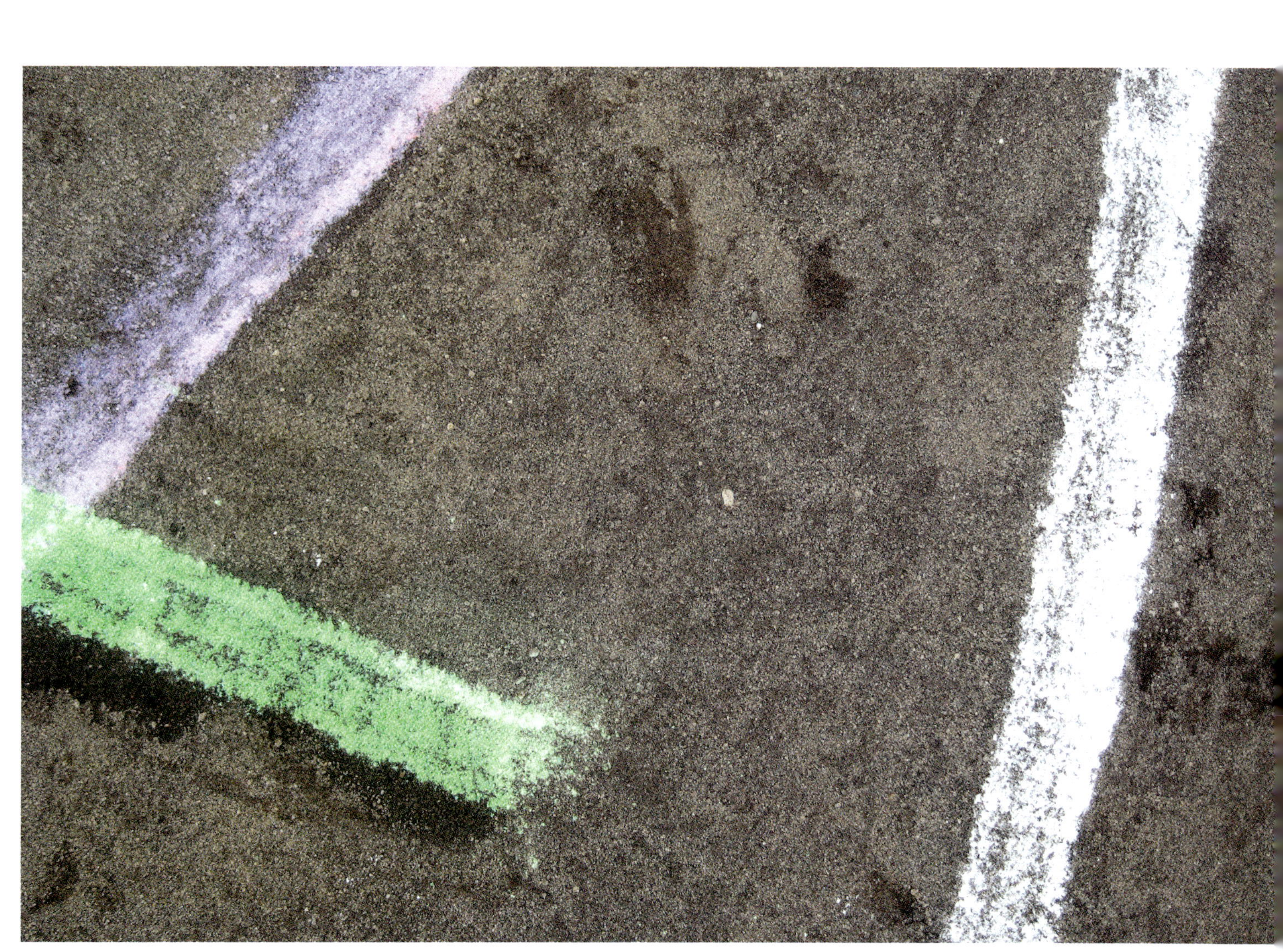

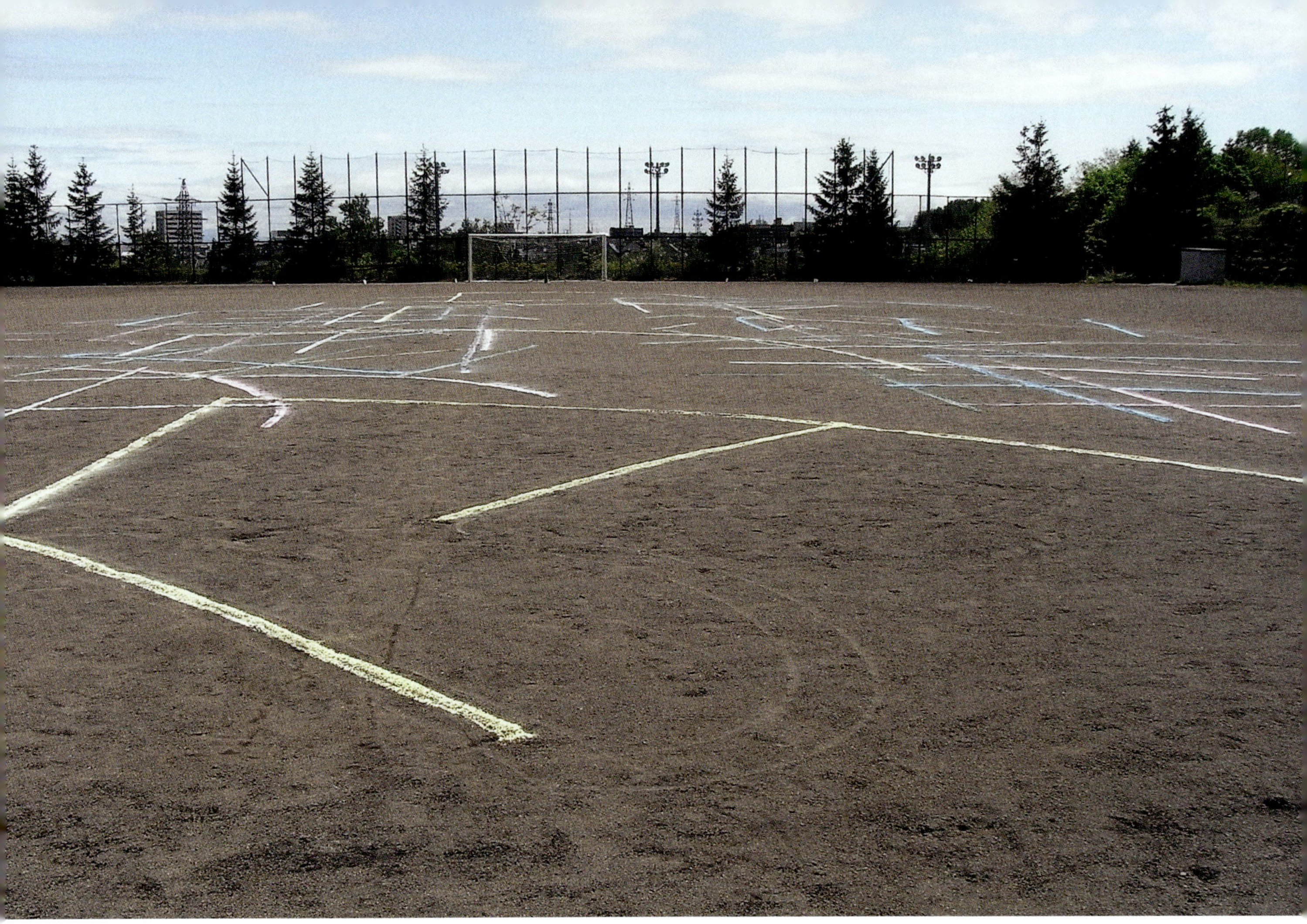

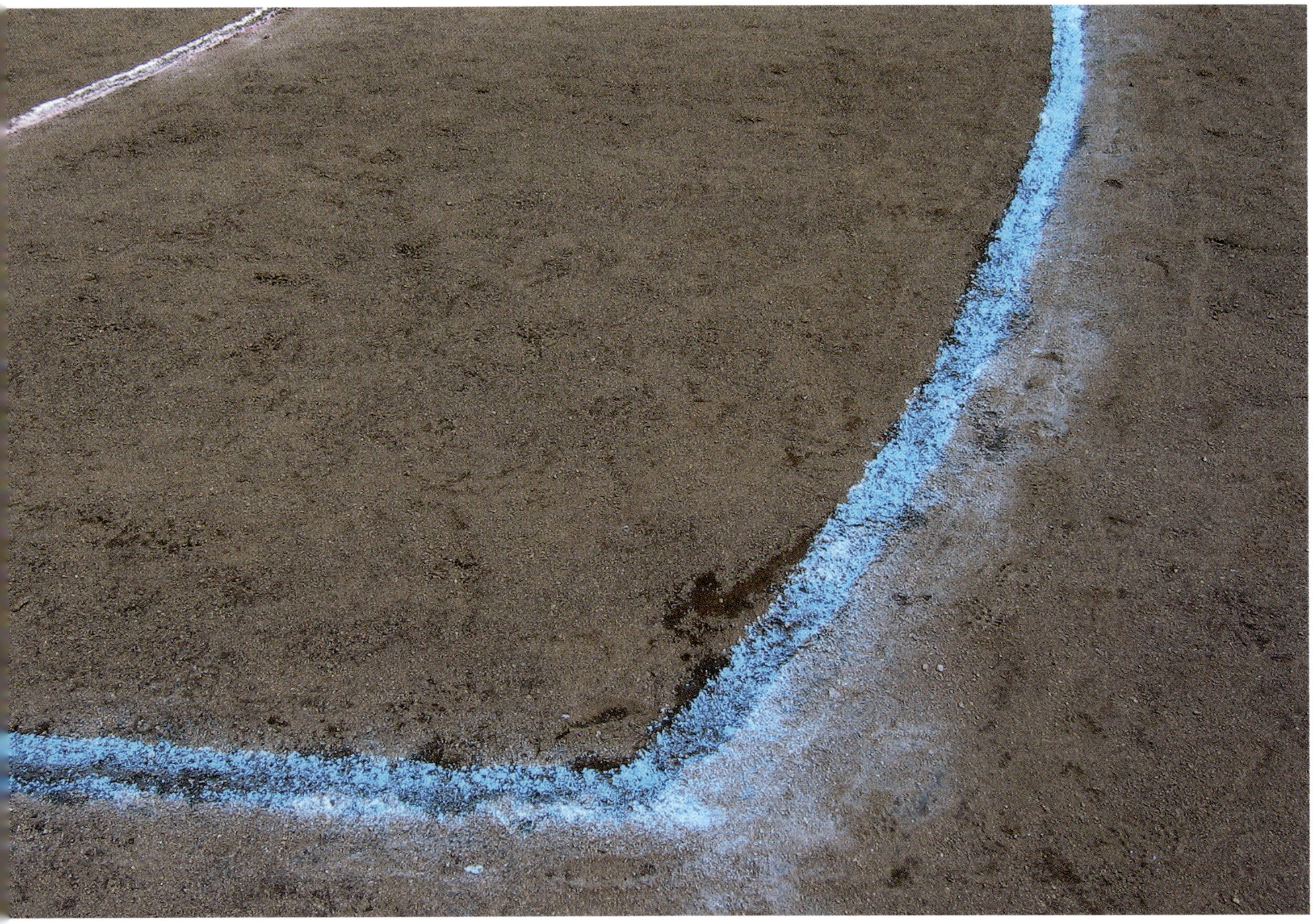

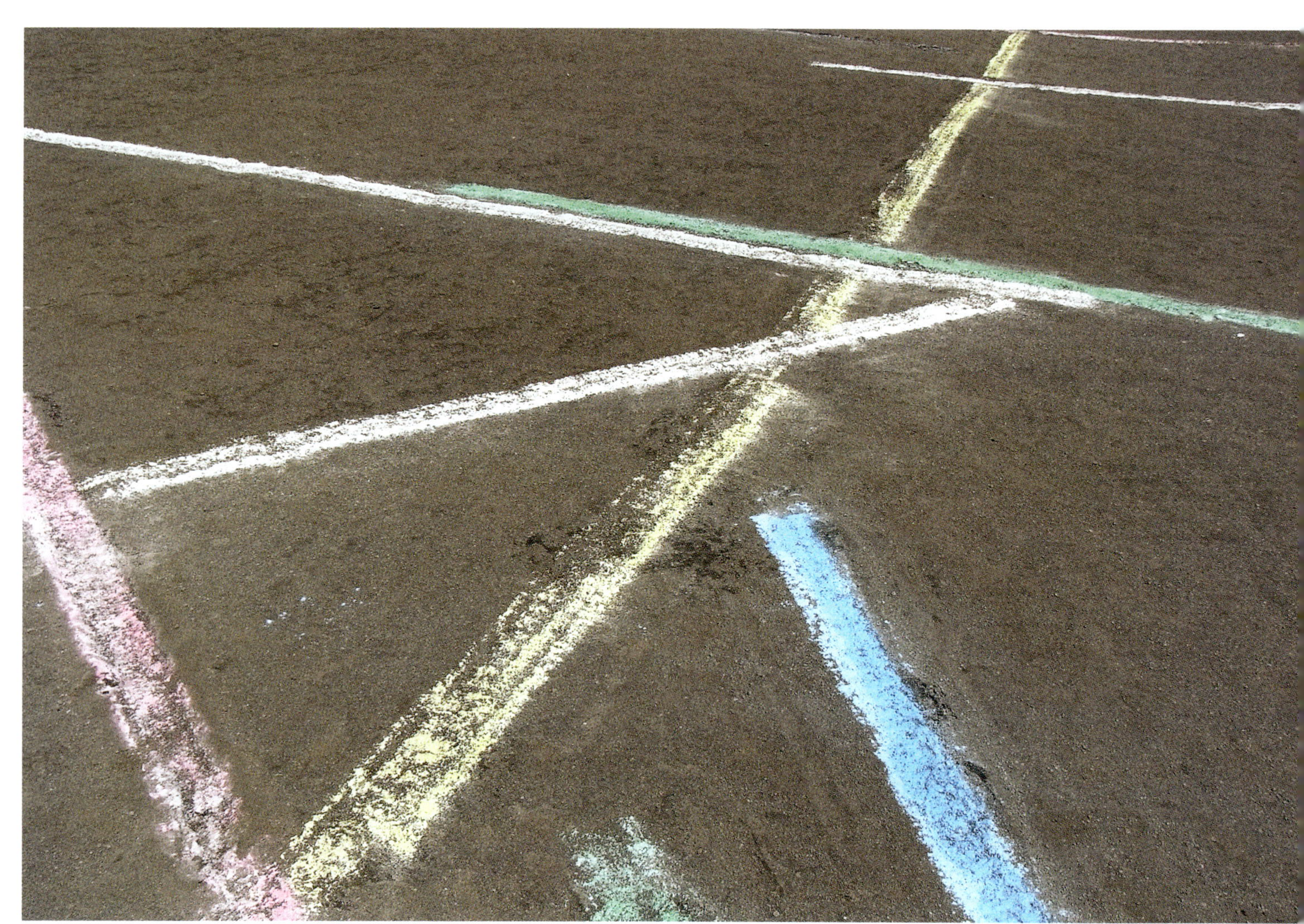

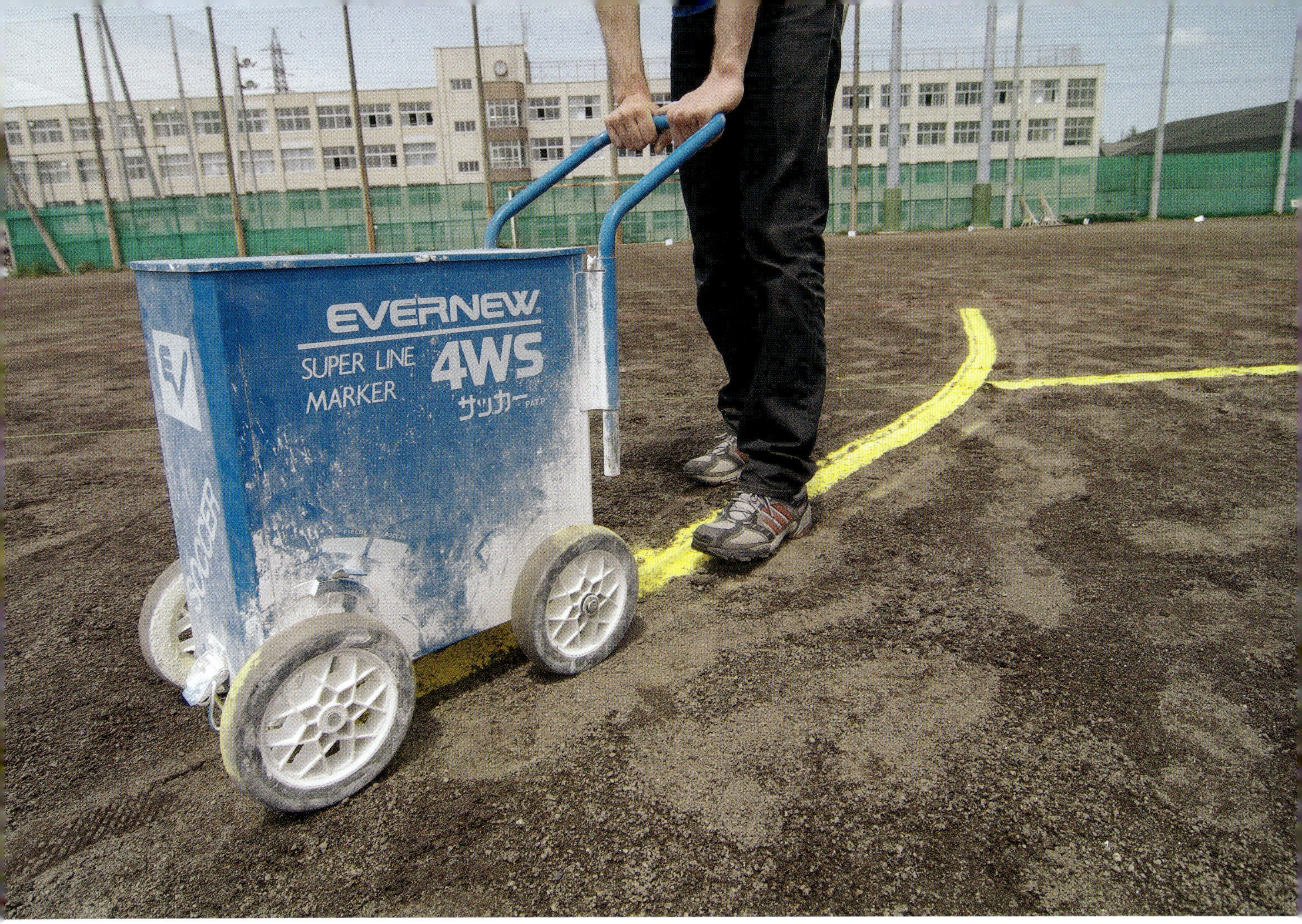

EVERNEW
SUPER LINE
MARKER
4WS
サッカー

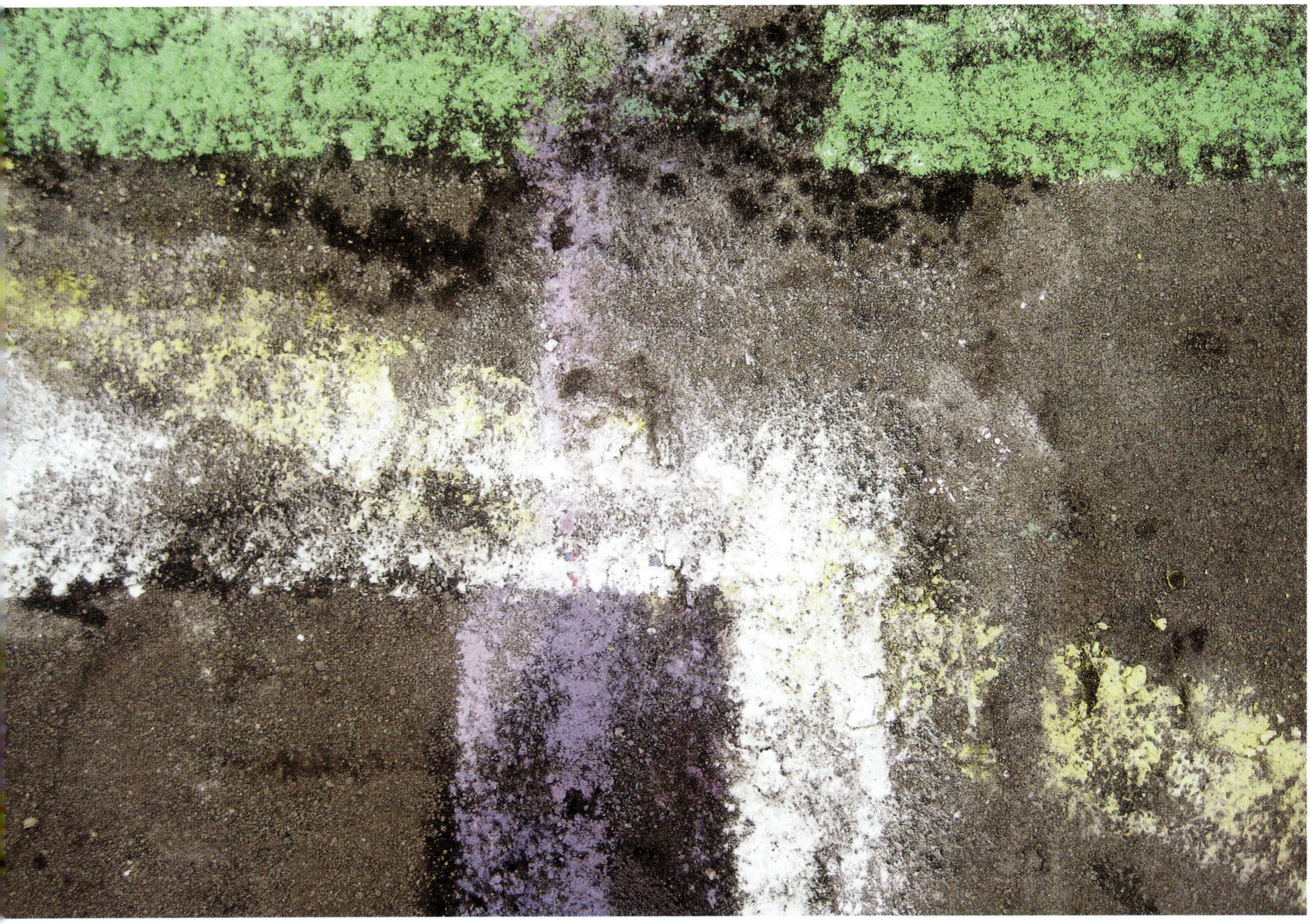

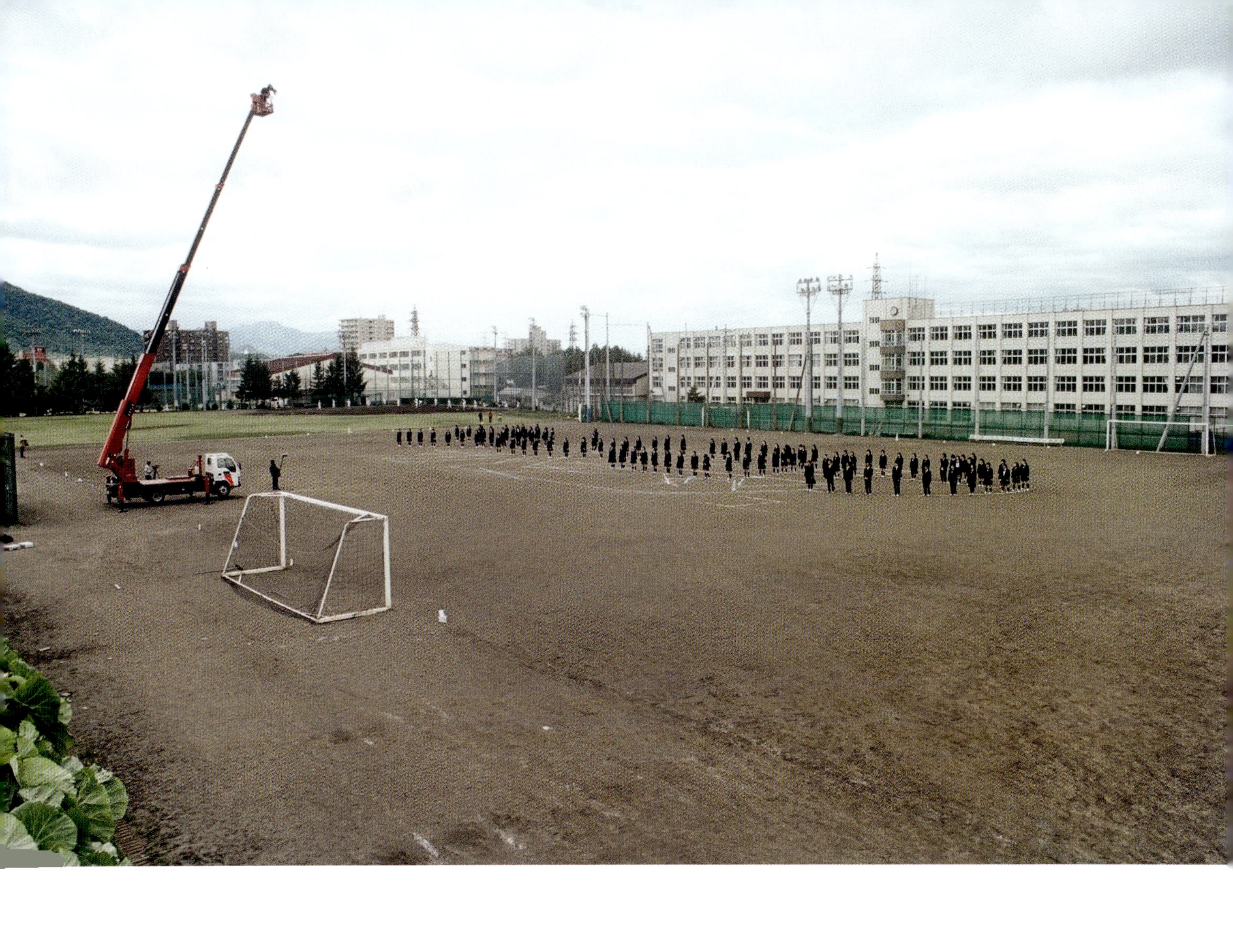

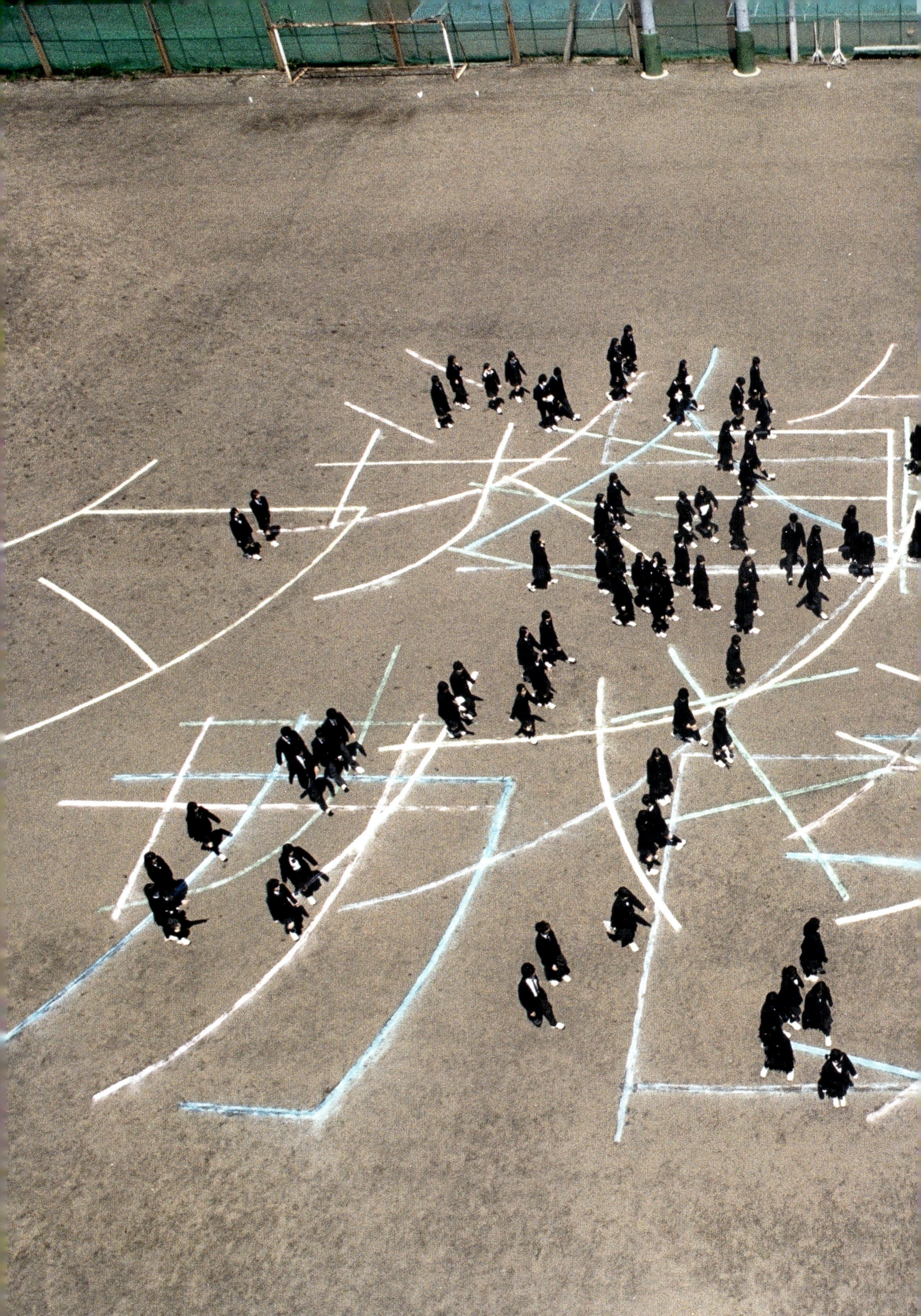

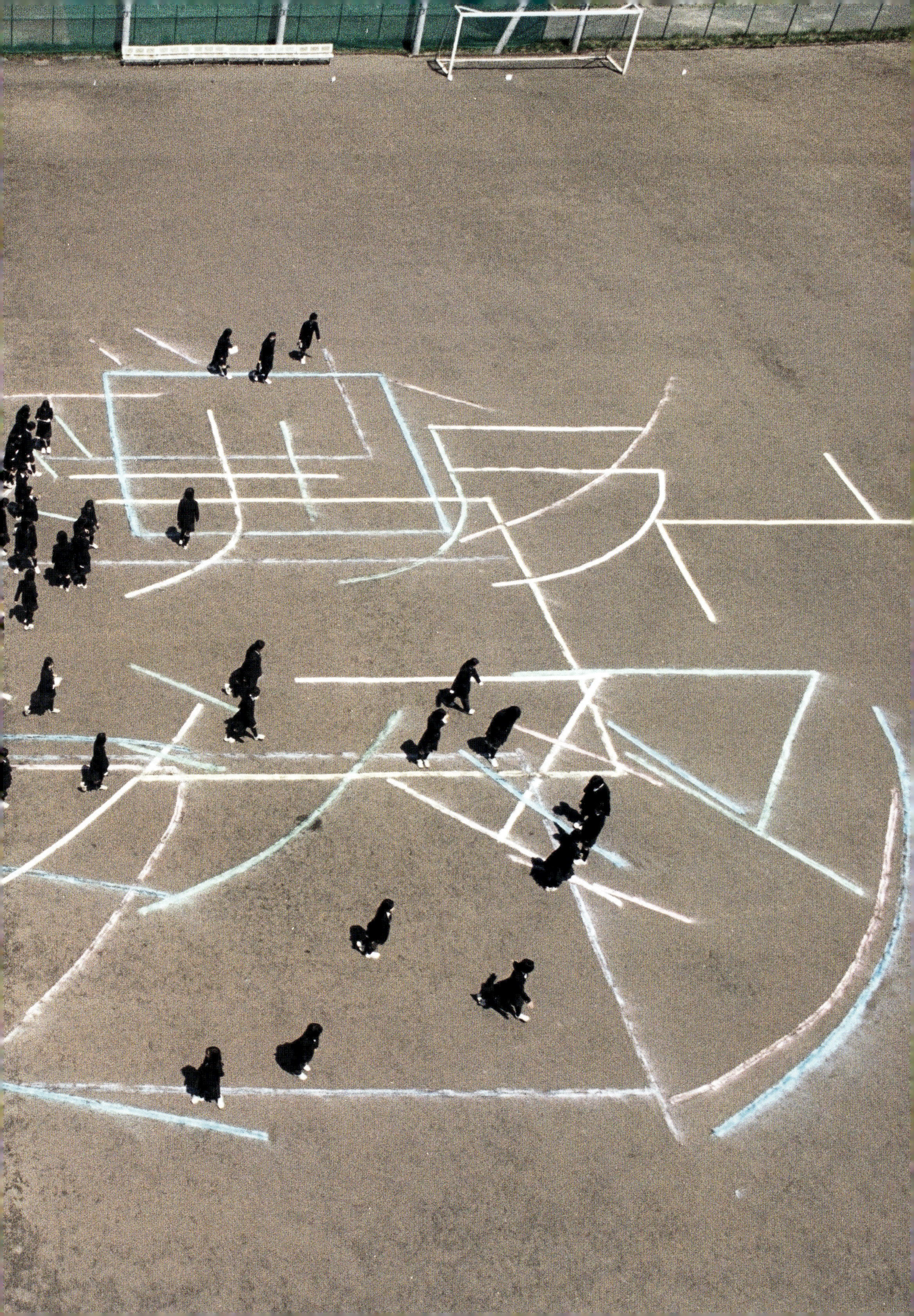

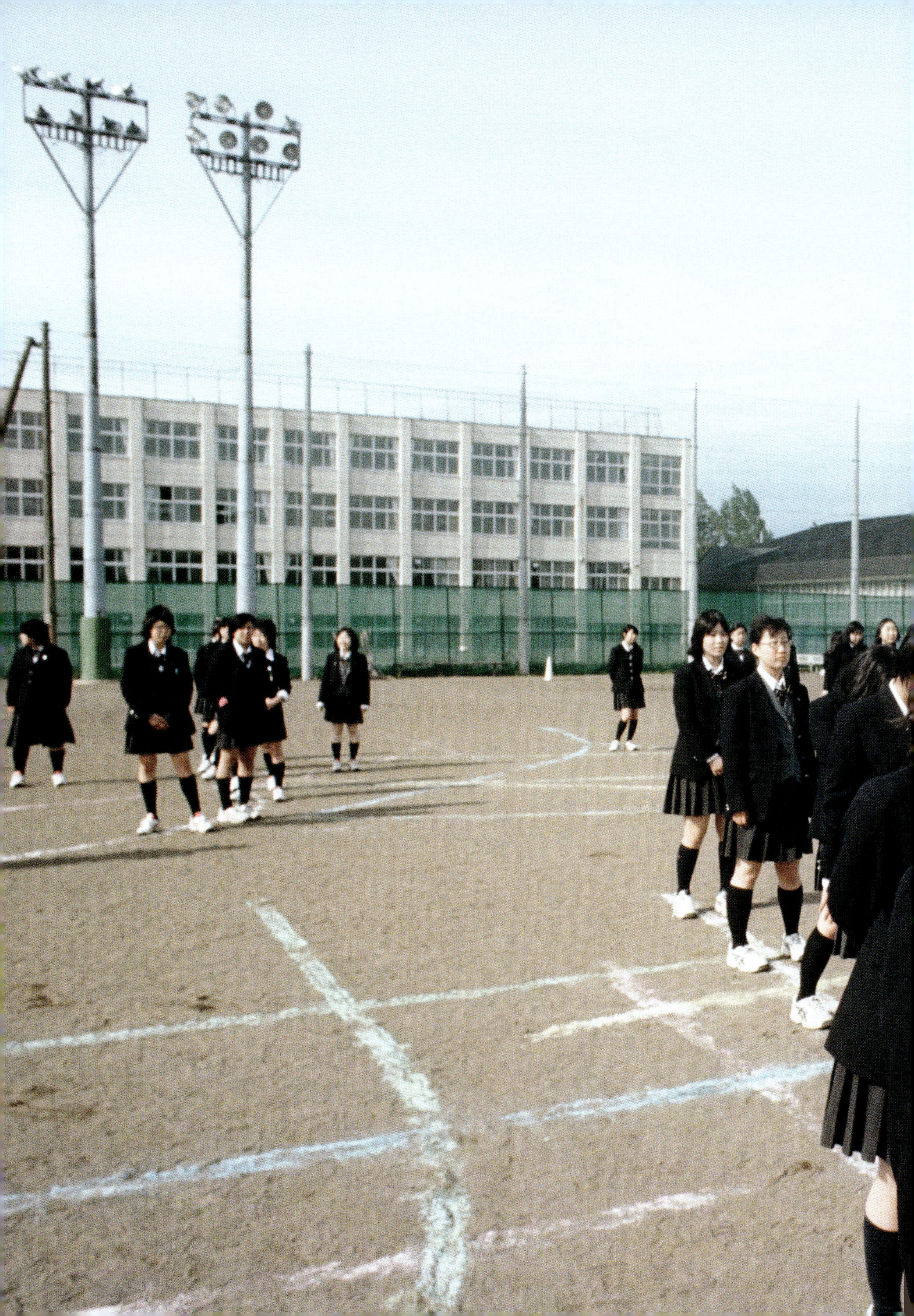

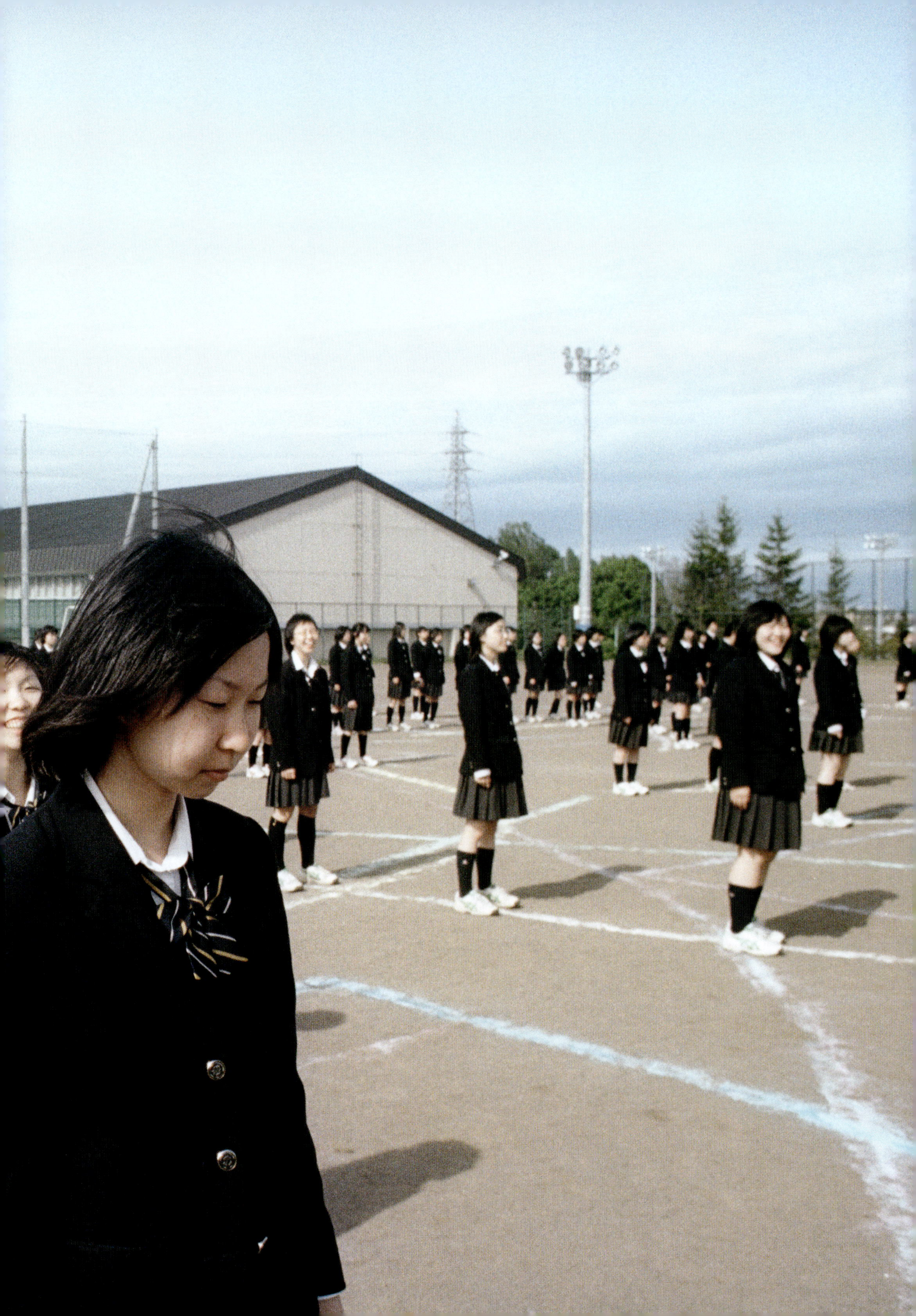

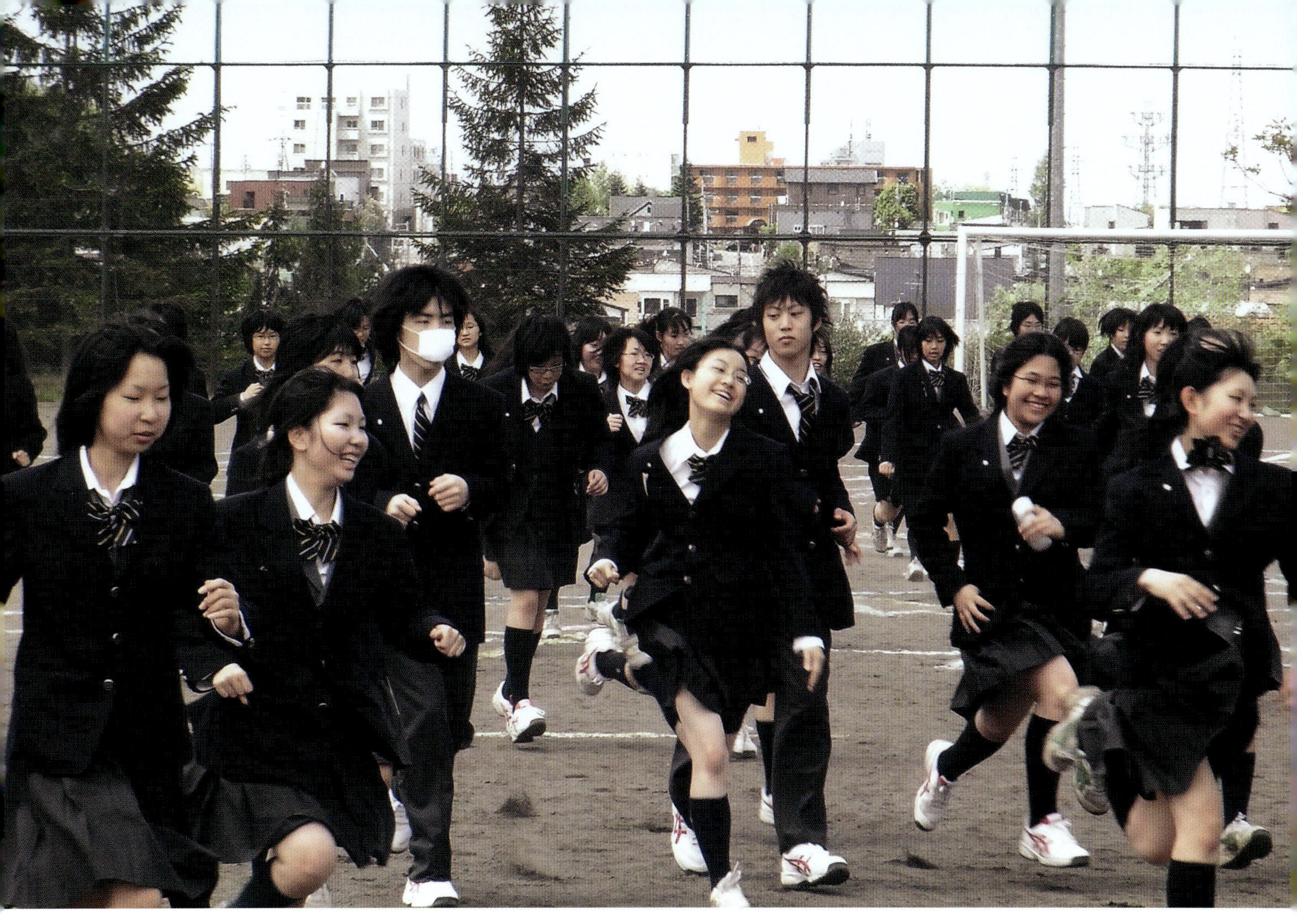

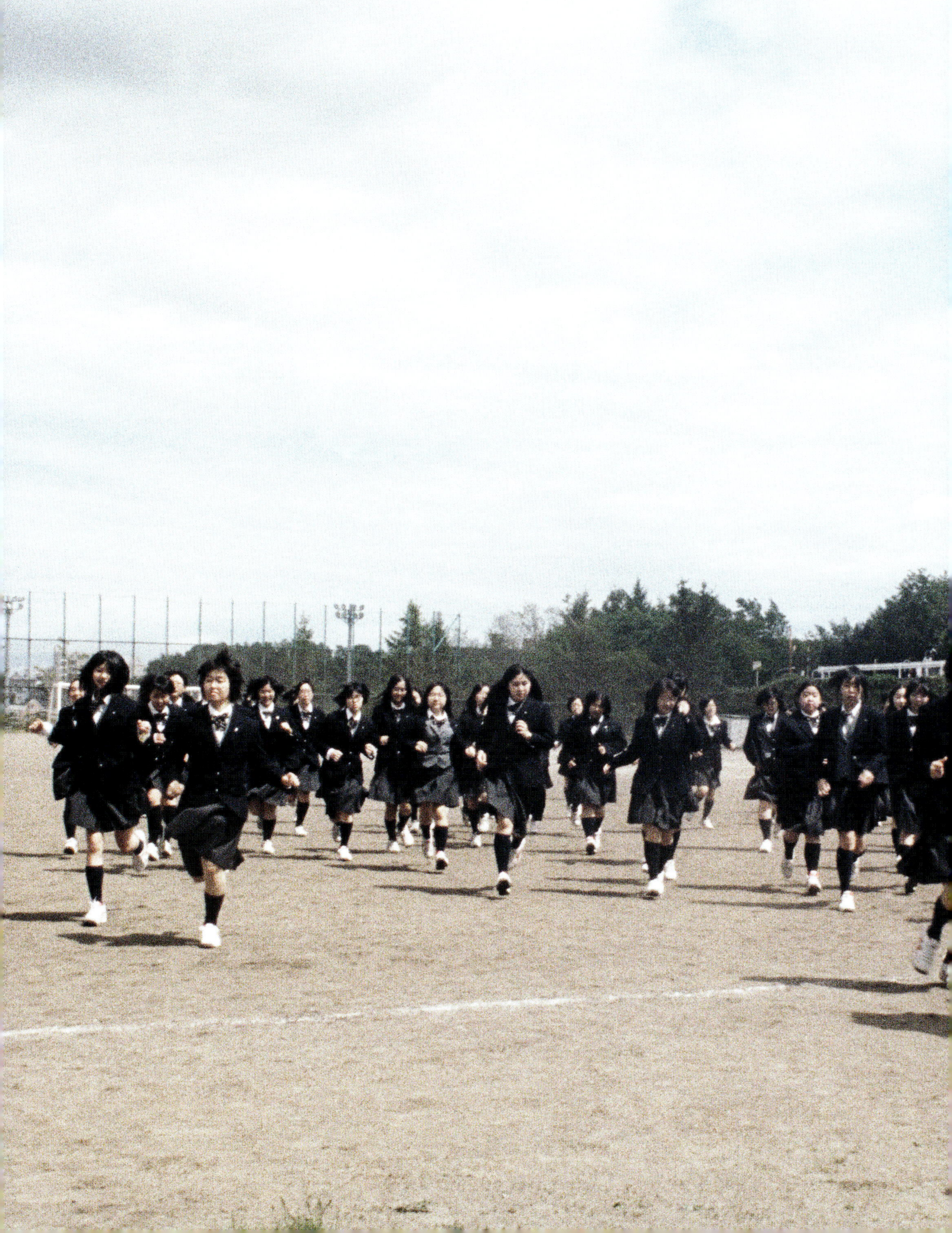

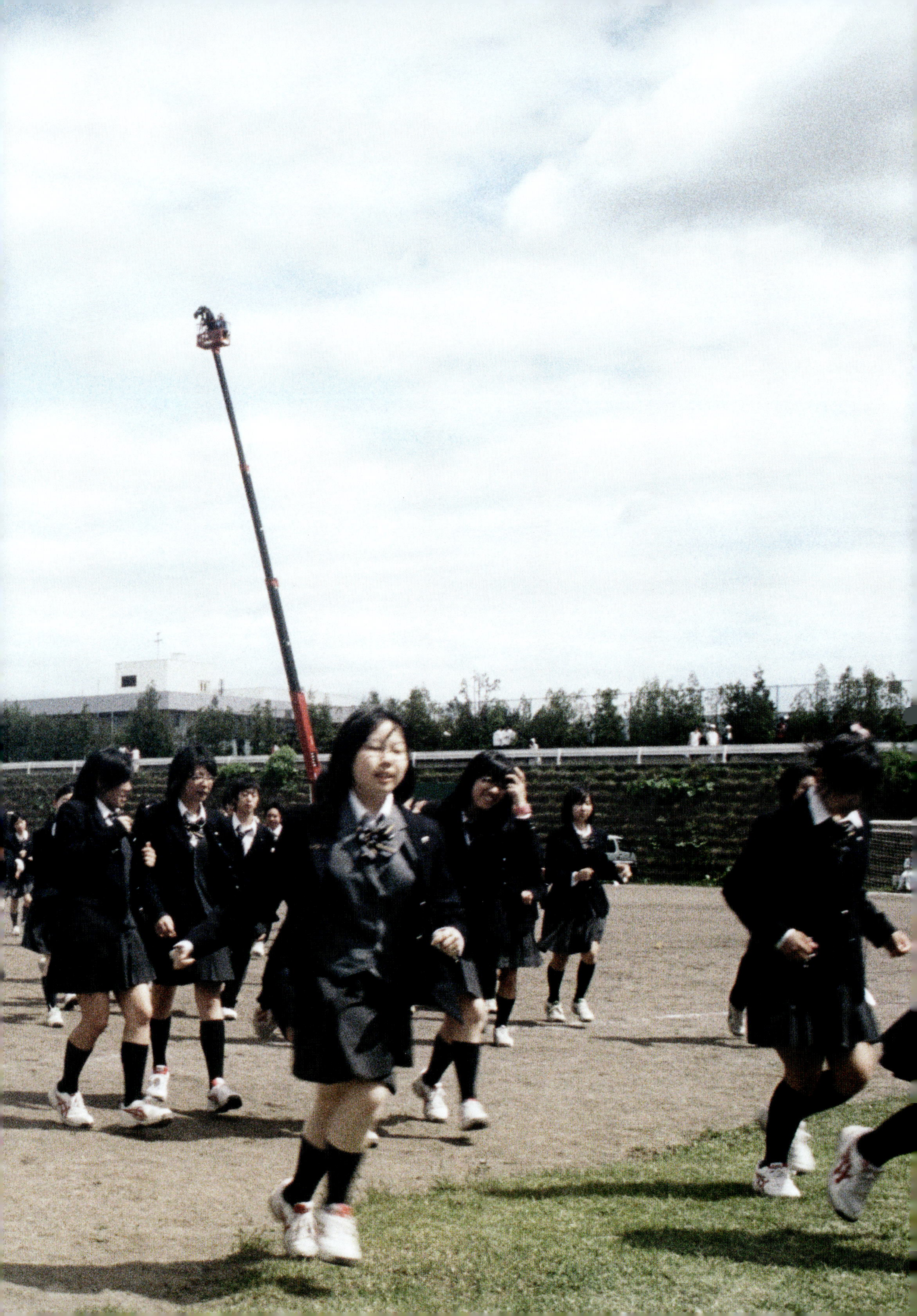

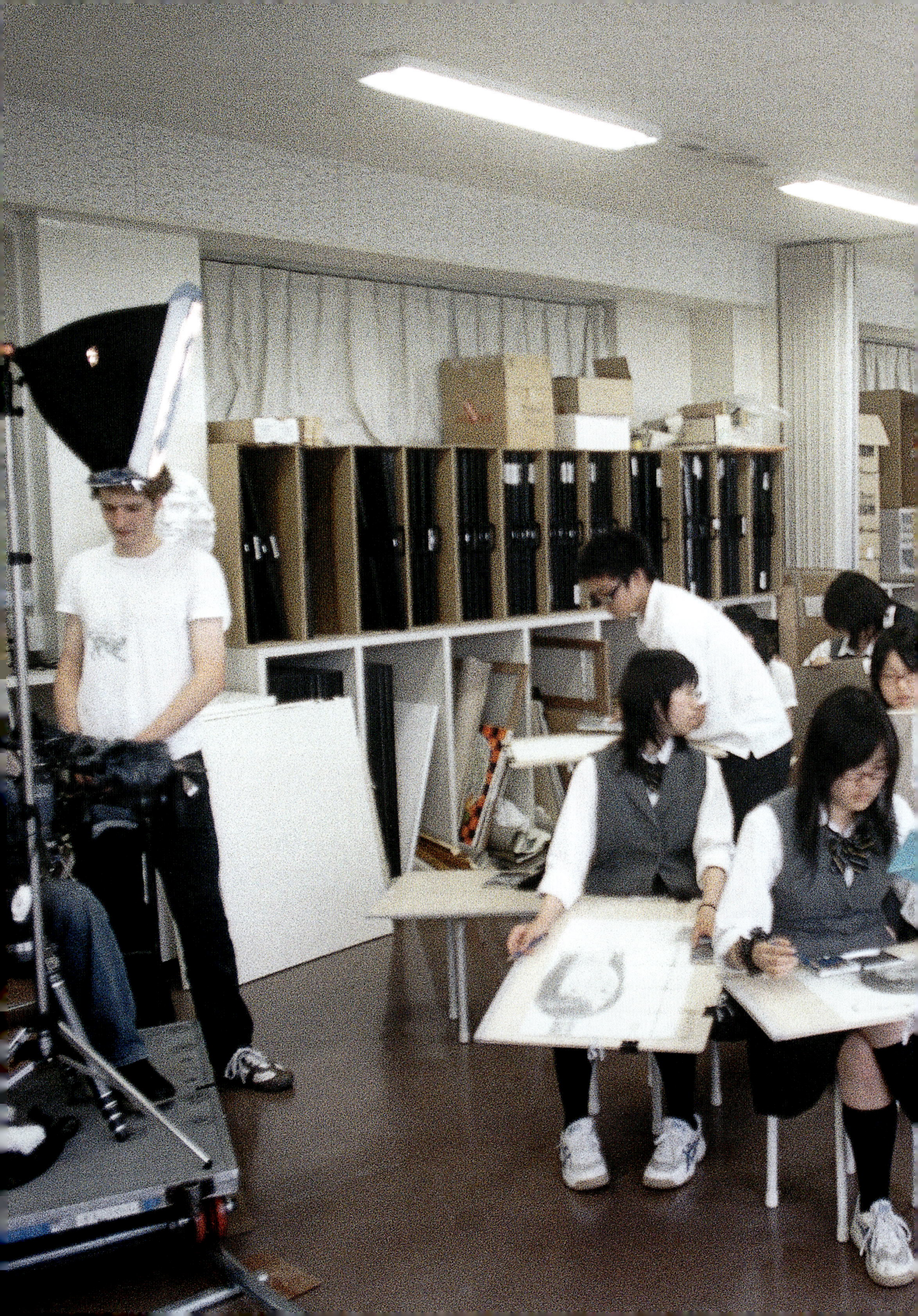

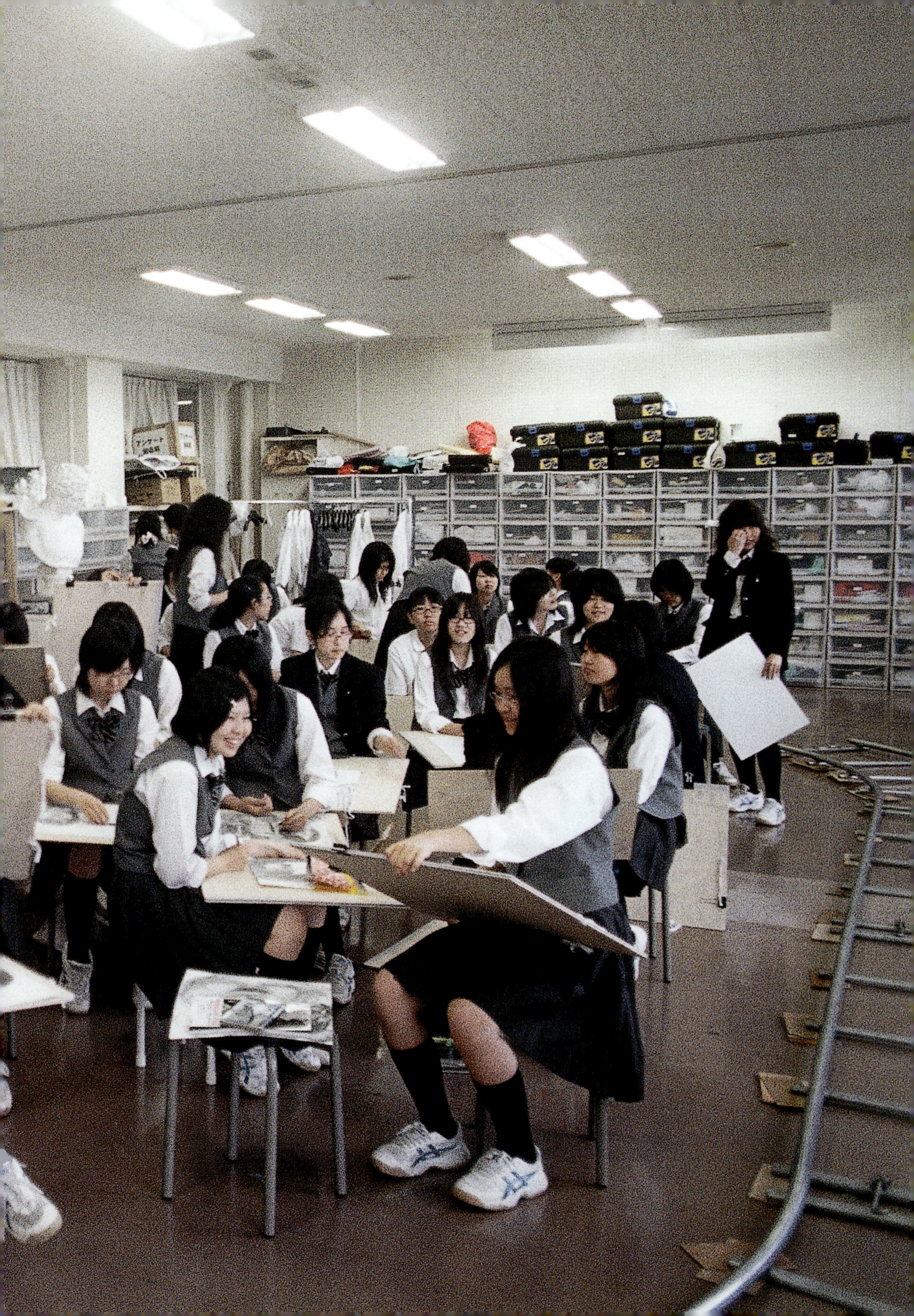

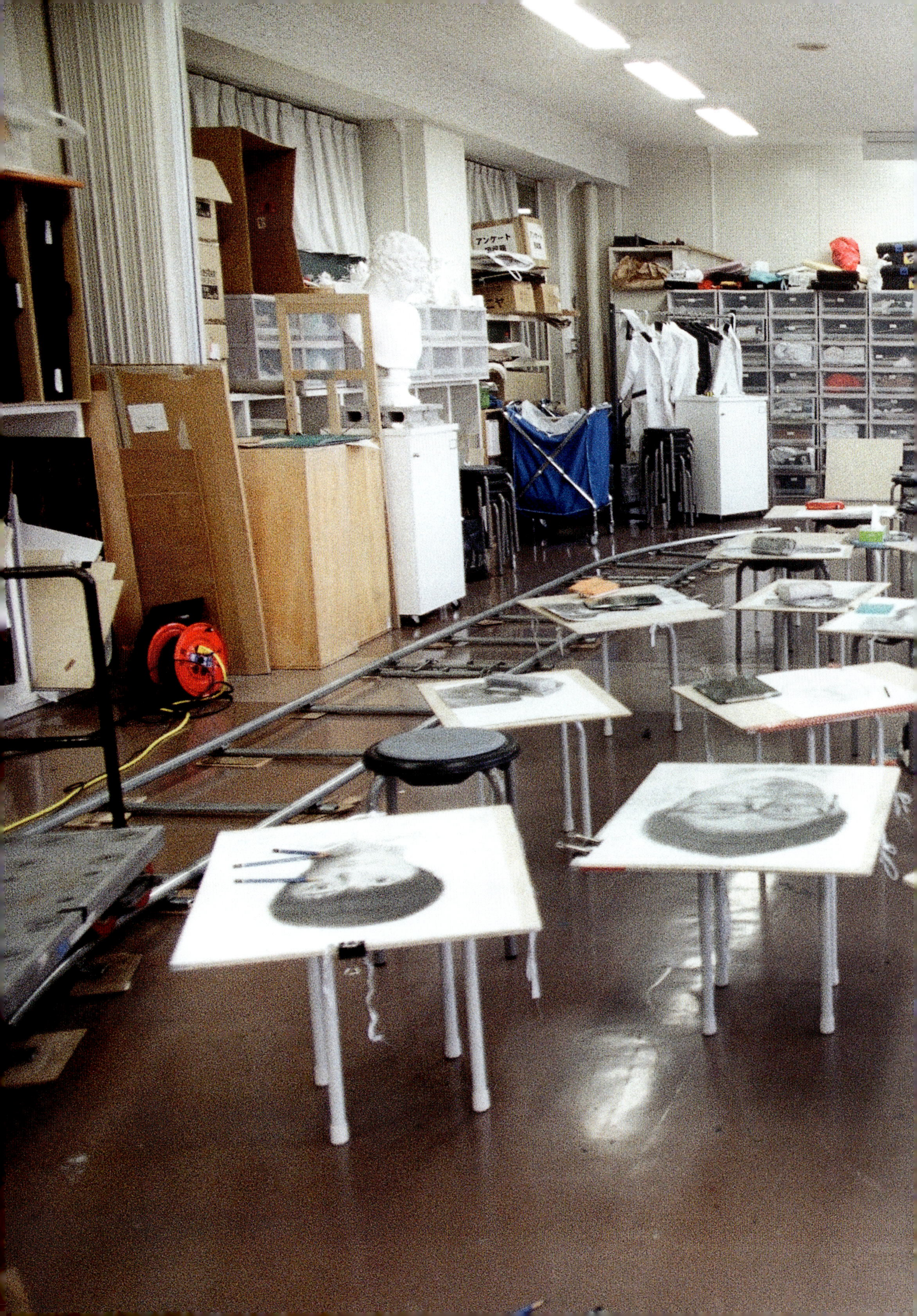
アンケート

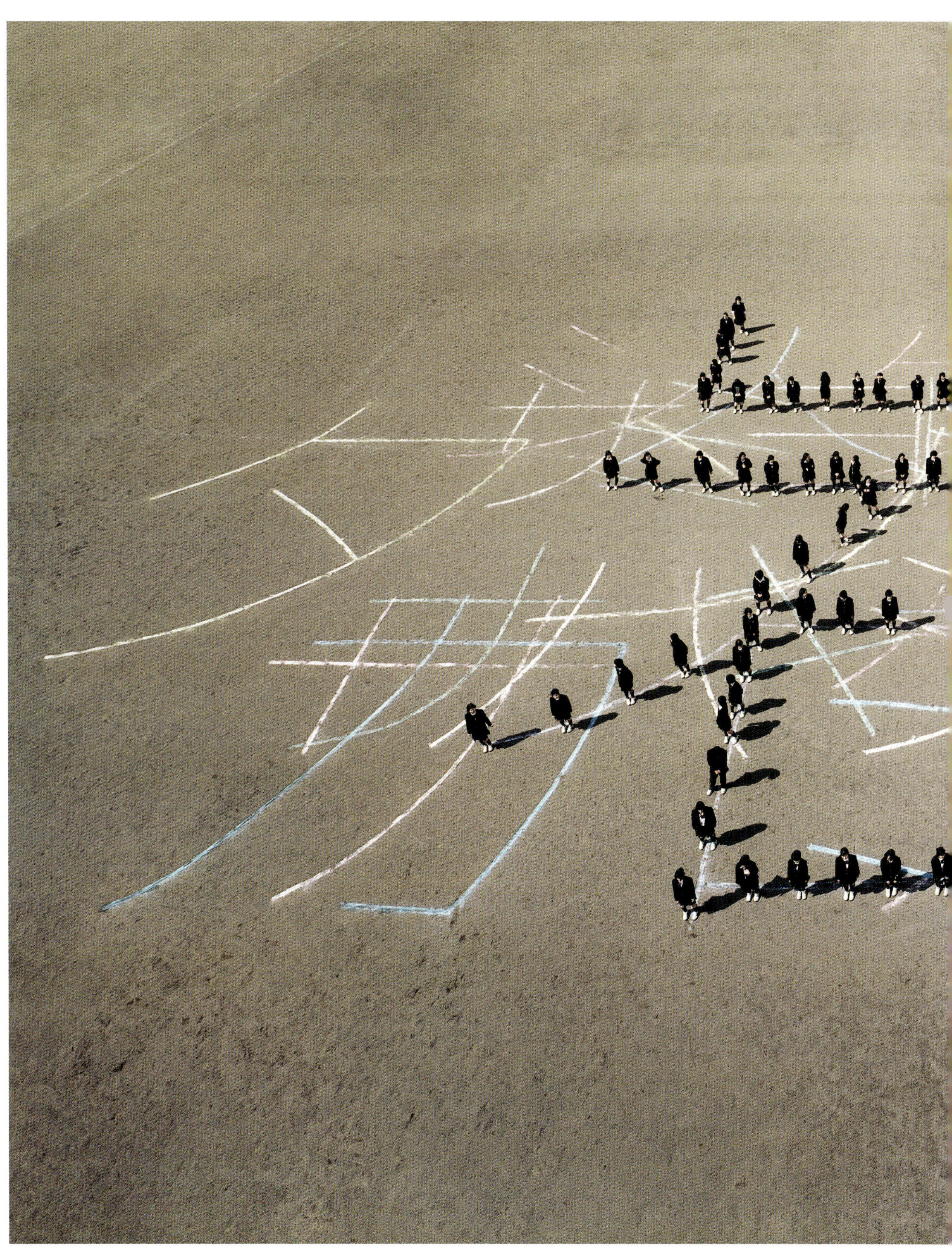

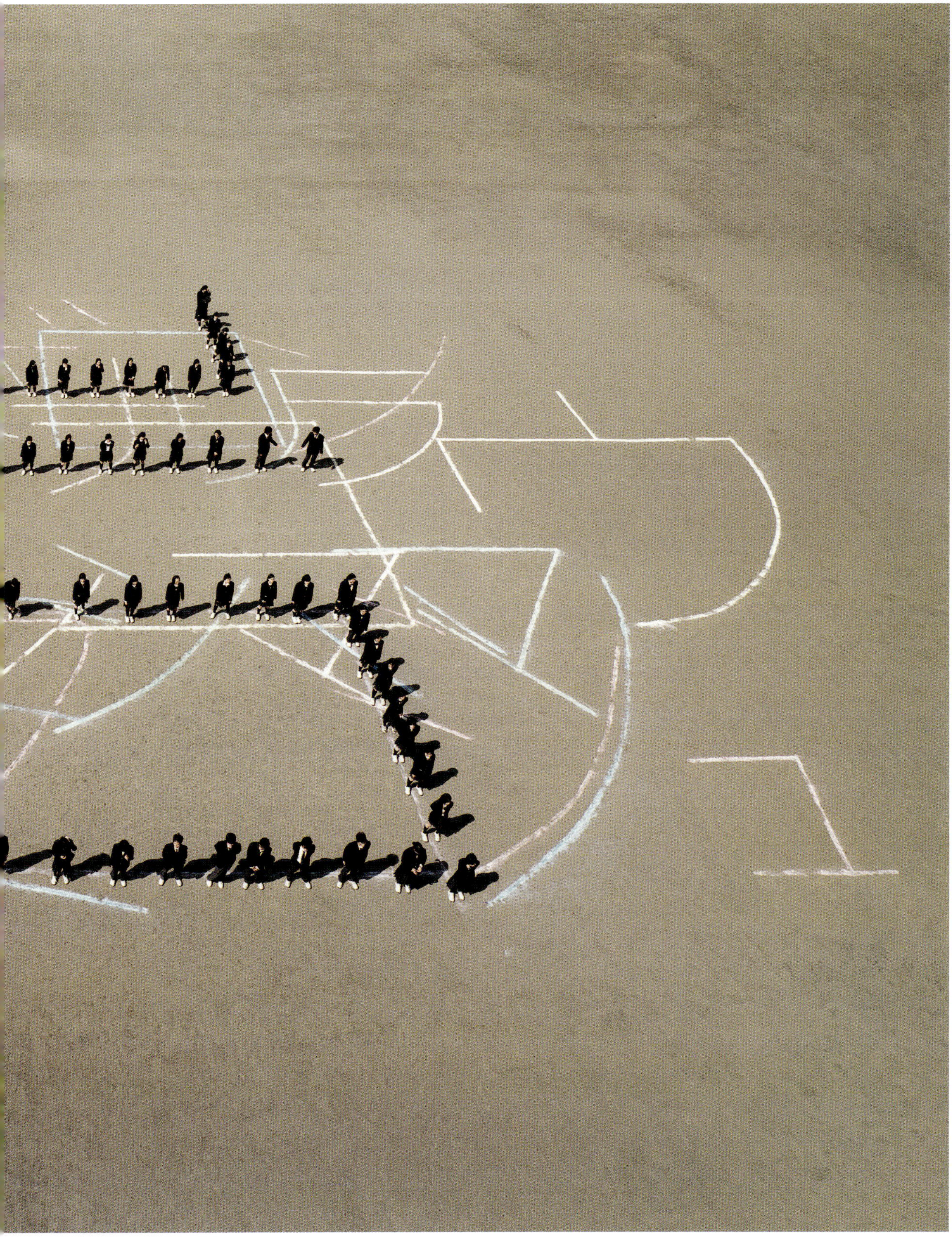

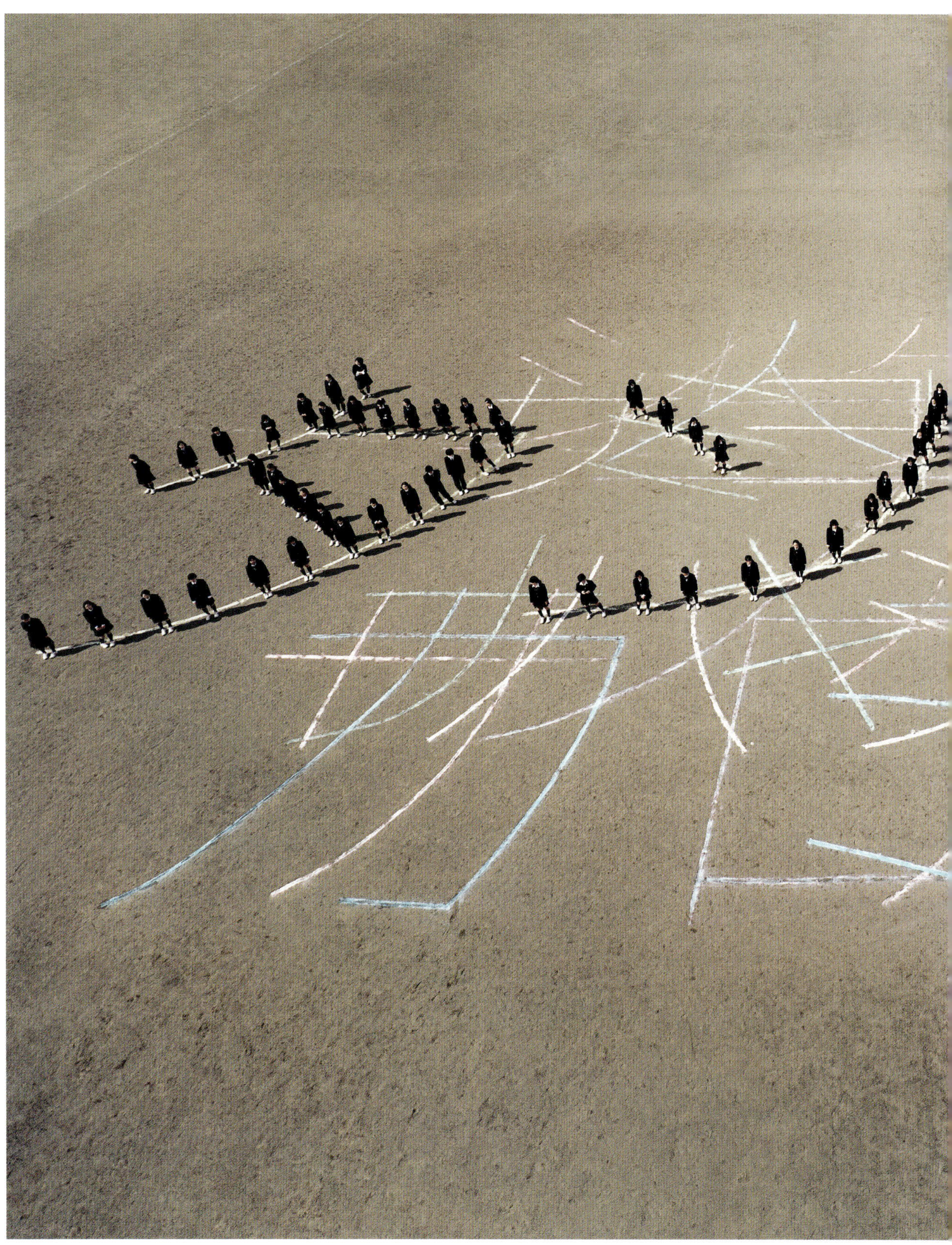

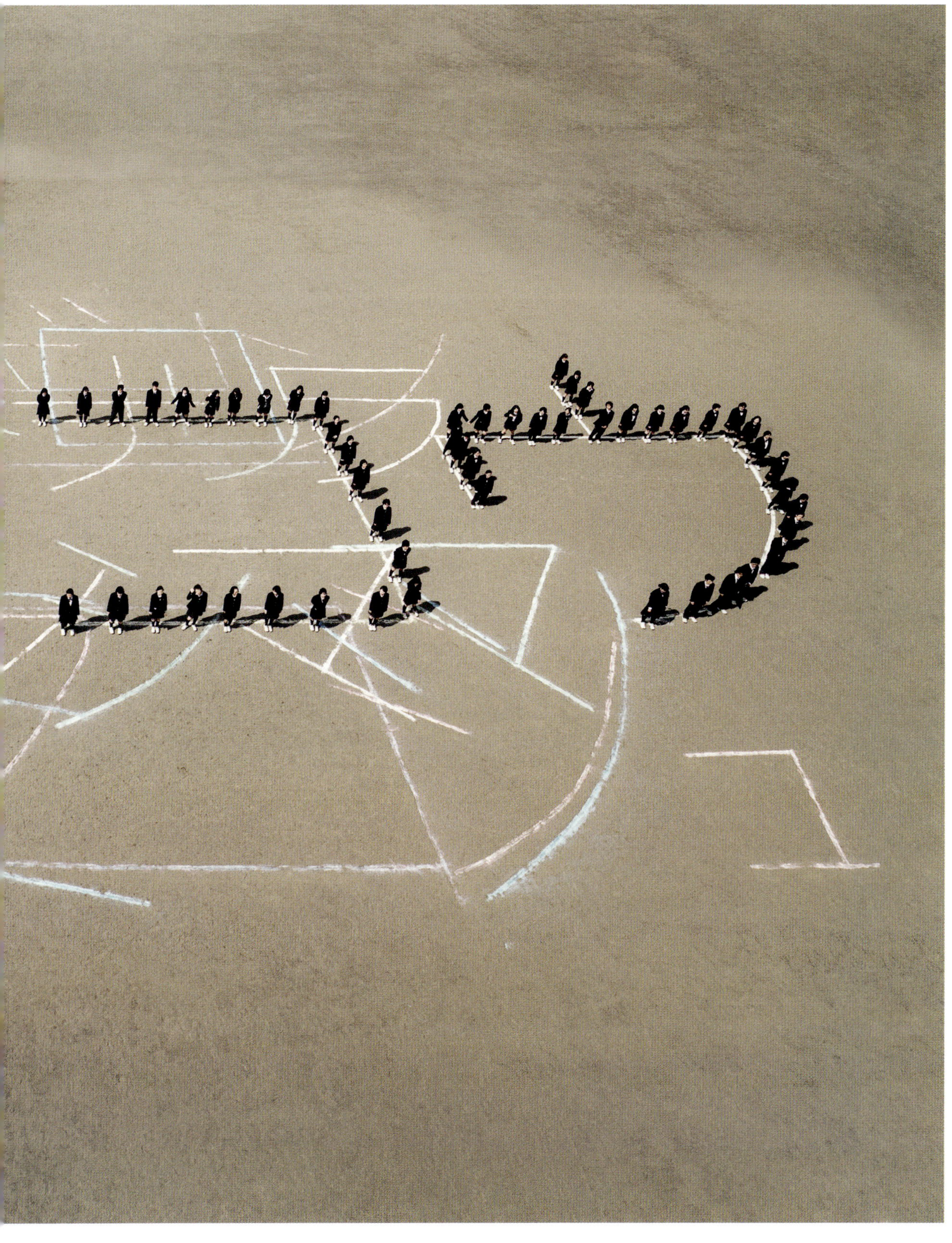

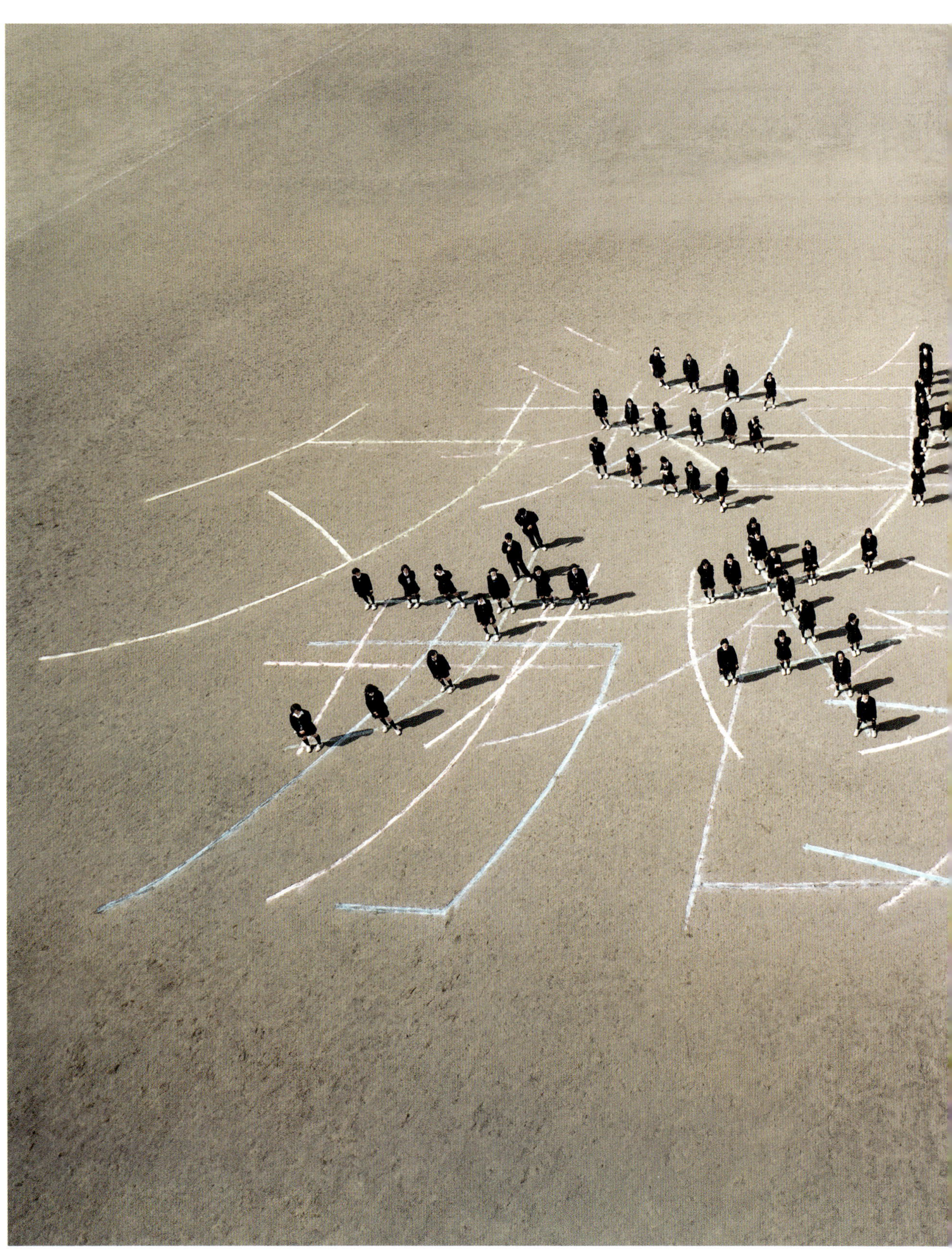

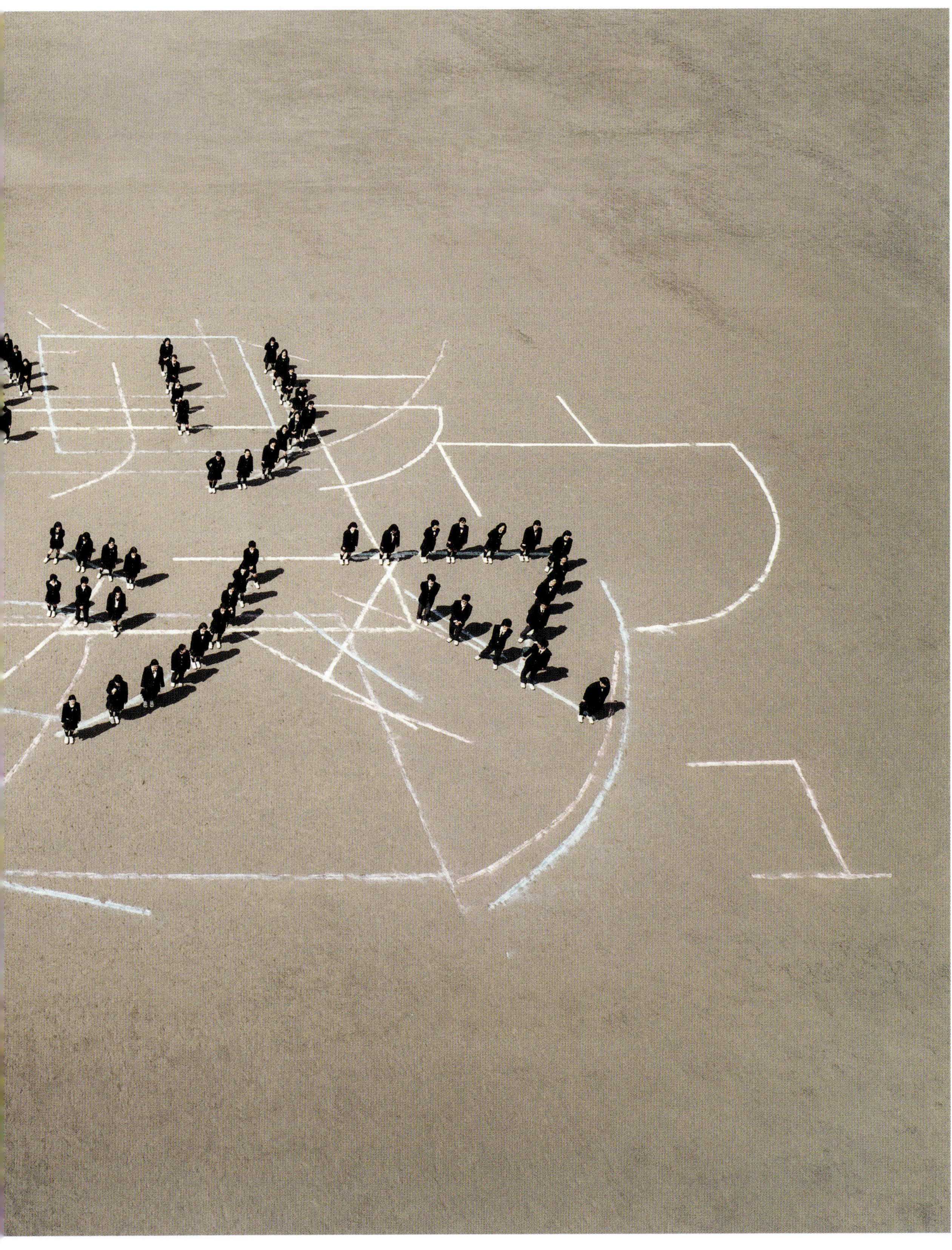

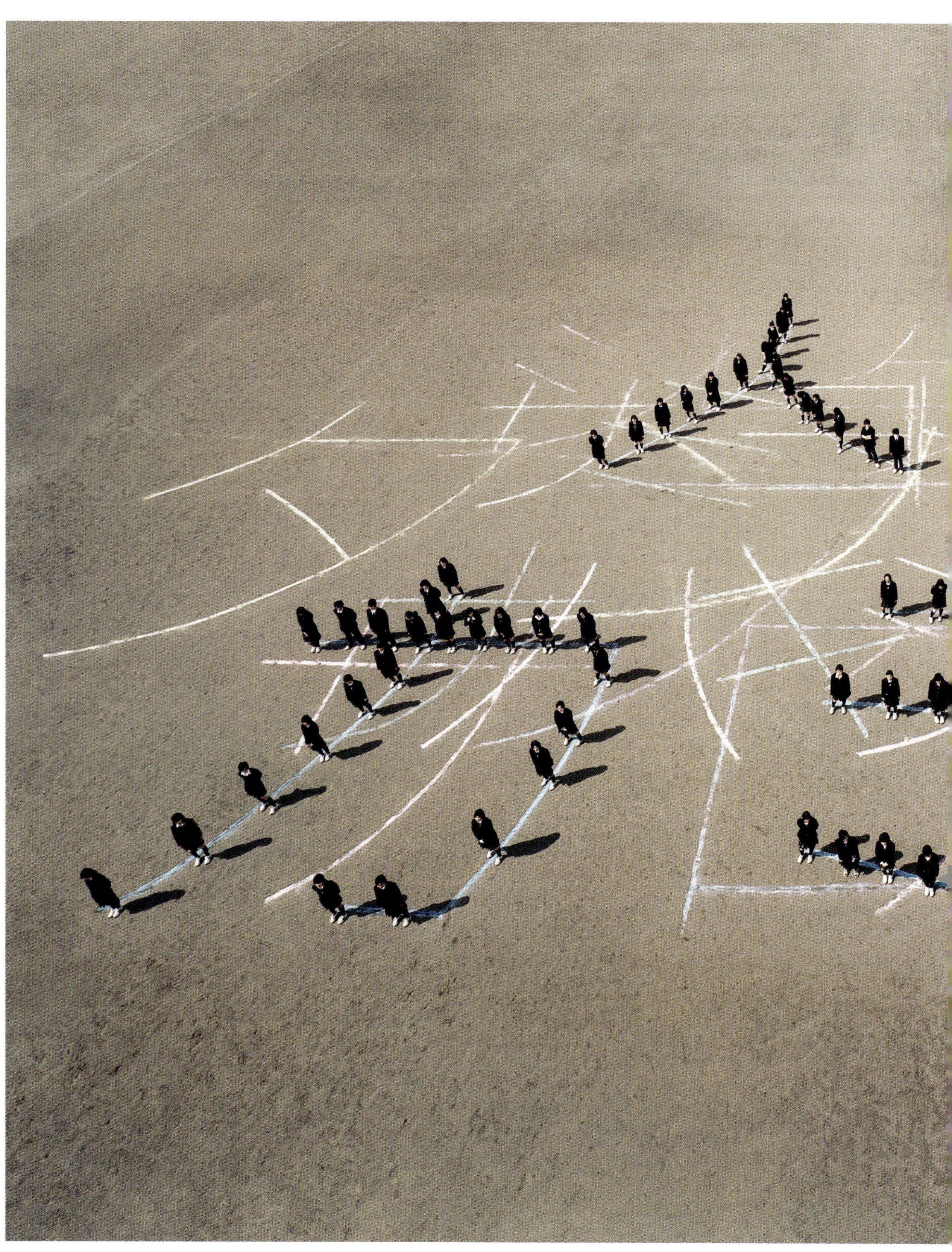

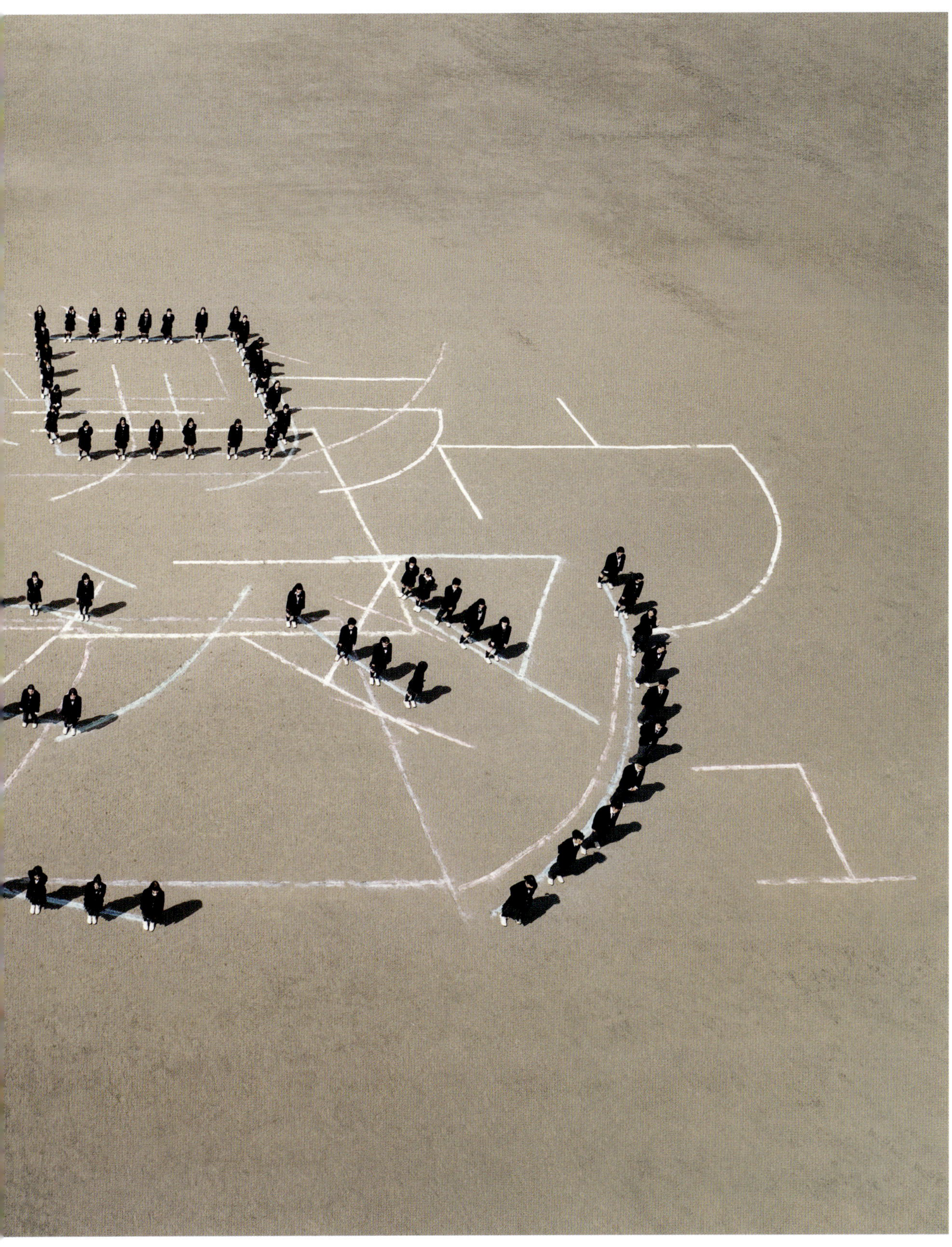

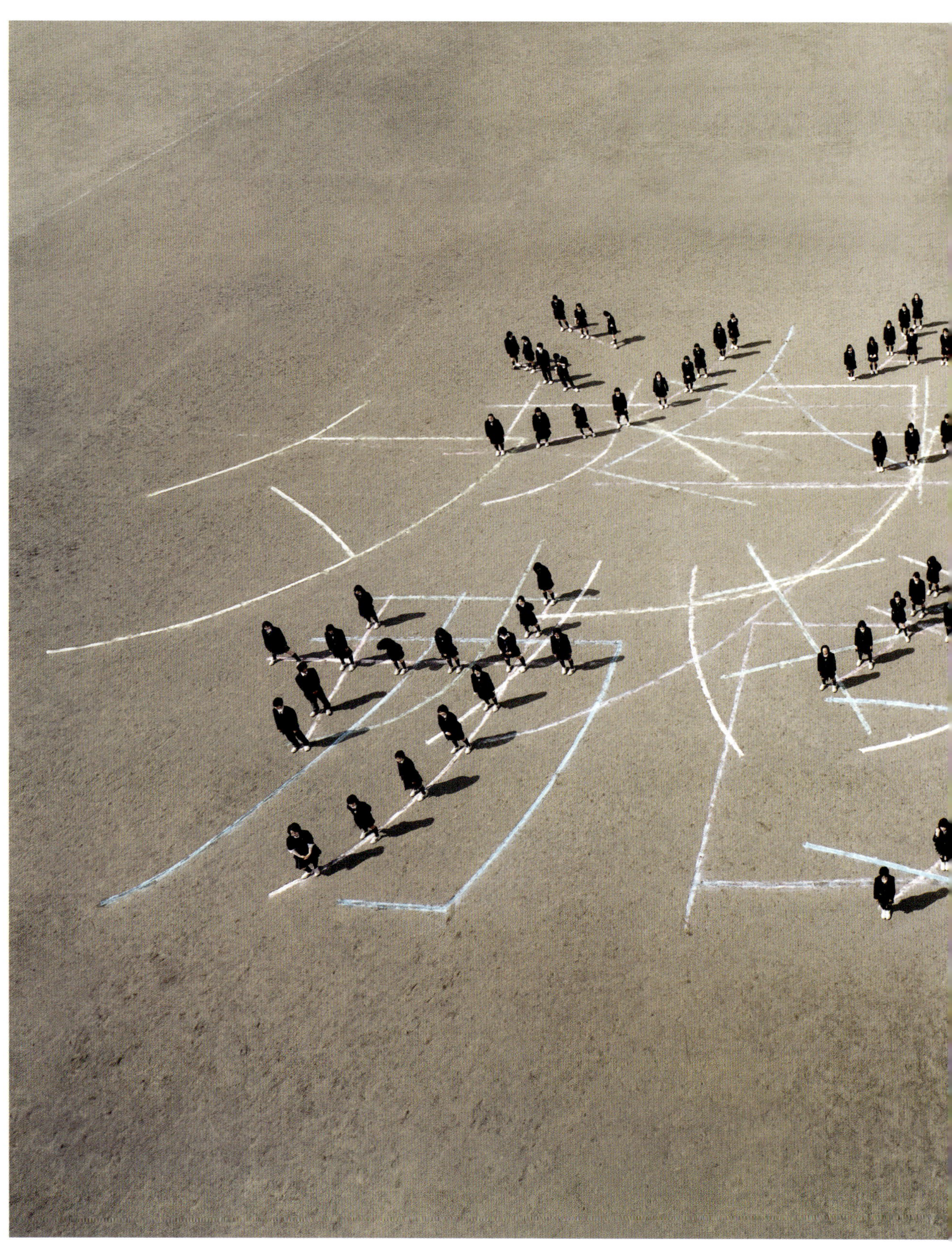

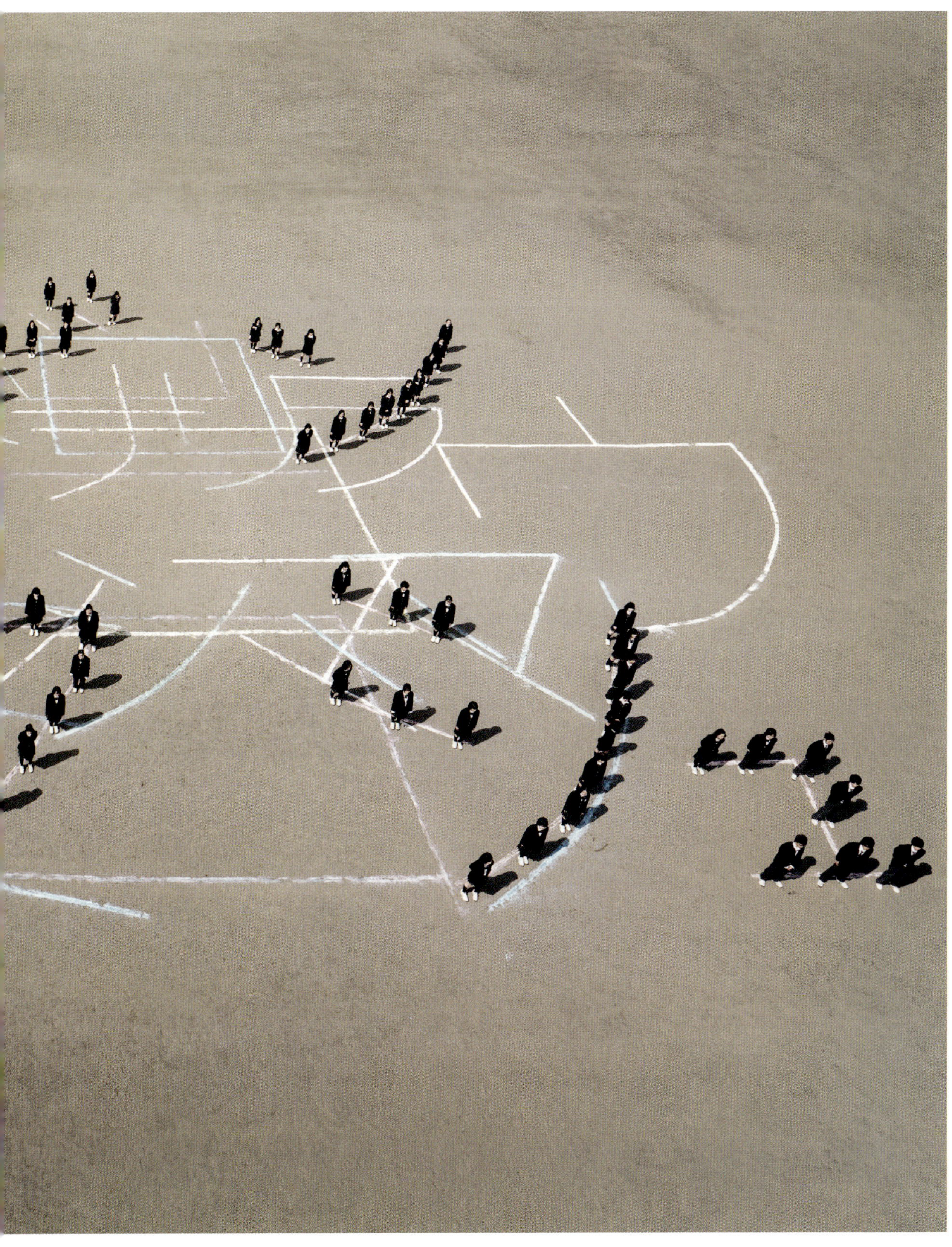

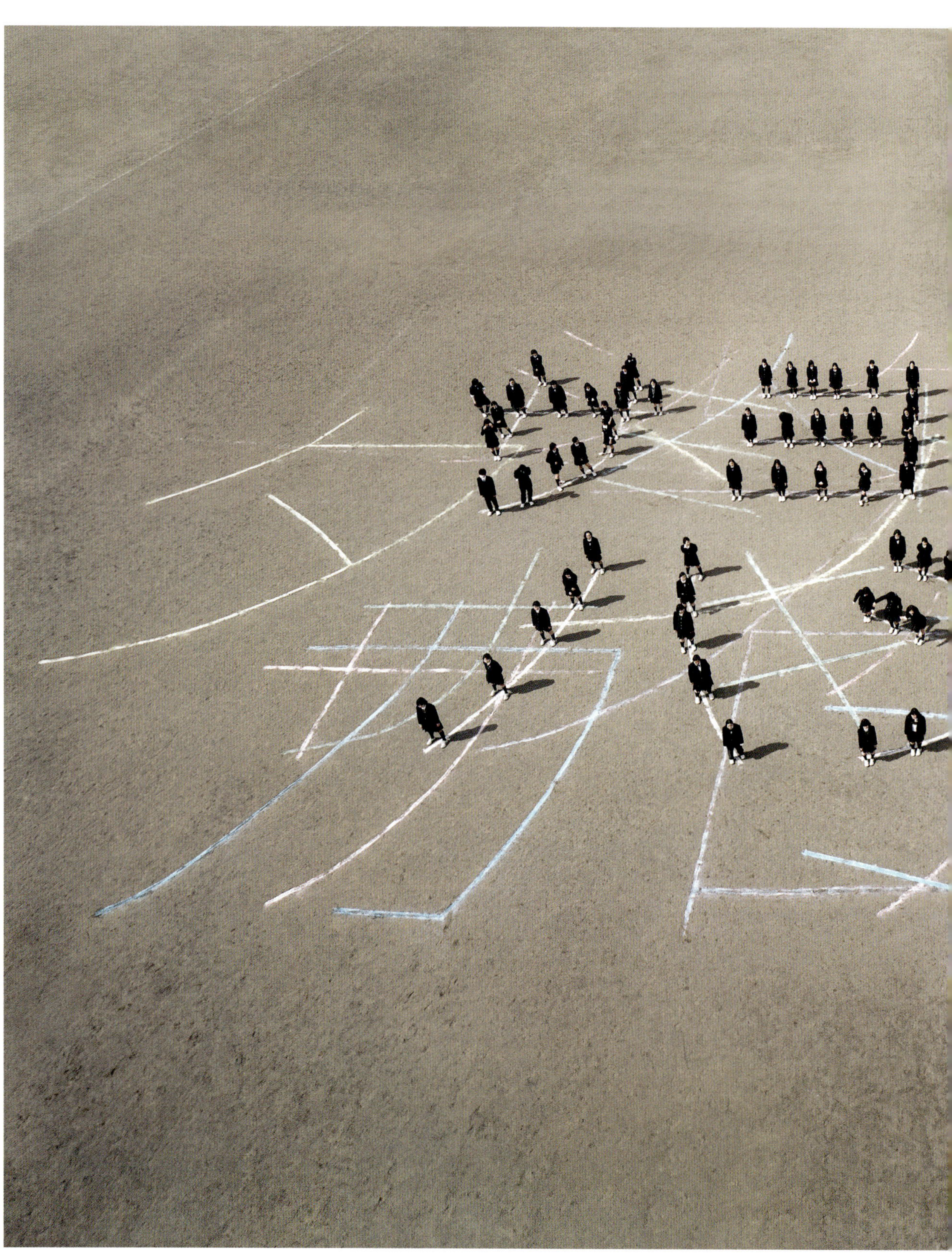

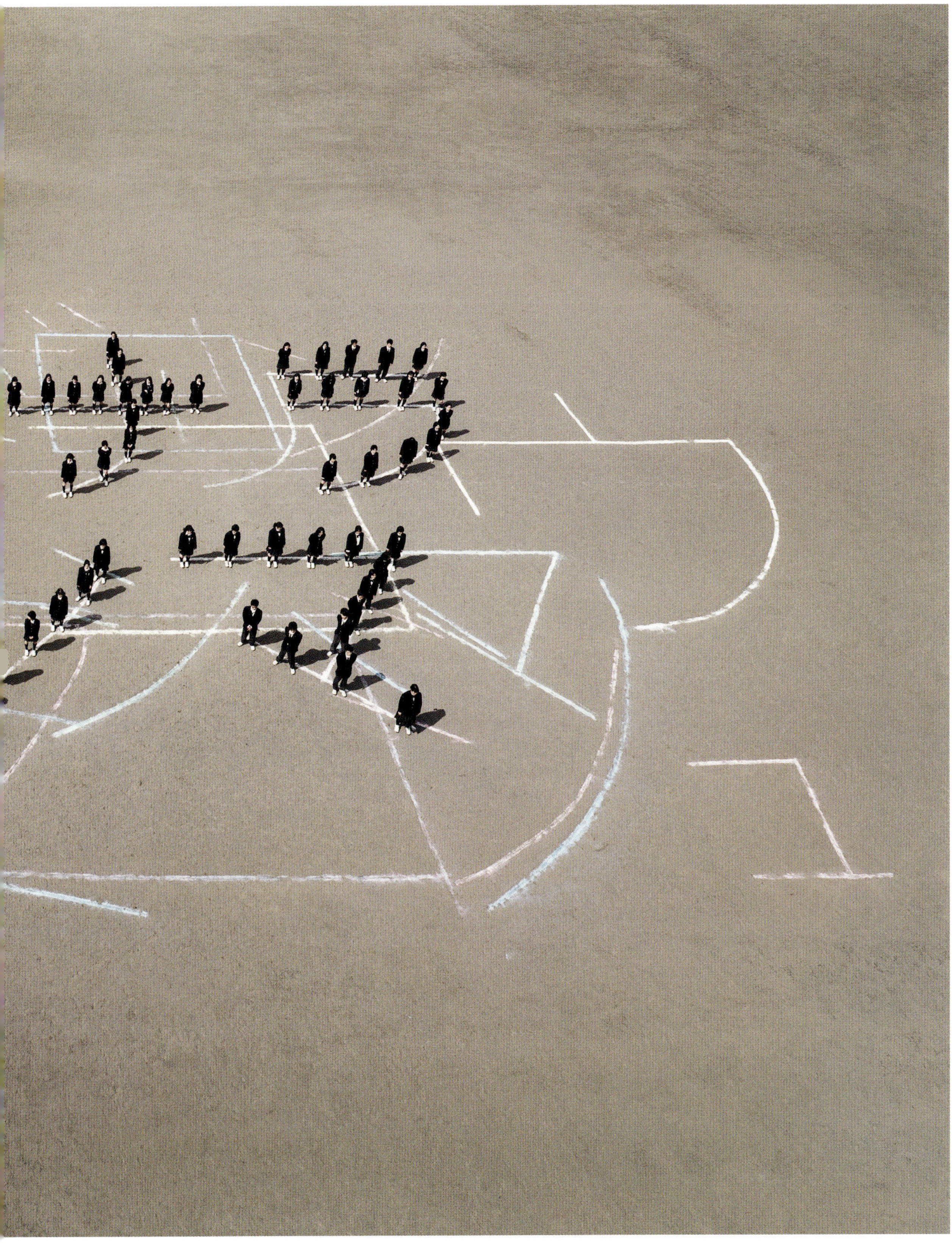

1 Solid Rock
2 Coal Mine
3 Greenless Island
4 Over Populated
5 Exploited Resources
6 Sayonara Hashima

1 岩
2 炭坑
3 緑なき島
4 人口過密
5 資源搾取
6 さよなら端島

Spelling Dystopia: Pages in history

Some 20 kilometers out to sea from Nagasaki harbor lies the island of Hashima, where the process of modernization and changes in the structure of industry in Japan since the Meiji period (1868–1912) are clearly spelled out. Coal was discovered on Hashima in 1810, and the island's coal mines were operated by members of the Nabeshima clan of the former Saga domain from the early Meiji period until Hashima was sold to Mitsubishi in 1890. The Hashima coal mines received a boost in the form of the Meiji policies of national prosperity and defense and the promotion of industry, and continued to develop both economically and physically, expanding to cope with the demand for coal generated by the Sino-Japanese War, the Russo-Japanese War, and the First World War. In 1916 Japan's first reinforced-concrete high-rise apartment building was built on Hashima, and the lifestyle on the island came to be regarded as a utopian one in which the latest electrical appliances were available in abundance. In 1921 the island came to be known as Gunkanjima (Battleship Island) after a local newspaper noted similarities between the silhouette of the island with its concentration of high-rise apartment buildings to that of the battleship Tosa. It is not difficult to imagine that the smoke billowing continuously from the island's smokestacks reinforced the image of a battleship in the minds of the public.

During the Second World War, the mass production of munitions further enhanced Hashima's prosperity, and the island's population continued to grow after the war, reaching over 5000 in the 1960s. This coincided with the period of rapid economic growth in Japan, with coal production reaching a postwar high in 1961. However, there was a major shift after the war from coal to petroleum as the country's mainstream energy industry, while the first nuclear power plant had been launched in Japan in 1963. As imports of coal increased and the overall structure of industry changed with the emphasis shifting from the "heavy and unwieldy" to the "light and compact," the Hashima coal mines, whose historical role had come to an end, closed in January 1974, and by April the same year Hashima had become an uninhabited island. The utopia had turned into a dystopia.

Since being abandoned on the high seas as a piece of industrial waste, the giant battleship that is Hashima has been used a number of times as a movie location, including for *Battle Royale*, which was shot in 2000. Directed by Kinji Fukasaku, the film is based on a horror novel by Koushun Takami, whose dystopian plot centers on a group of junior high school classmates under government orders to take part in a survival game in which they must kill each other until only one is left. The novel was also turned into a manga series. The younger generation is aware that Hashima served as the film's location, but among the general population there is a large gap between the generation that know Hashima as an island of coal mines and the generation that know it through this movie.

Meanwhile, two thirds of the structure of Japanese industry came to be taken up by tertiary industries, with creative industries such as design, anime, fashion, and movies becoming important strategic industries. This shift in the structure of industry in Japan alone speaks volumes for people's awareness and consciousness of Hashima.

The shift of collective memory is a focal point of Nina Fischer and Maroan el Sani's work *Spelling Dystopia—Sayonara Hashima*. In their film they combine real and fictive stories that happened on the island Hashima, by intertwining voice-overs of a former inhabitant of the coal mining island who shares his childhood memories, with a girl's voice that recalls fragments of the blockbuster movie *BR*, which was filmed on the island. Both oral story lines use the same images as a backdrop. A walk through the island's abandoned streets and houses, a boat-trip around the island. These images are accompanied by a choreography of high school students, who practice the formation of 6 different Japanese kanji and katakana characters on the sport field [Solid Rock, Coal Mine, Greenless Island, Over Populated, Exploited Resources, Sayonara Hashima], spelling out the islands history from utopia to dystopia. By blurring the boundaries of reality and fiction, Fischer and el Sani also raise the questions of how we remember history, which memory we keep or care about and which memory we abandon instead.

"For kids today, who spend a lot of time in front of their computer, history often appears as fiction, made up by the media. They start having difficulties adapting to the real world."

In Japan, as an aftermath of the March 11 Tohoku earthquake and tsunami, particularly after the Fukushima nuclear accident, strong interests and concerns about the nation's energy policy have been emerged. All those devastating images of earthquake, tsunami, and nuclear accident which are unimaginable, are broadcast through global media and have had a strong impact and influence on energy and nuclear policies of many countries around the world, including some countries that have already made some political decisions. These are certainly the new pages being written in man's history. At this time, *Spelling Dystopia* particularly sharpens the awareness of these mechanisms of the shift in cultural values and memories in society everywhere.

Mami Kataoka,
Mori Art Museum,
Tokyo, 2011

スペリング・ディストピア：歴史のページ

長崎港から20キロほど沖にある端島には、日本における明治以降の近代化や産業構造の変化が綴られている。1810年に石炭が発見されて以来、旧佐賀藩の鍋島氏が明治初頭から炭礦を経営し、1890年に三菱へ売却。その後の端島炭礦は、明治の富国強兵、殖産興業政策の追い風を受け、日清戦争、日露戦争、第一次世界大戦を経て拡大し、経済的にも物理的にも発展を続ける。1916年には日本初の鉄筋コンクリート構造の高層アパートが建てられ、端島の生活は最先端の電化製品が溢れるユートピア的なものだった。この島が軍艦島と呼ばれるようになったのは、1921年、限られた土地に高層ビルが林立する姿を地元の新聞が軍艦「土佐」に見立てたことに由来する。煙突から途切れることなく吹き上がる煙が、島をさらに軍艦のイメージと重ねあわせたことは想像に難くない。

第二次大戦中は軍需品が量産されて隆盛を極め、終戦後も1960年代には島の住民が5000人以上を数えた。それは石炭生産量が戦後最高を記録した1961年など日本の高度経済成長期と重なり合う。一方で、戦後のエネルギー産業の主流は石炭から石油へと大きく移行、1963年には日本初の原子力発電も実現する。輸入炭も増加しつつあり、産業構造全体も重厚長大から短小軽薄へと移行するなか、歴史的役割を終えた端島炭礦は、1974年の1月に閉山、4月には無人島になる。ユートピアはディストピアに転換した。

巨大な軍艦がまさに産業廃棄物として海上に放置されて以降、端島は何度か映画のロケ地に使われているが、2000年にこの島で撮影された「バトル・ロワイアル」もそのひとつだ。もともと高見広春のホラー小説で、国家命令を受けた中学校のクラスメートが最後の一人までお互いに殺し合うサバイバルゲームをする現代のディストピア的ストーリーが漫画化され、さらに深作欣二監督によって映画化された。若い世代は端島をこの映画のロケ地として知っているが、一般の日本人で端島を炭礦として知る世代と映画として知る世代の間には大きな空洞がある。その間、日本の産業構造は第三次産業が3分の2を占め、デザイン、アニメ、ファッション、映画などのクリエイティブ産業が重要な戦略産業となった。この産業構造の転換が、そのまま端島に対する人々の認識や意識を物語っているのだ。

このような集合的記憶の推移は、ニナ・フィッシャーとマロアン・エル・ザーニの《スペリング・ディストピア　さよなら端島》における中心的な関心である。そこでは炭鉱の島としての端島で幼少期の記憶を共有する元住人の声と、大ヒット映画「バトル・ロワイアル」の場面を彷彿させるような女子高生の声が絡み合うことで、端島で起こった現実と虚構の物語が融合されている。双方の語りの背景に、廃虚や荒廃した通り、船から見た島の外観など同じ風景が使われていることで、その重なり合いが強調されている。これらの映像にはそれらは、「岩」、「タンコウ」、「ミドリナキシマ」、「人口カミツ」、「シゲンサクシュ」、「サヨナラハシマ」、など高校生による人文字の映像が挿入され、この島のユートピアからディストピアへの変遷を綴っている。現実と虚構の境界を曖昧にすることによって、われわれがいかに歴史を記憶するのか、どの記憶を残し、どの記憶を忘却の彼方へ葬っているのかを問い掛けるフィッシャーとエル・ザーニは、「コンピュータやスマートフォンとともに多くの時間を過ごしながら育った現代の若者には、歴史さえも、メディアが作りあげた虚構だと思えてくる。虚構を前提とした世界に現実を適応させることに難しさを感じ始めているのだ」と指摘する。

3月11日の東日本大震災を経た日本では、福島原発事故を受けて新しいエネルギー政策への関心が高まっている。地震も津波も原発事故も、グローバルなニュース映像で伝えられたイメージは、想像を絶する現実だった。それは世界各国のエネルギー政策、核戦略にも影響を及ぼし、すでにさまざまな政策等の形で顕在化している。人類の歴史にとってまた新たなページが綴られている今、《スペリング・ディストピア》は、改めてわれわれの社会における文化的価値や記憶の推移のメカニズムに対する自覚や意識を研ぎ澄ませてくれるものである。

片岡真実
森美術館チーフ・キュレーター
東京、2011年

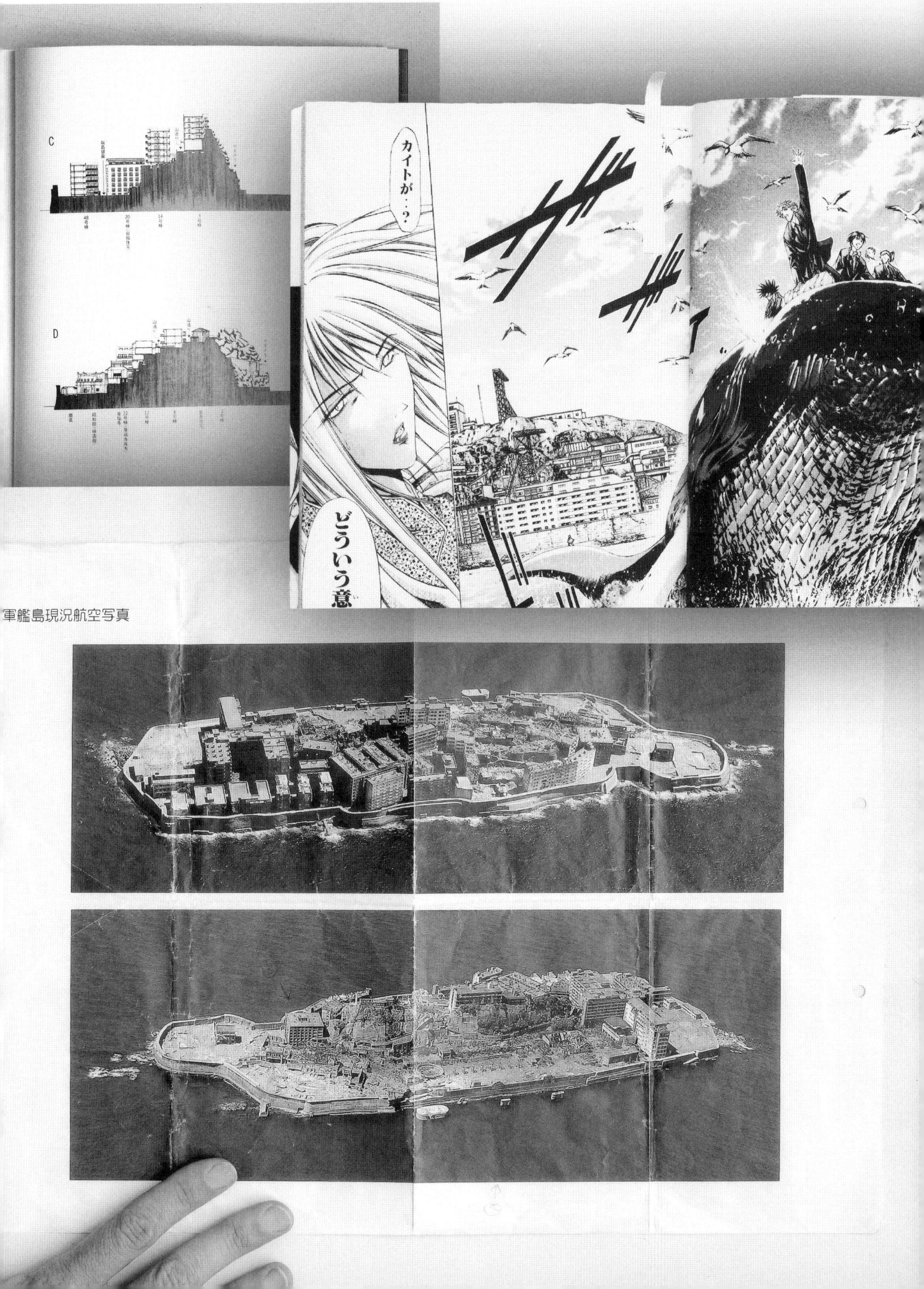

C

端島銀座

山通り

48号棟

20号棟（日給住宅）

14号棟

3号棟

D

山通り

山通り

商店

昭和館（映画館）

泉福寺

12号棟

8号棟

カイトが・・？

どういう意

軍艦島現況航空写真

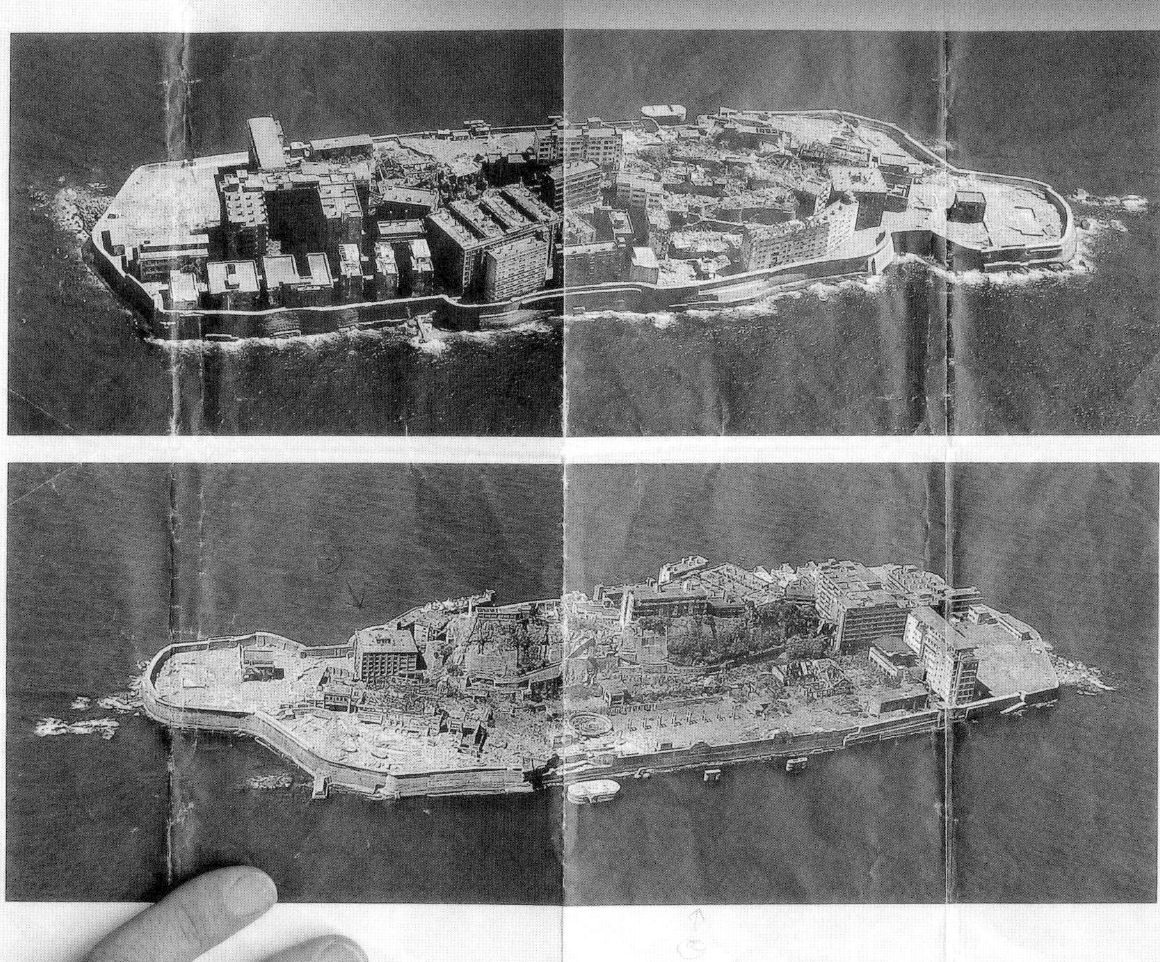

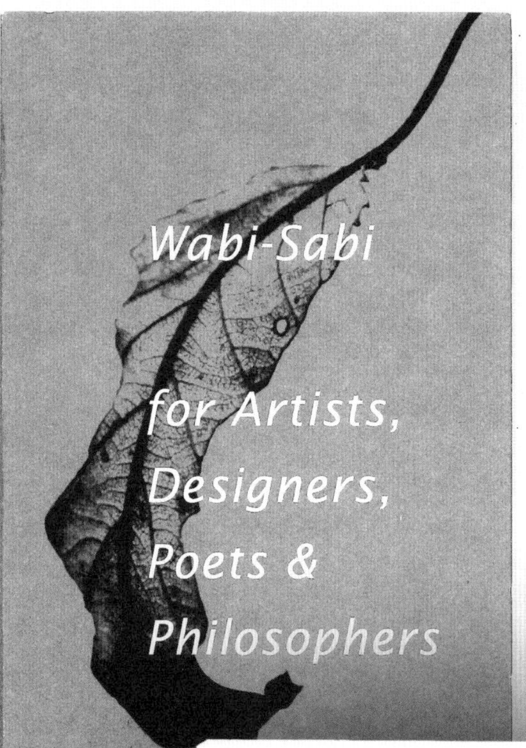
Wabi-Sabi
for Artists,
Designers,
Poets &
Philosophers

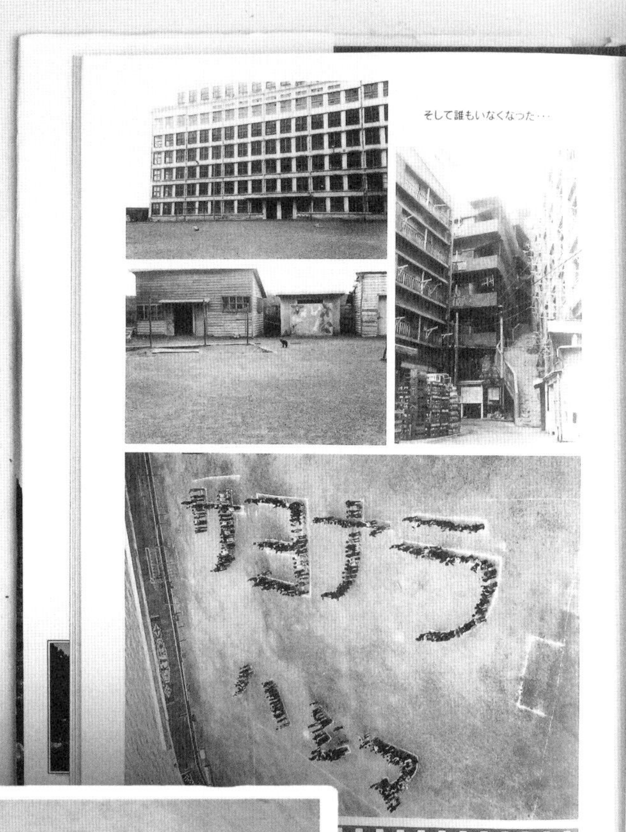
そして誰もいなくなった…
サヨナラ

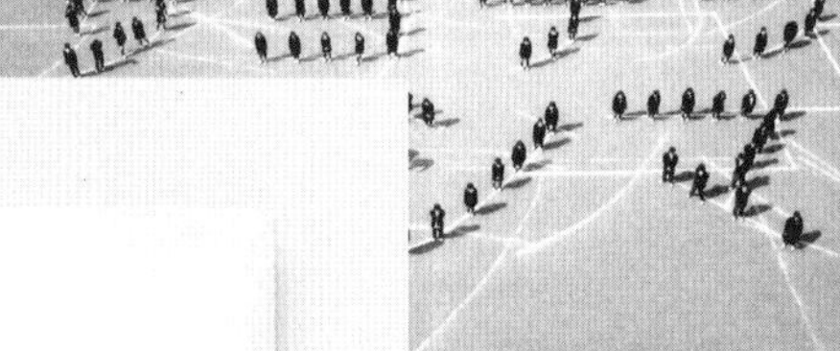

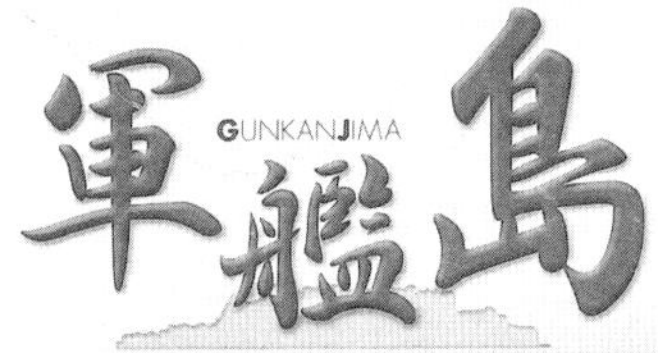
軍艦島
GUNKANJIMA

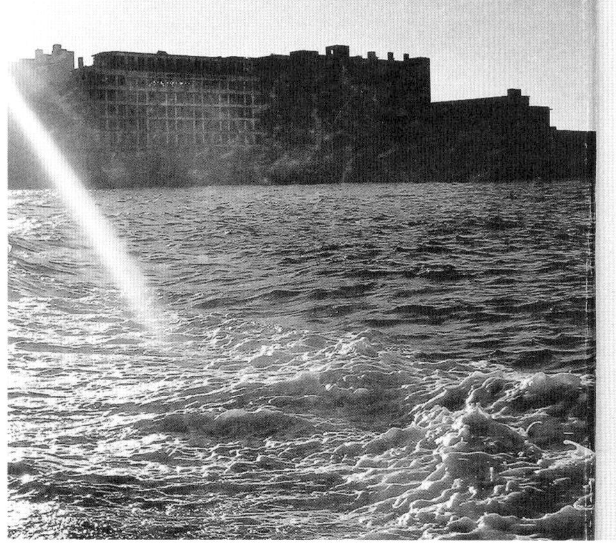

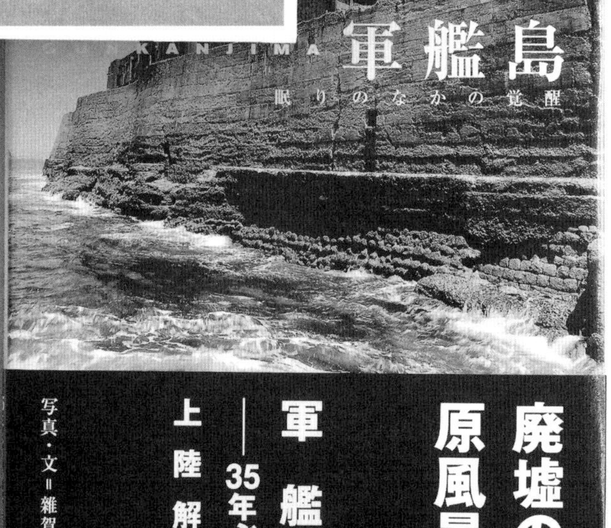
軍艦島
眠りのなかの覚醒
廃墟の原風景へ
軍艦島
—35年ぶりの
上陸解禁!
写真・文＝雑賀雄二

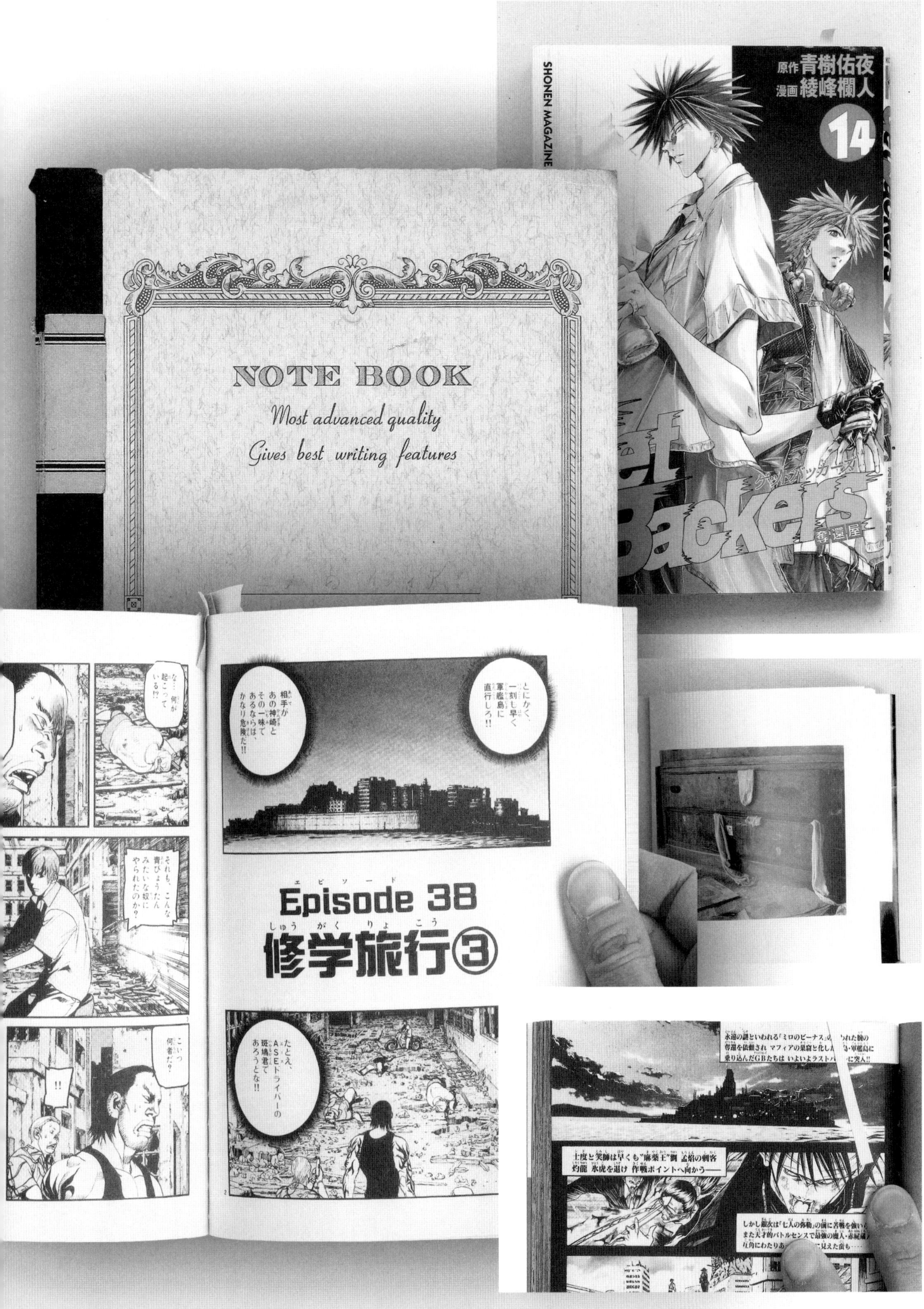

SHONEN MAGAZINE
原作 青樹佑夜
漫画 綾峰欄人
14
GetBackers
ゲットバッカーズ
奪還屋
NOTE BOOK
Most advanced quality
Gives best writing features
な…何が起こっている!!
それも、こんな青びょうたんみたいな奴にやられたのか!?
とにかく、一刻も早く軍艦島に直行しろ!!
相手があの神崎とその一味であるならば、かなり危険だ!!
Episode 38
修学旅行③

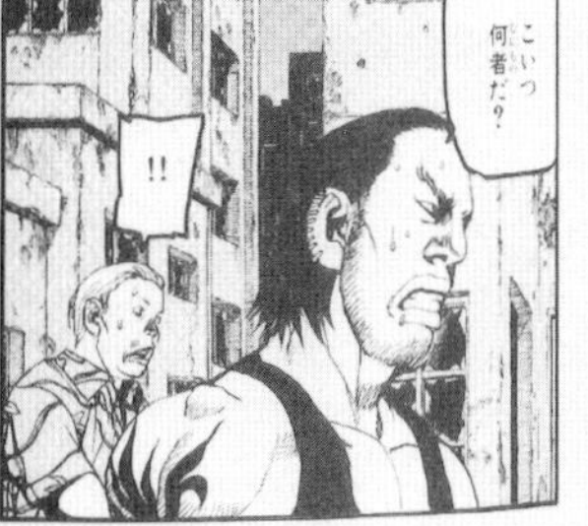
こいつ何者だ!?
!!

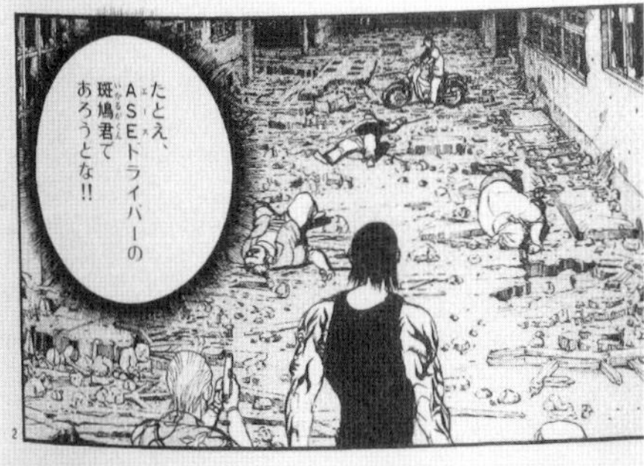
たとえ、ASEドライバーの斑鳩君であろうとな!!

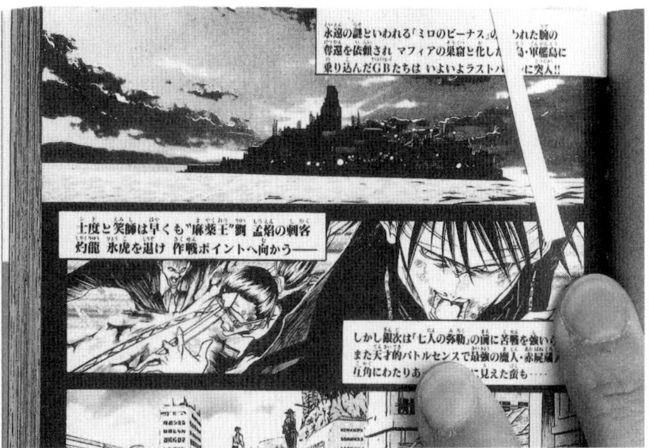
永遠の謎といわれる「ミロのビーナス」の
奪還を依頼され マフィアの巣窟と化した
乗り込んだGBたちは いよいよラスト
士度と笑師は早くも"麻薬王"劉 孟焔の刺客
灼龍 氷虎を退け 作戦ポイントへ向かう——
しかし銀次は「七人の弥勒」の前に苦戦を強い
また天才的バトルセンスで最強の魔人・赤屍蔵
互角にわたりあ
に見えた蛮も……

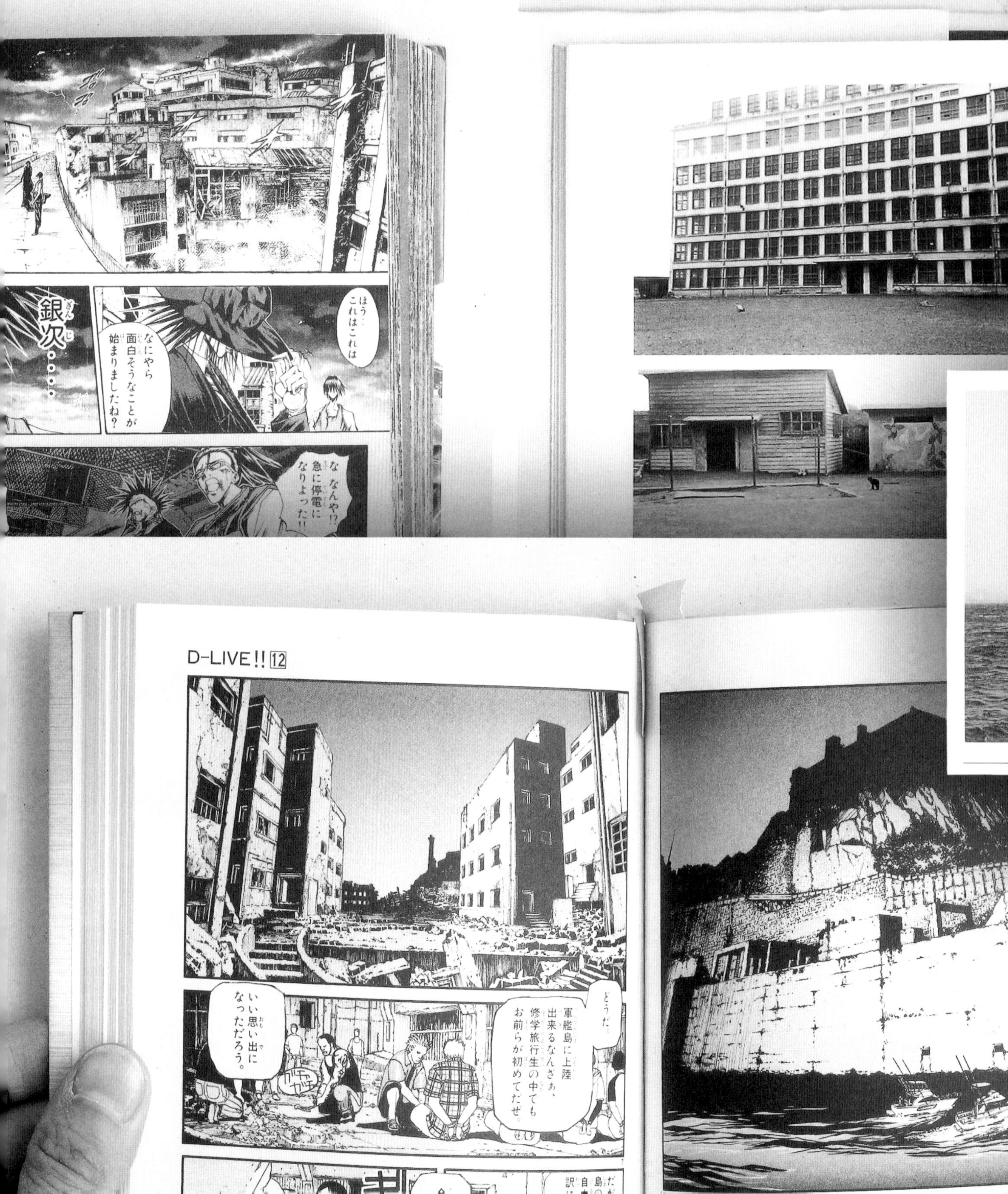

ほう…
これはこれは
なにやら
面白そうなことが
始まりましたね？
銀次……
な なんや!?
急に停電に
なりよった!!
D-LIVE!! 12
別名
軍艦島はな!!
どうだ。
軍艦島に上陸
出来るなんざぁ、
修学旅行生の中でも
お前らが初めてだぜ。
いい思い出に
なっただろう。
だが、
島の中を
自由に観光させる
訳にはいかねぇ。
今回の…
取引が
終わるまでな。

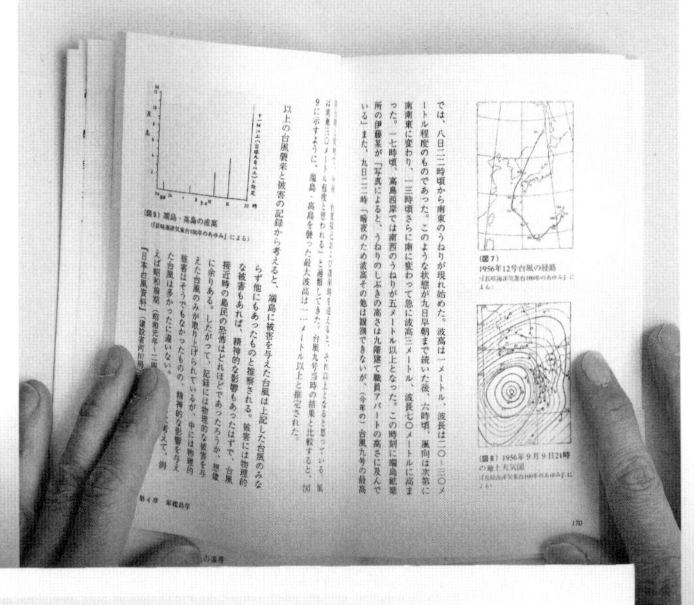
では、八日二二時頃から南東のうねりが現れ始めた。波高は一メートル、波長は二〇～三〇メートル程度のものであった。このような状態が九日早朝まで続いた後、六時頃、風向は次第に南南東に変わり、一三時頃さらに南に変わって急に波高三メートル、波長七〇メートルに高まった。一七時頃、高島西岸では南西のうねりが五メートル以上となった。
(図7) 1956年12号台風の経路
(図8) 1956年9月9日21時の地上天気図
(図9) 端島・高島の波高
170
第4章 軍艦島学

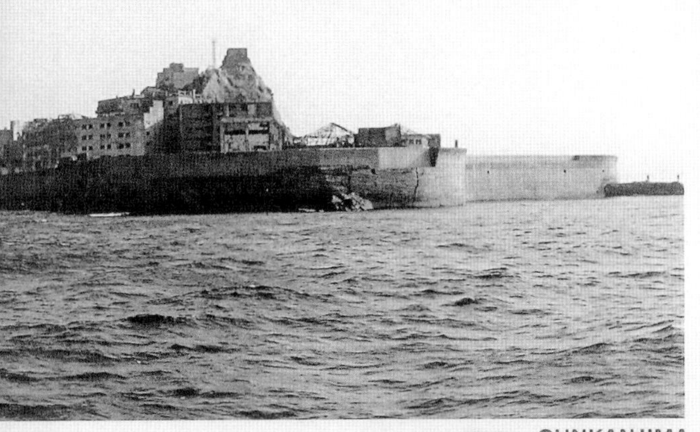
GUNKANJIMA

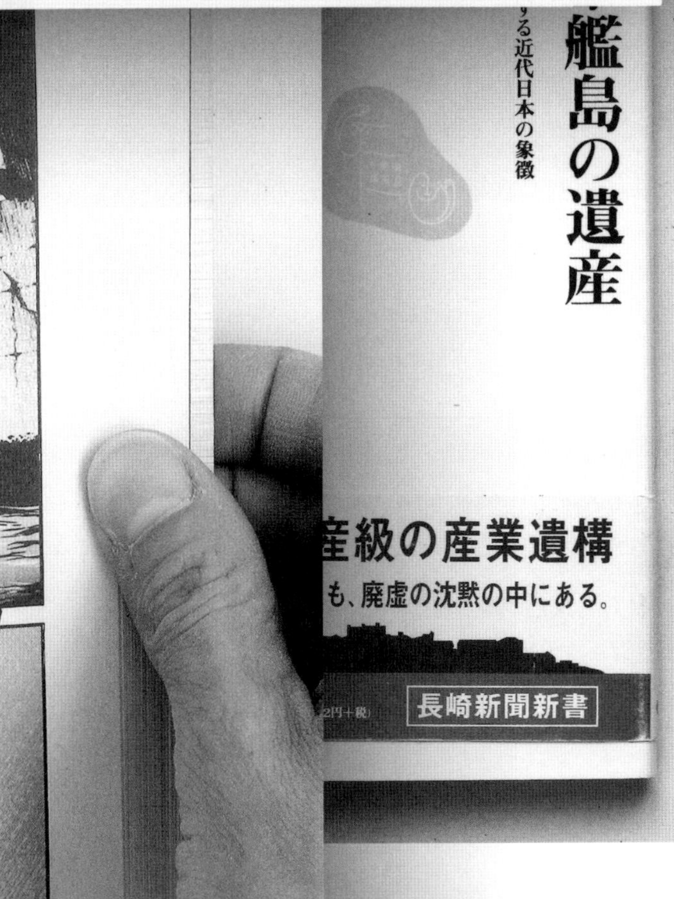
艦島の遺産
る近代日本の象徴
産級の産業遺構
も、廃虚の沈黙の中にある。
長崎新聞新書

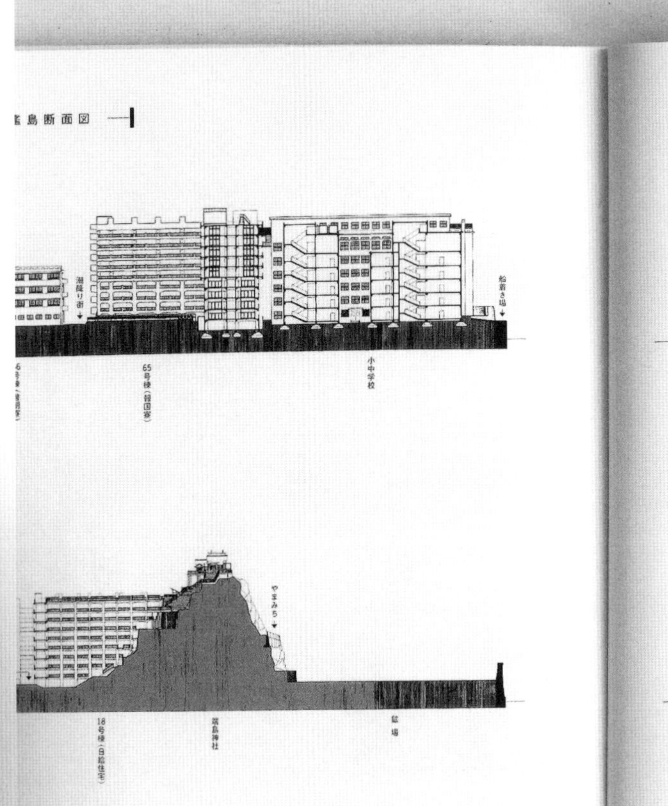
艦島断面図
船着き場
65号棟（報国寮）
小中学校
やまみち
18号棟（日給住宅）
端島神社
広場

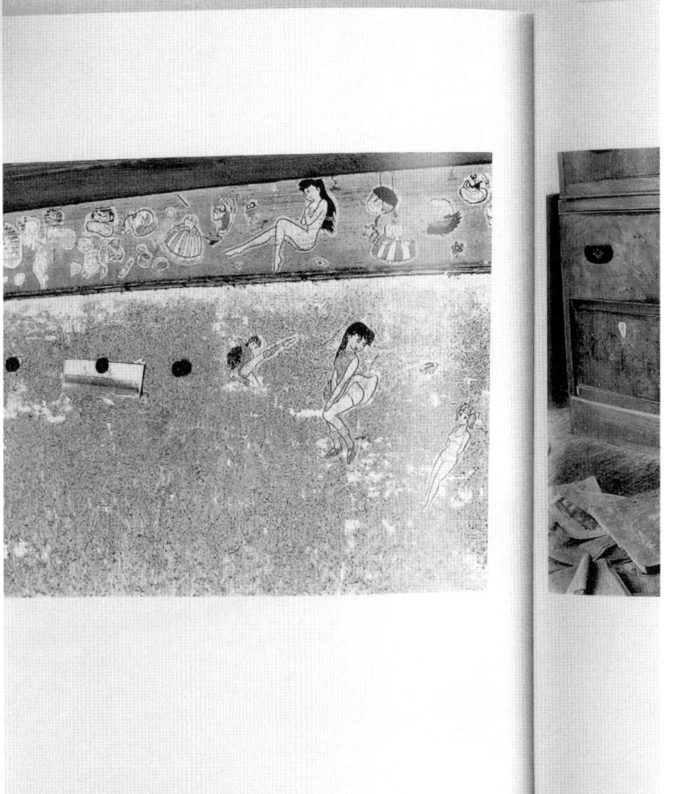

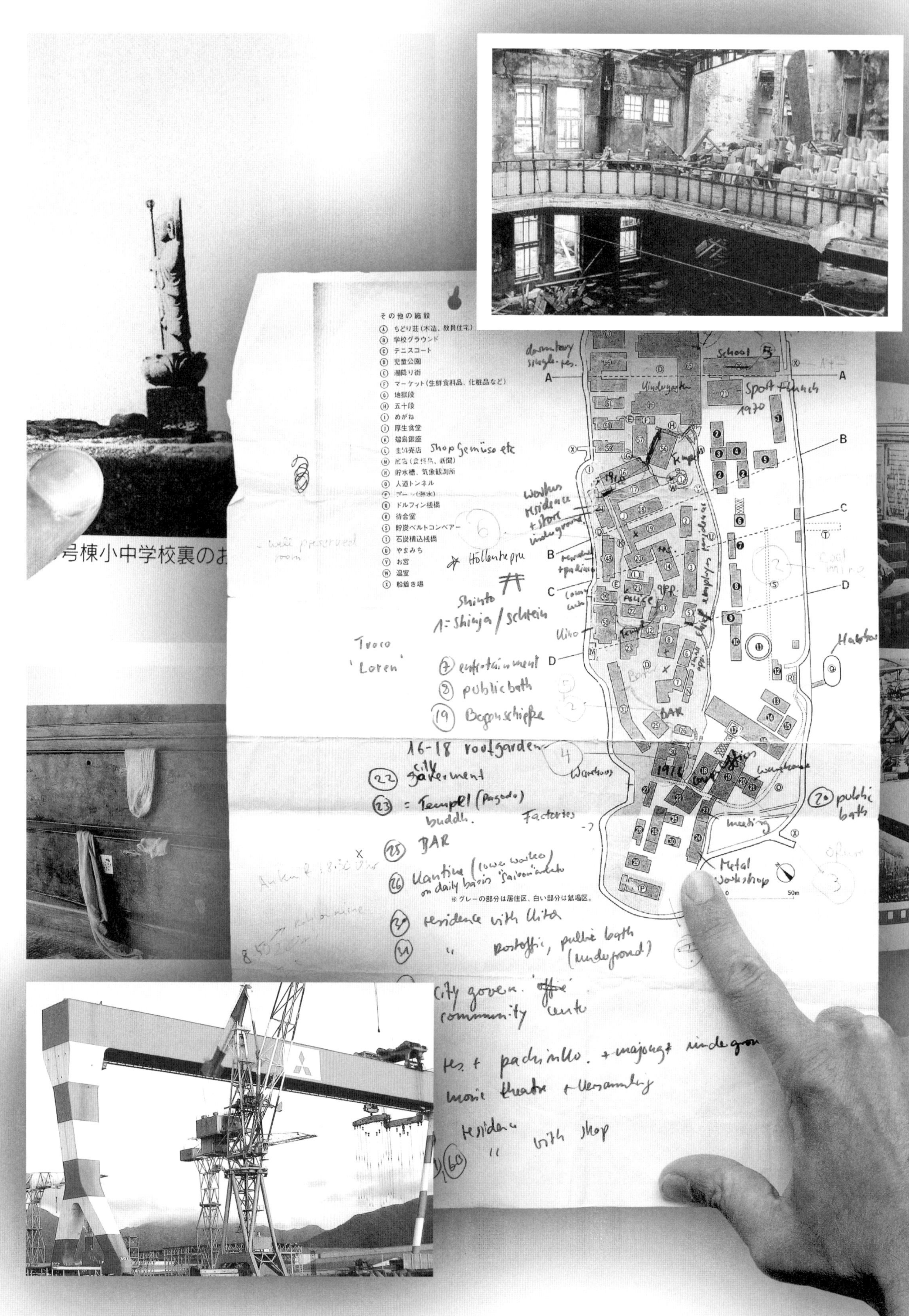
その他の施設
Ⓐ ちどり荘（木造、教員住宅）
Ⓑ 学校グラウンド
Ⓒ テニスコート
Ⓓ 児童公園
Ⓔ 潮降り街
Ⓕ マーケット（生鮮食料品、化粧品など）
Ⓖ 地獄段
Ⓗ 五十段
Ⓘ めがね
Ⓙ 厚生食堂
Ⓚ 端島銀座
Ⓛ 主婦売店
Ⓜ 売店（食料品、新聞）
Ⓝ 貯水槽、気象観測所
Ⓞ 人道トンネル
Ⓟ プール（海水）
Ⓠ ドルフィン桟橋
Ⓡ 待合室
Ⓢ 貯炭ベルトコンベアー
Ⓣ 石炭積込桟橋
Ⓤ やまみち
Ⓥ お宮
Ⓦ 温室
Ⓧ 船着き場
※グレーの部分は居住区、白い部分は鉱場区。
50m
号棟小中学校裏のお

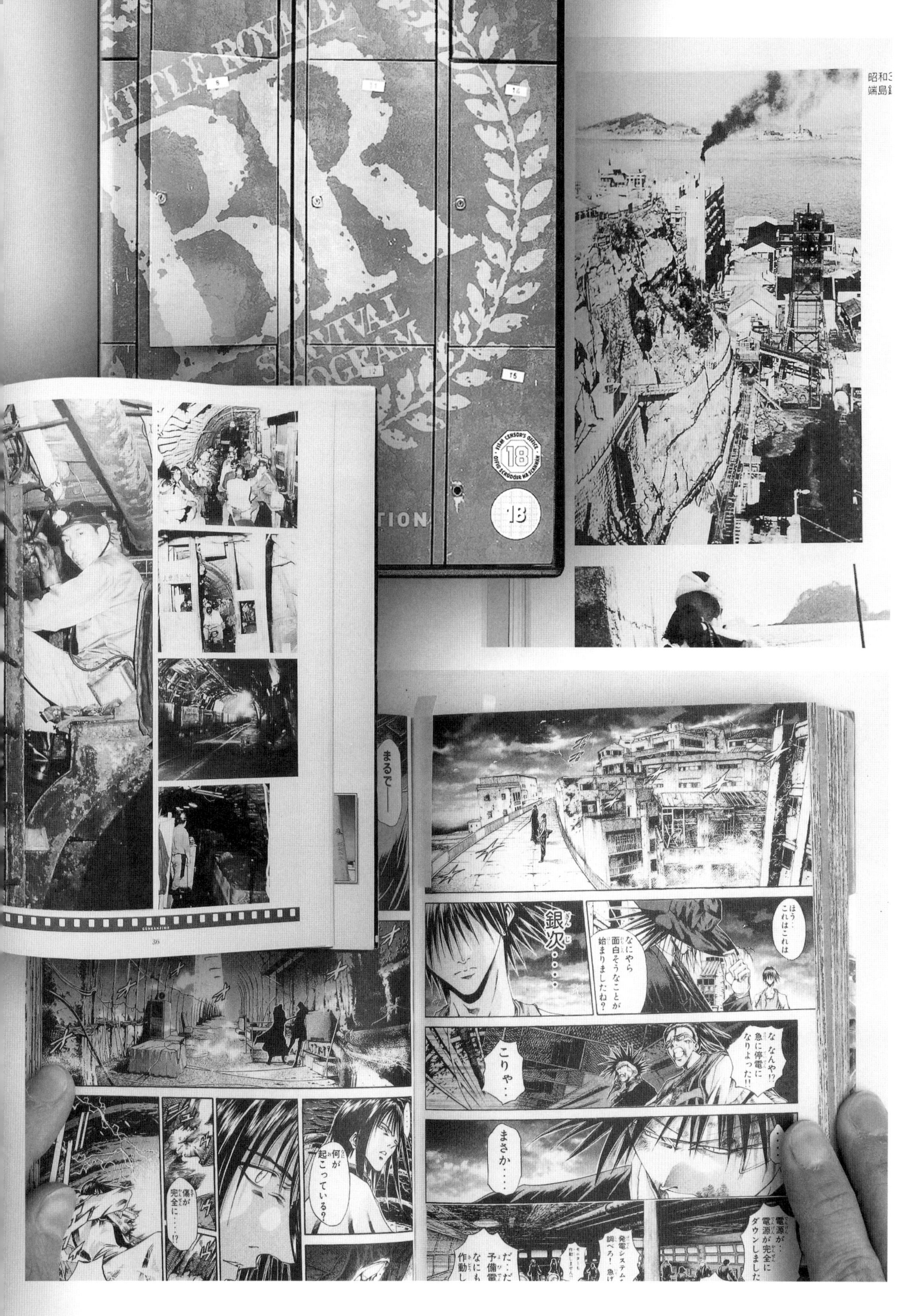

18
18
まるで──
ほう…これはこれは
なにやら面白そうなことが始まりましたね?
銀次……
な なんや!? 急に停電になりよった!!
こりゃ…
まさか……
何が起こっている?

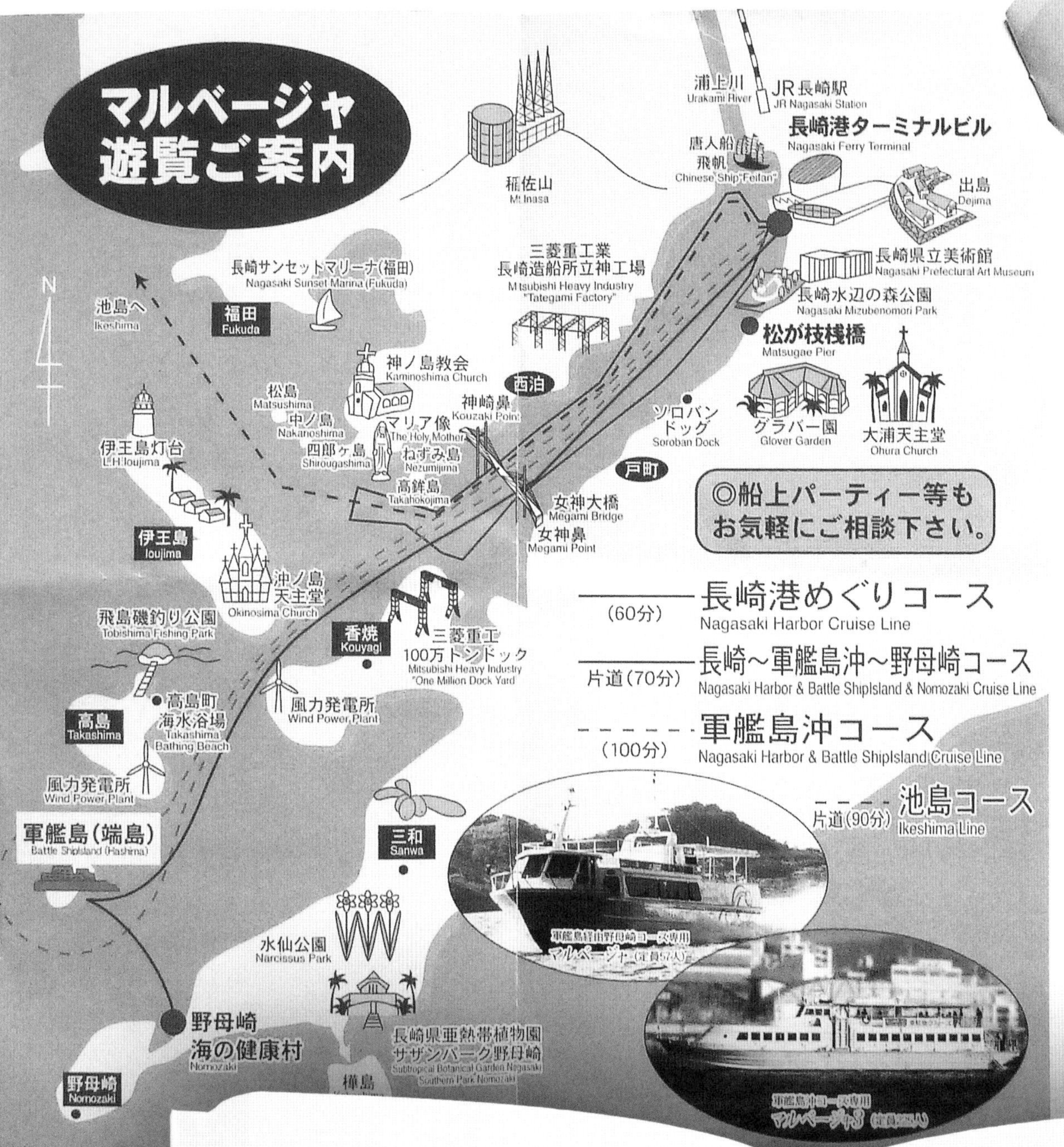

まして仲の良い家族のような付き合いをしてきた人たち
れから三〇年、端島はその悲しみをまだ知っている島なので

六五号棟の生活

私が最後に住んでいた六五号棟の九階は、棟の最上階にあ
ばれ、昭和三三年（一九五八）に新六五号（一〇階建）が建設
上には端島幼稚園（保育園含む）があった。島の中では一番
約三四〇世帯が暮らしていた。コの字型の建物下には公園が
こえ賑やかな場所だった。

コの字型だから互いの部屋のベランダが向き合い、私の住
各世帯のベランダが全部見えるような位置にあり、夜に

（写真5）学校と65号棟

Doutoku Sakamoto, former inhabitant of Hashima

00:04:40 The size of the island is just 480 meters long and 160 meters wide. This side of the island was the coal mining area, so there is not much remaining now. When we go further, there's a round asphalt area, that is the entrance to the island. People call it Dolphin Pier. They would dock the ship there, and then go onto the island.

この島の大きさはね、この長さが480メートル、幅が160メートルしかない。こちら側は炭坑地帯があった所で、今ほとんど残っていません。しばらく行くと丸っこいアスファルトのものがあります。あれがここの入り口、ドルフィン桟橋。あそこに横付けして上陸してたんです。

000:05:03 The building you see on the right hand side, that's the school. That's the elementary school and the junior high school where we all studied. Up to the 4th floor it was the elementary school, and from the 5th to the 7th was the junior high school. It took so much courage to go up from the 4th floor to the 5th floor and the 6th floor, and you also had to shave your head.
I hated the idea, so if I could avoid it I would rather not go up to the 5th floor. In the end, I had to shave my head and went to the 5th floor. But, for an elementary school kid, it took so much courage even just to step up those stairs. Because junior high school students are, to a certain degree, already adults, and they had different atmosphere. There was this feeling that they were scary big brothers.
Our elementary and junior high school is still there, and if I look at it even now, I can still see students waving from the school.

右の方に見えてきた白い建物、これが学校です。僕らが学んだ小学校、中学校がありました。4階までが小学校、5階と7階が中学校だった。4階から5階に行くというのはものすごく勇気が要った。上には中学生がいるから。4階から5階、6階にあがるためには、頭を坊主にしなければいけない。それがもう嫌でね、できたら5階に上りたくないなんていう思いがあった。まあ仕方なく坊主にして上がったんだけどね。小学生の時はやっぱりその階段を上るだけでも勇気が要るんだよね。中学生になればある程度大人だから、やはりちょっと雰囲気が違う。怖いお兄さんがいるっていう雰囲気があった。小学校中学校も今まだ残ってますけど、いまでもこうやって見ると向こうから手を振ってる姿が見えるんですよ。

00:05:48 When it got to this time of the day, everybody came home from school, and it was the most lively time of the day for the island. People would also gather for bathing around this time. The big hole you see from here, that's the way into the seabed watercourse. There were water pipes from Nomozaki, which is the opposite shore, through the seabed to the island. The building just next to where the lighthouse is, that's the water tank in which they kept the fresh water, and there are still some bits of the steel pipes left in there. That tank supplied all the water on this island. After the pier, you see the bridge with two pillars, that's where they docked the ship and loaded coal onto it.

この時間になるとだいたいみんな学校から帰ってきて、一番にぎやかな時間帯だった。それとまた、島の中の風呂場に集まる時間だったわけです。
ちょうど今、大きな穴が見えてるけど、あれが海底水路の入り口。だから対岸の野母崎からその海底を通って水道管が入ってたんです。今灯台のあるところのすぐ右にある建物、あれが水を貯めてた貯水タンク。あそこに今まだ少し、鉄管が残ってますよね。あれがこの島の水を供給してたところです。
それと今桟橋を過ぎて2つの橋脚、橋が見えますよね、あれが石炭を積み出すための橋脚。その横に船が停まって石炭を積みこんでいた。

坂本道徳、端島に当時住んでいた島民

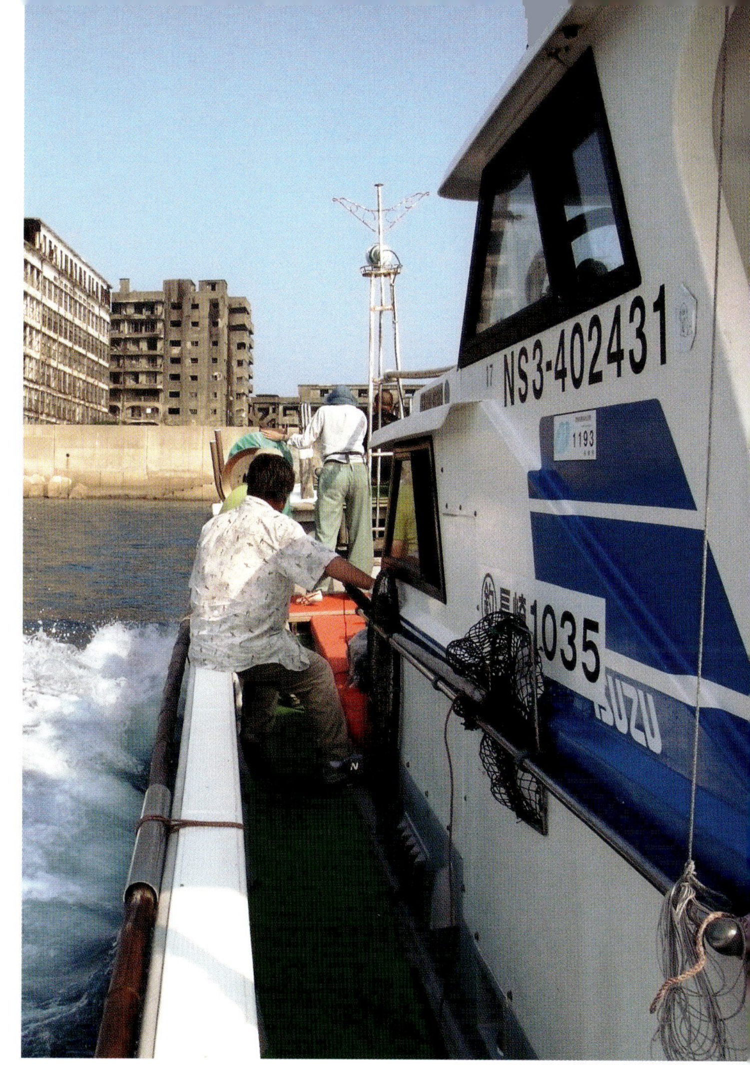
NS3-402431
1193
1035

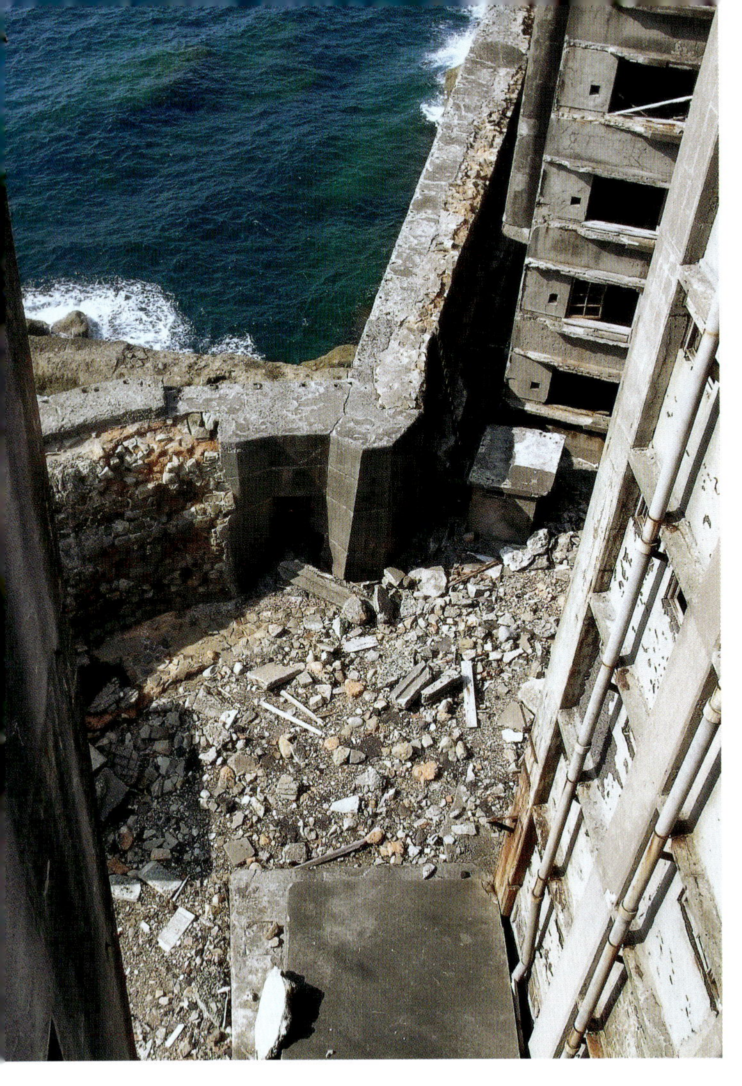

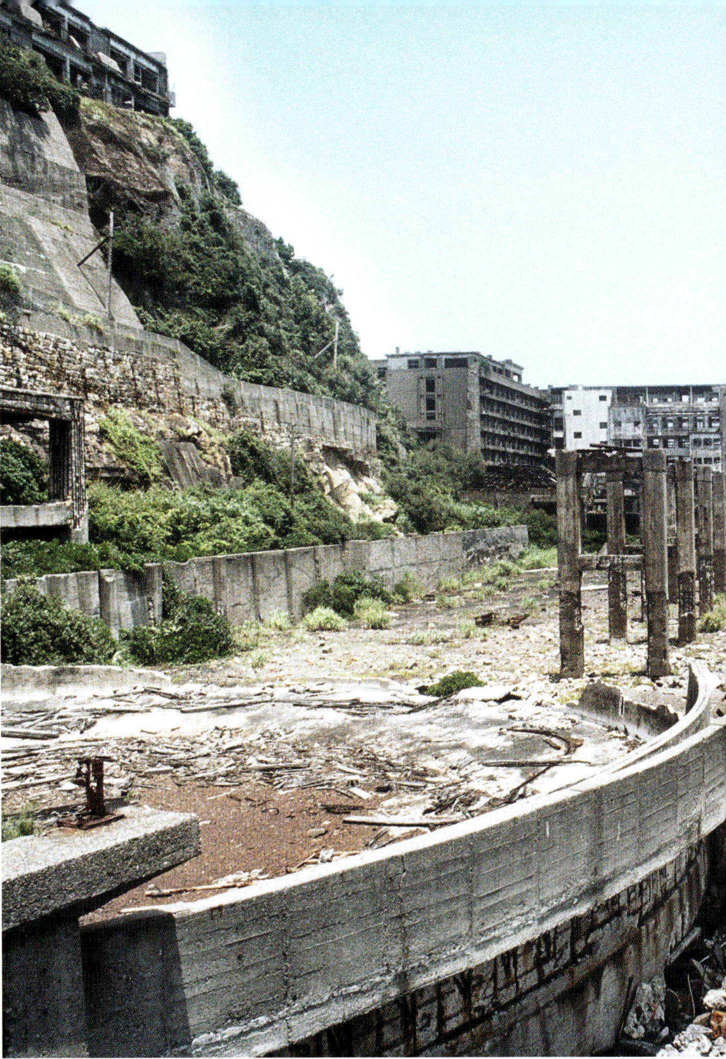

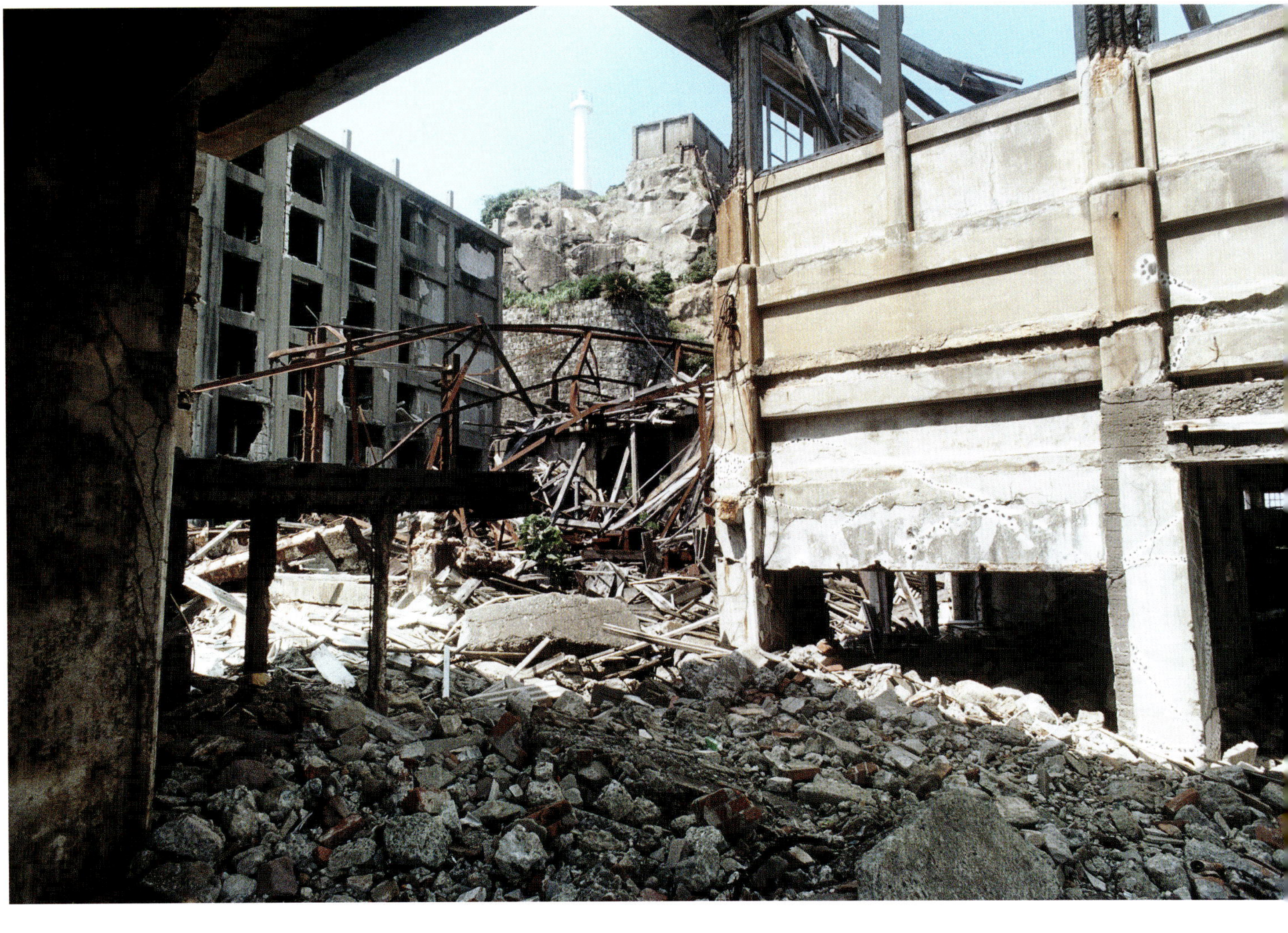

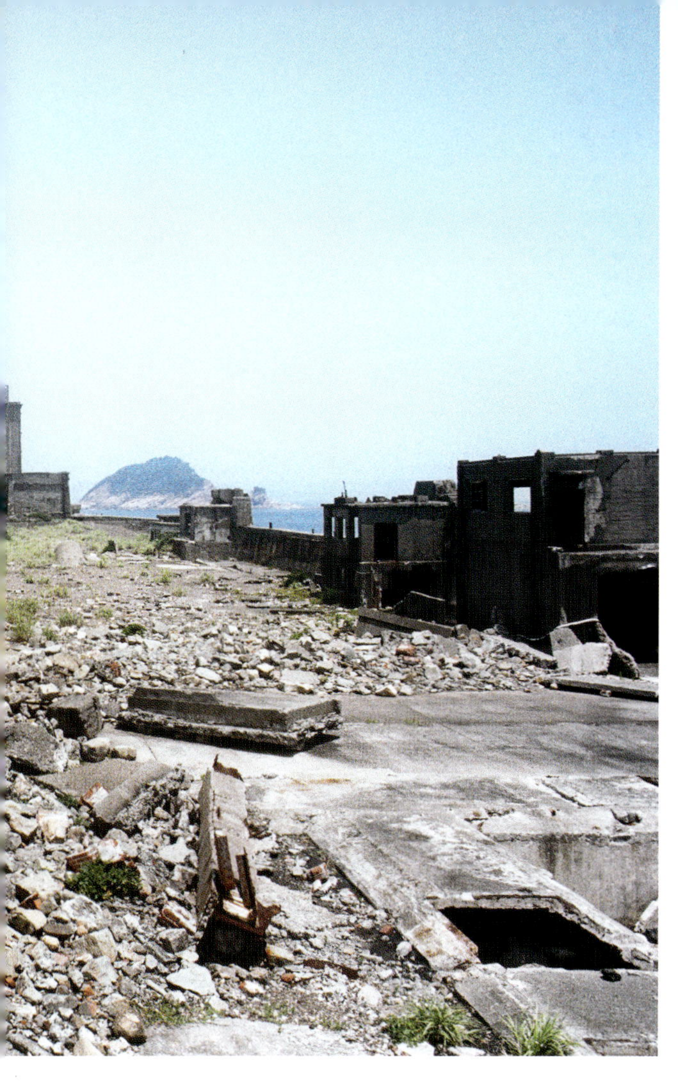
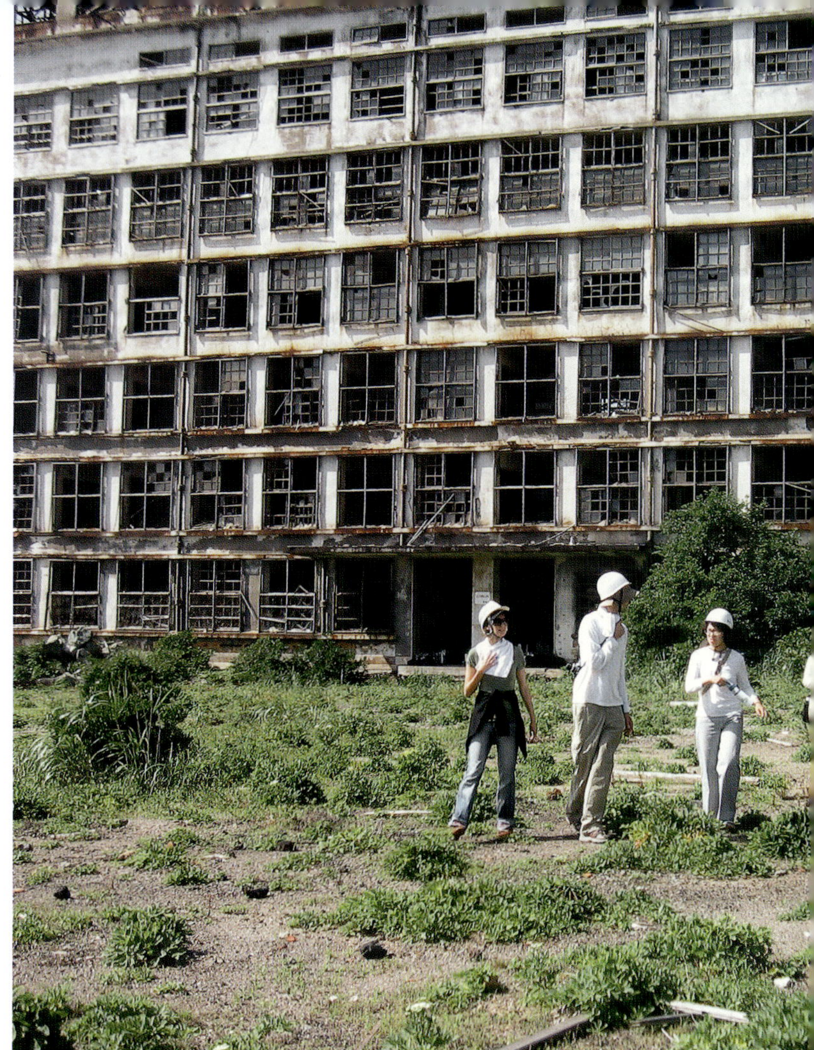
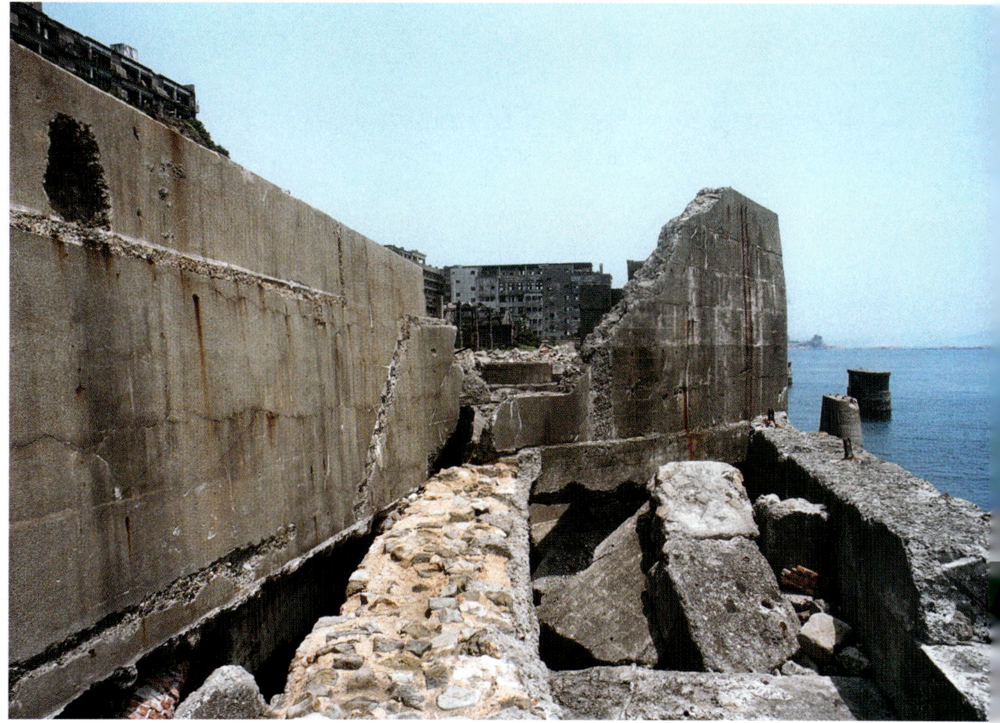

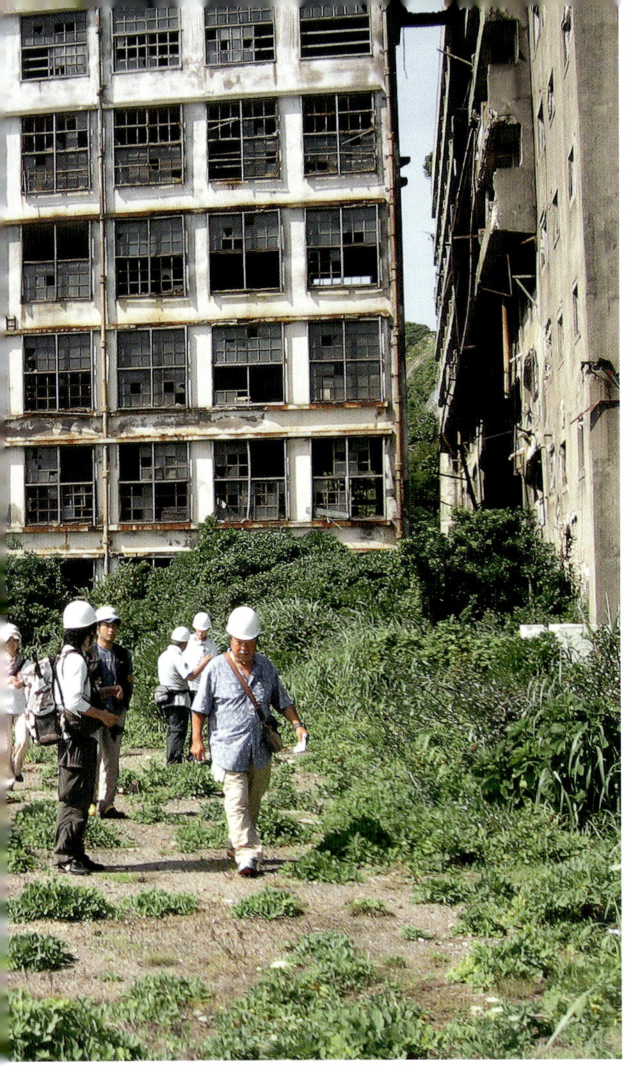
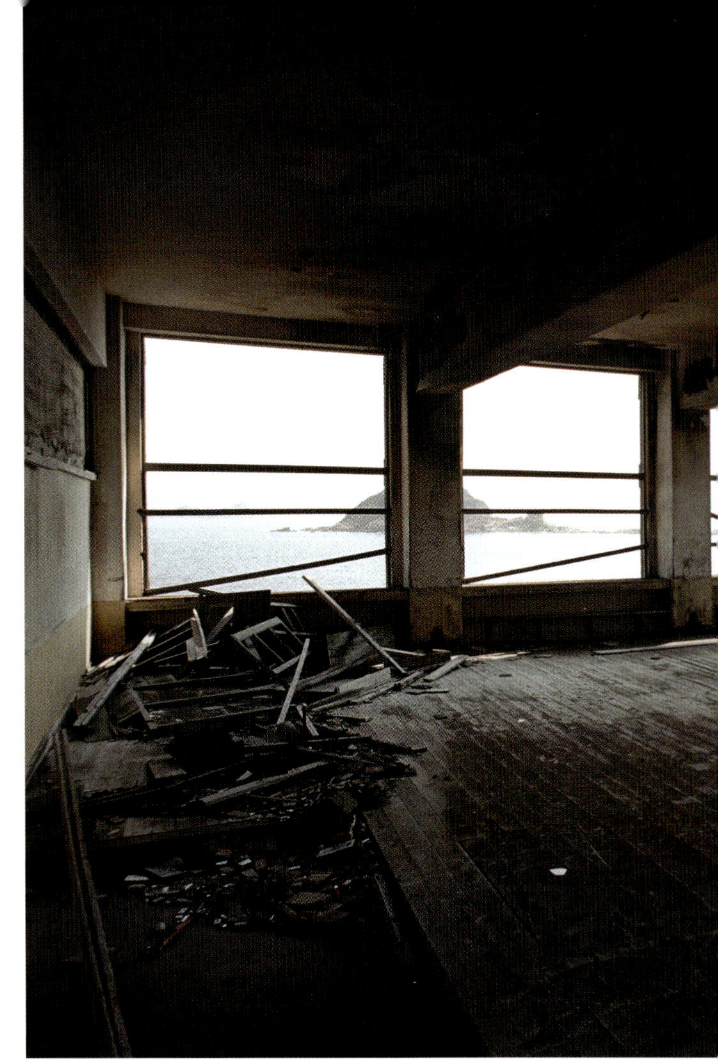
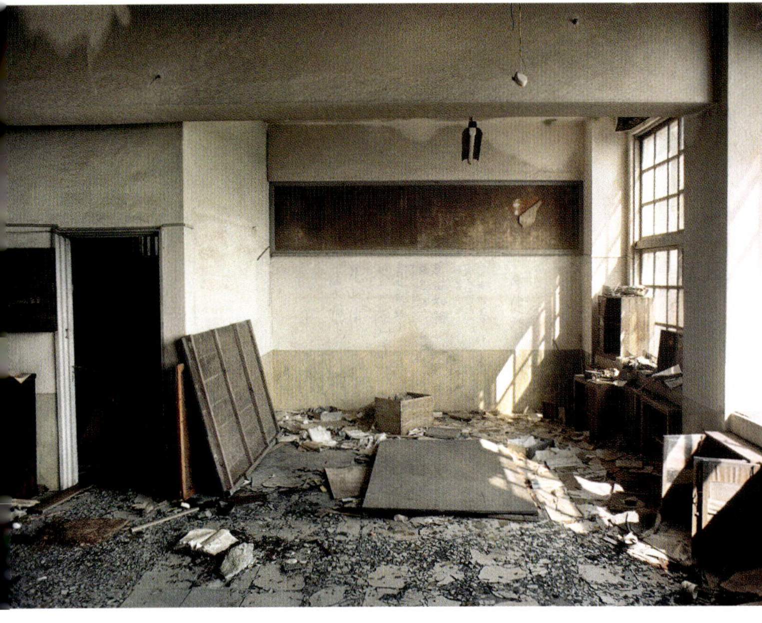
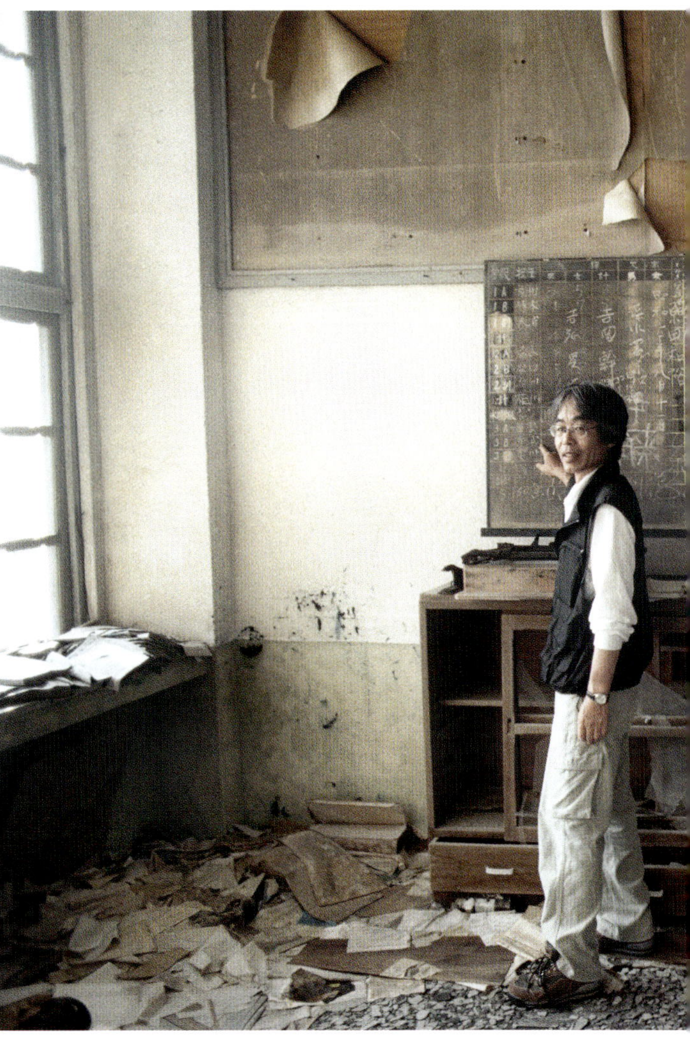

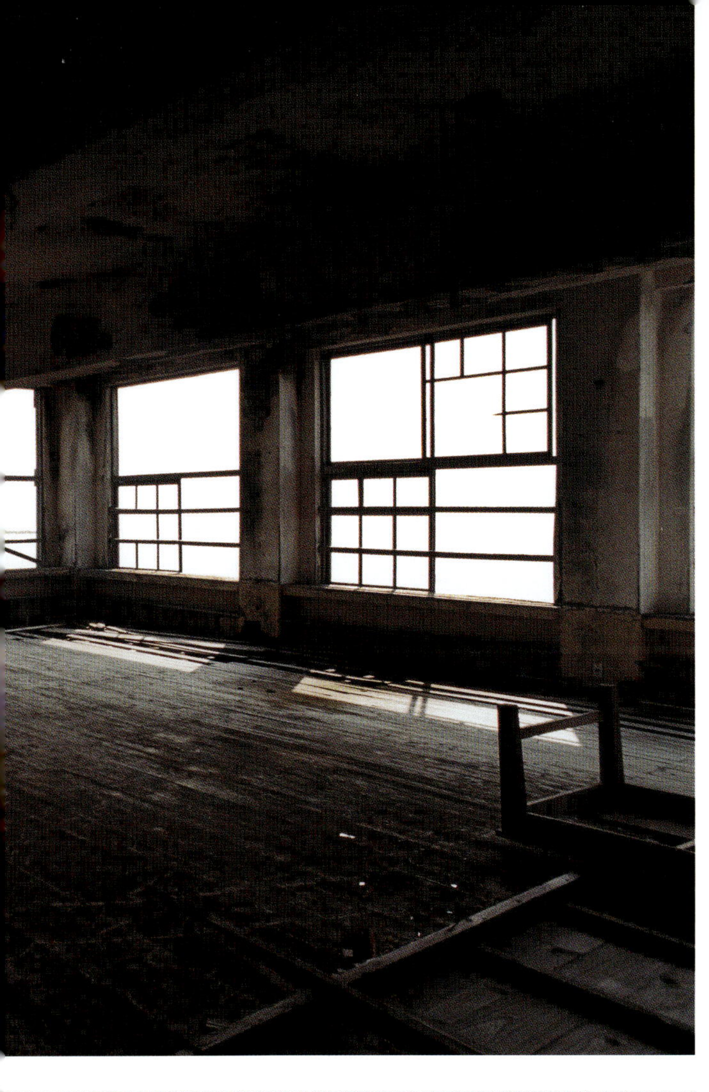

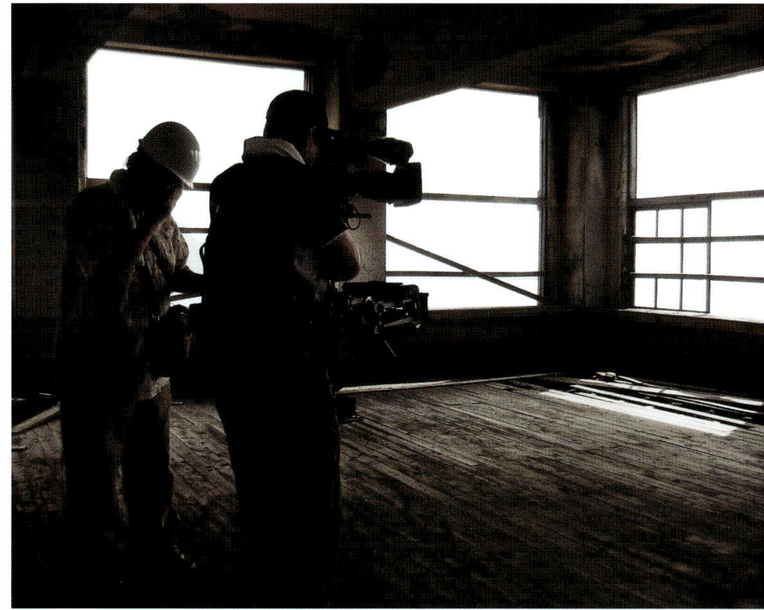

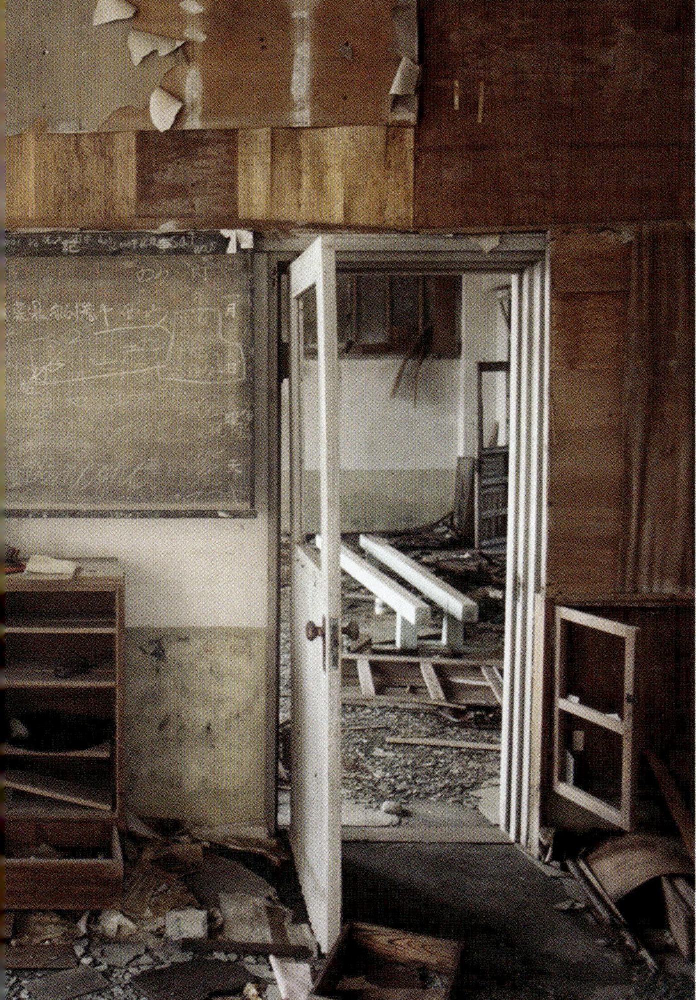

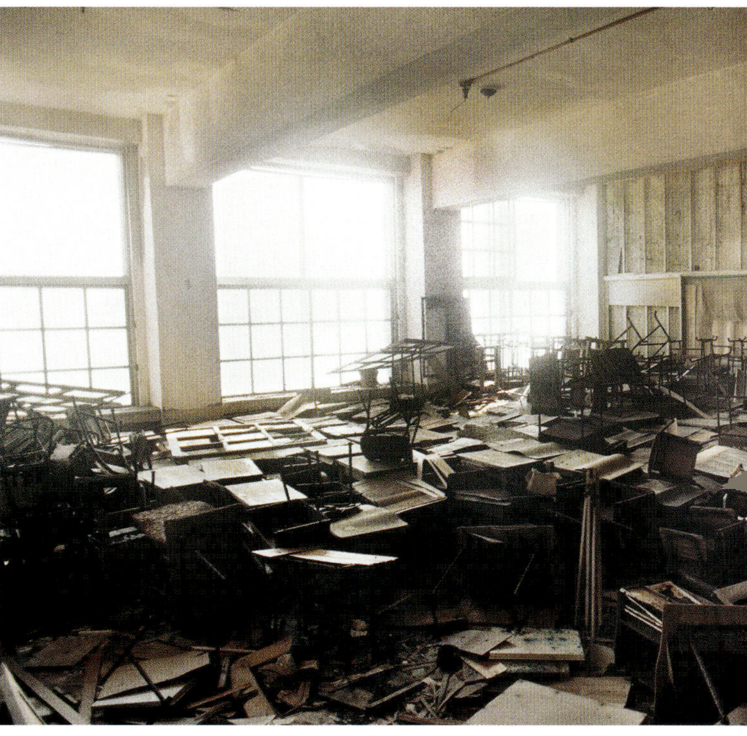

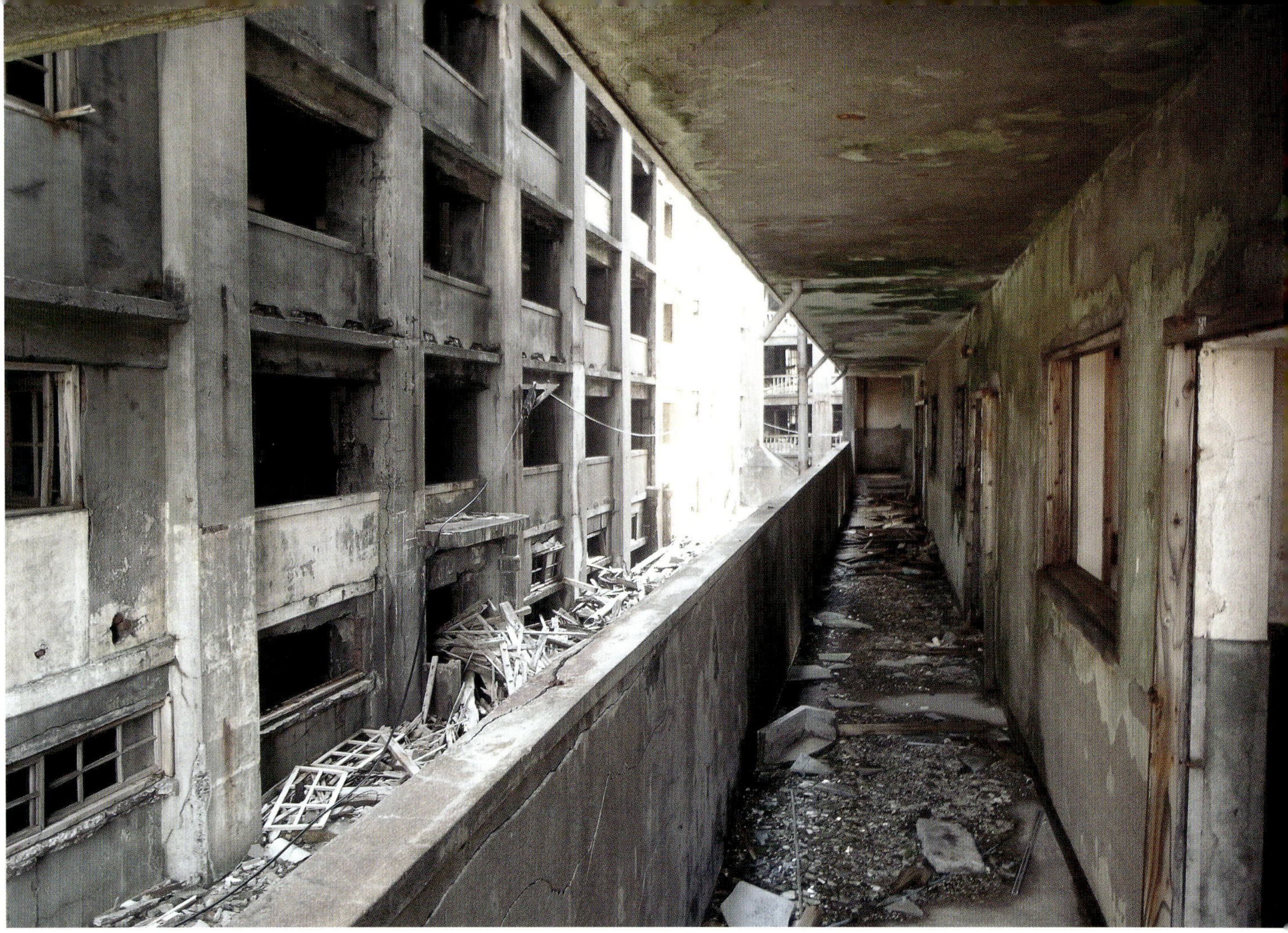

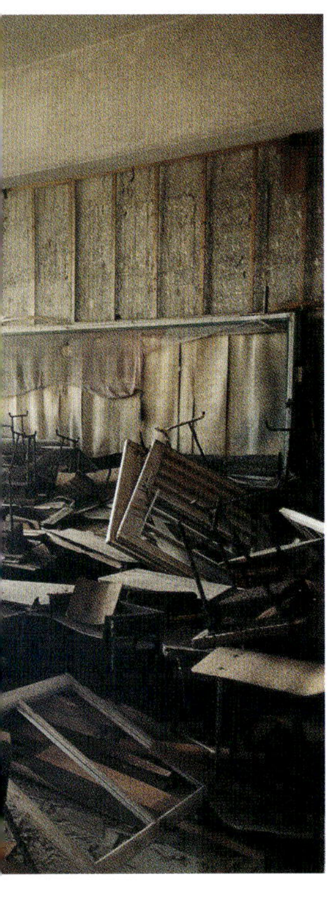

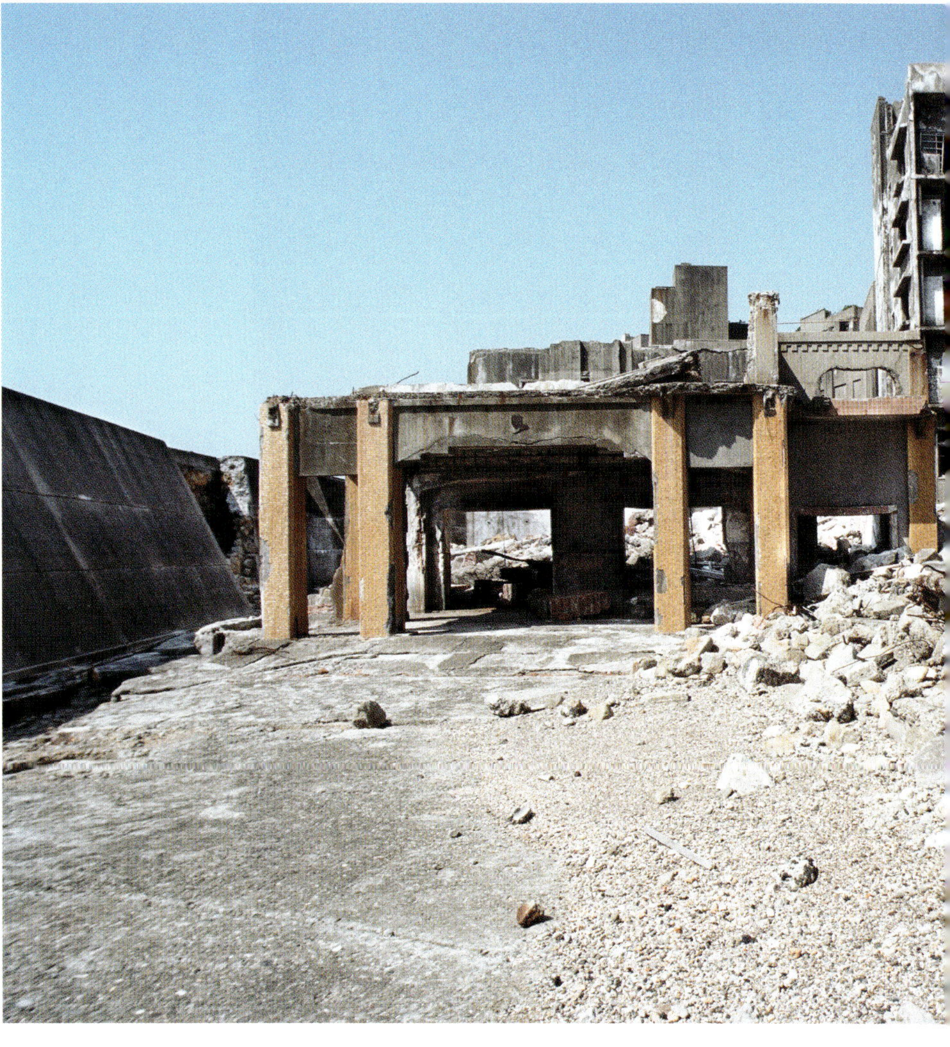

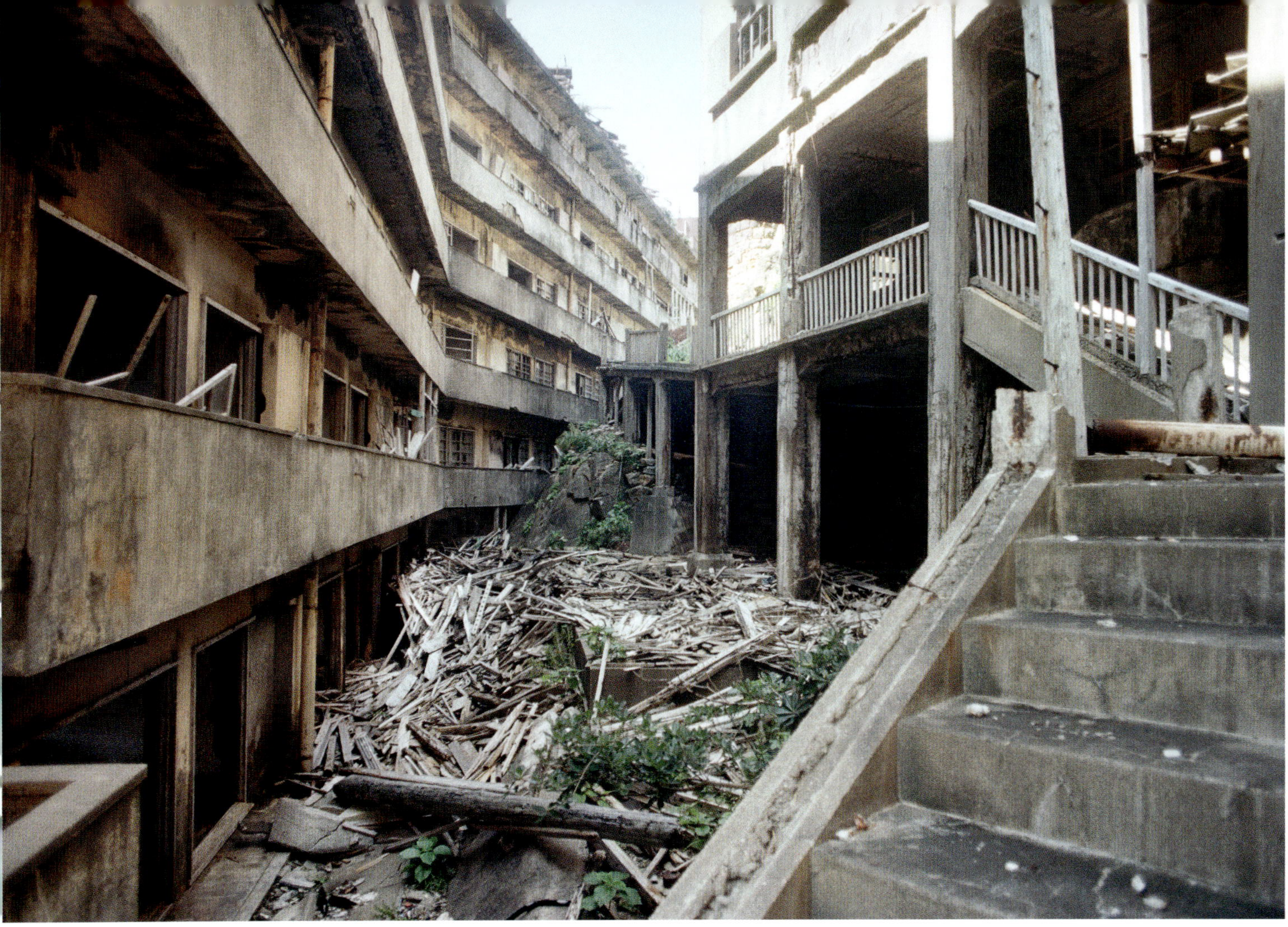

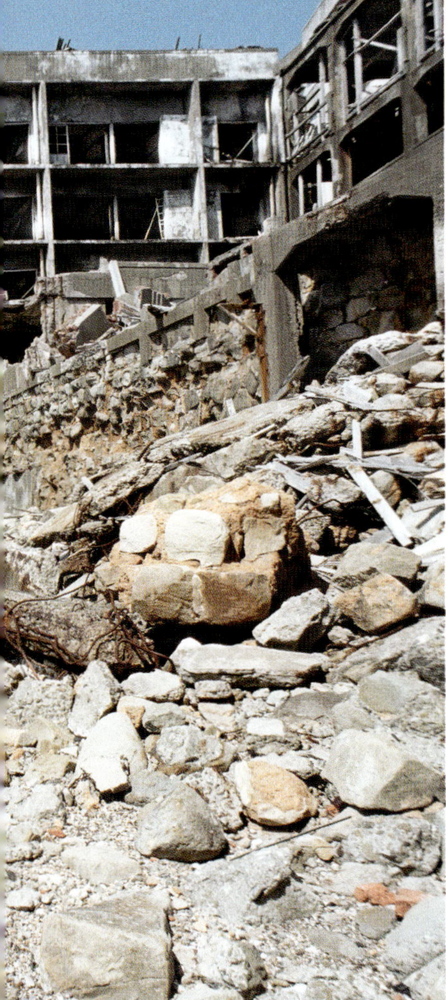

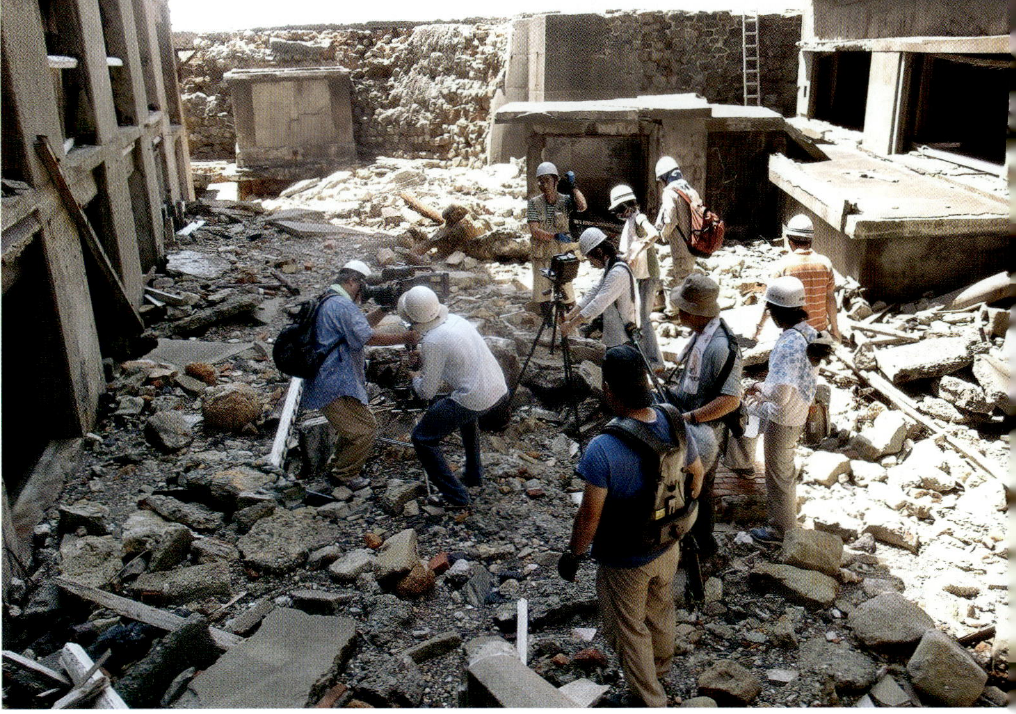

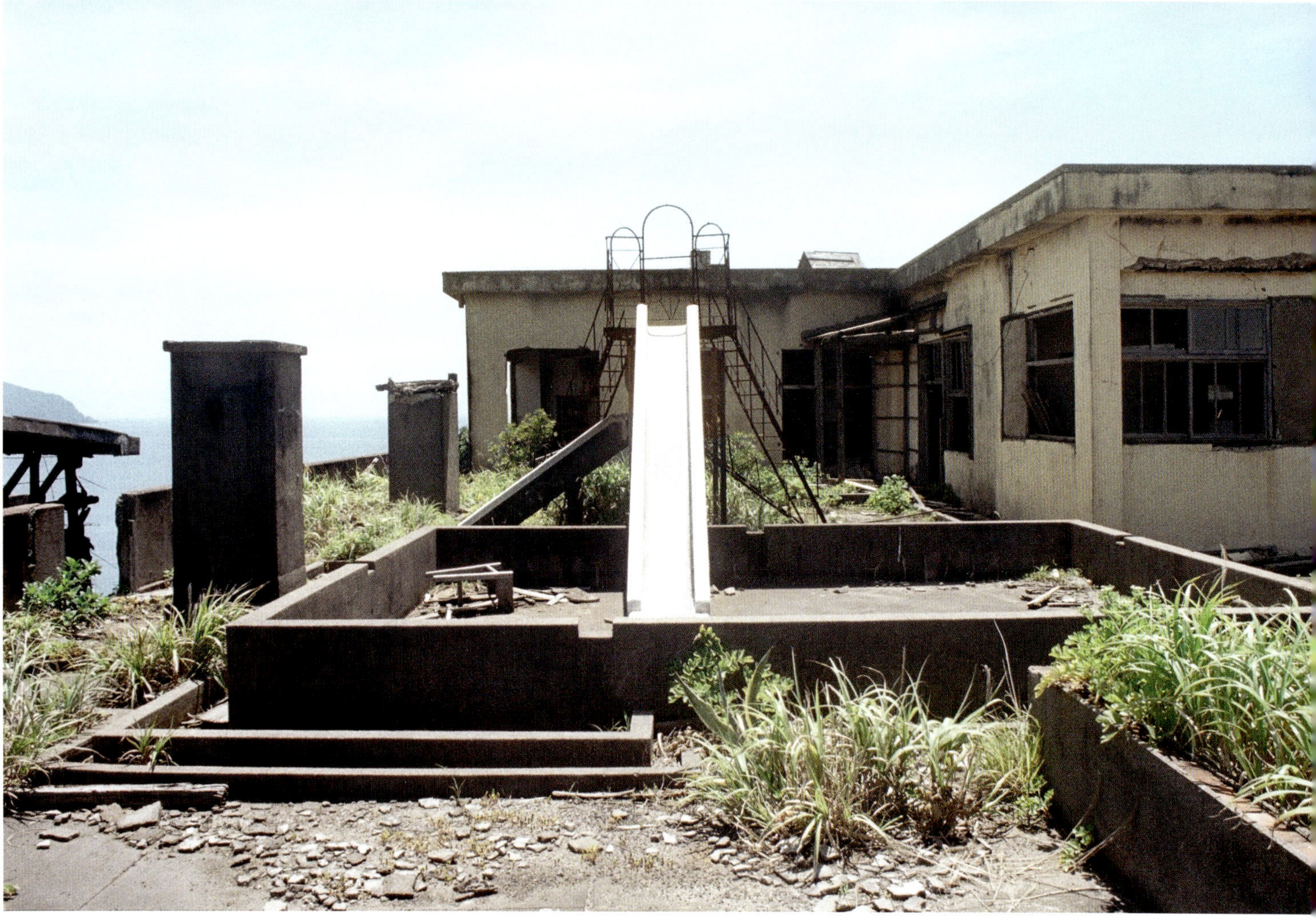

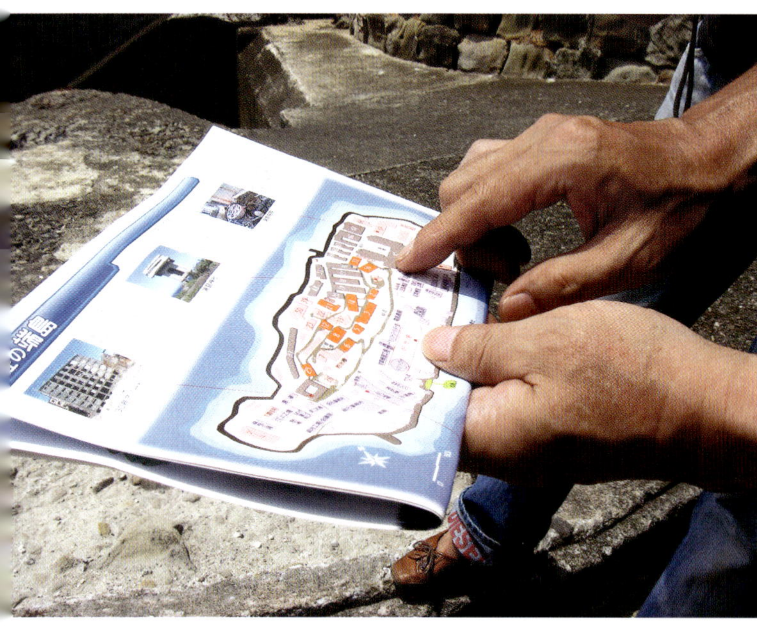

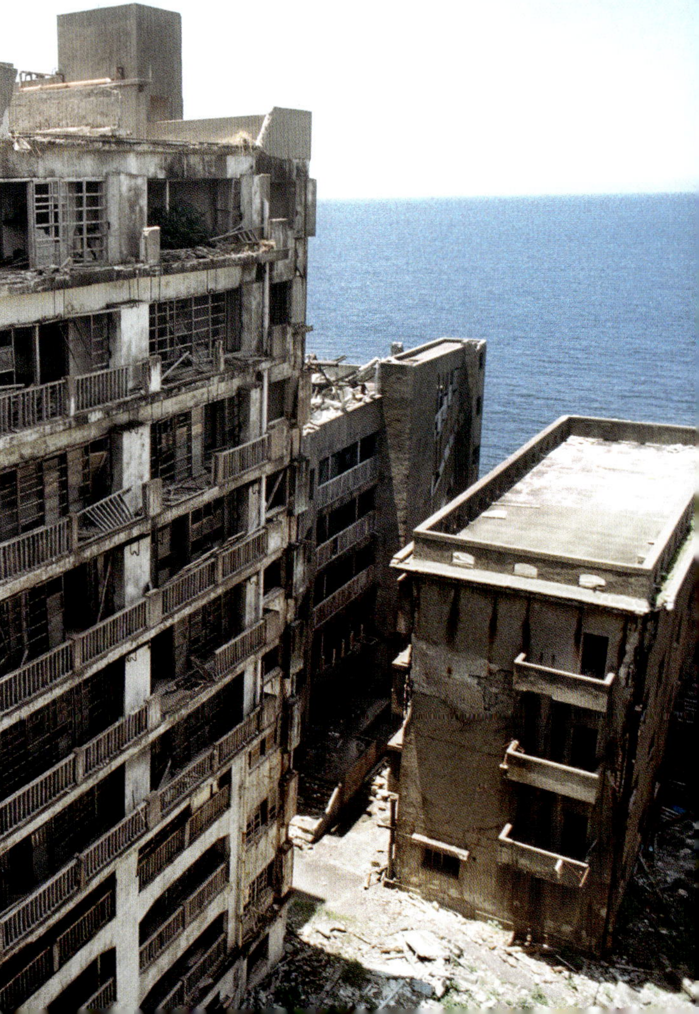

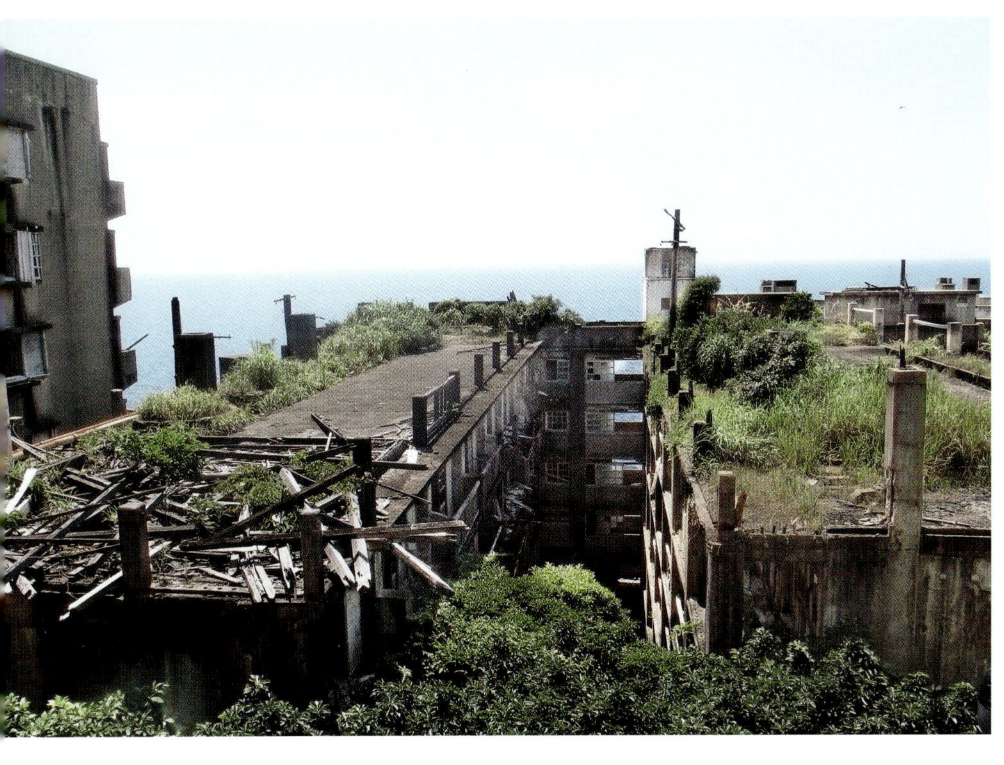

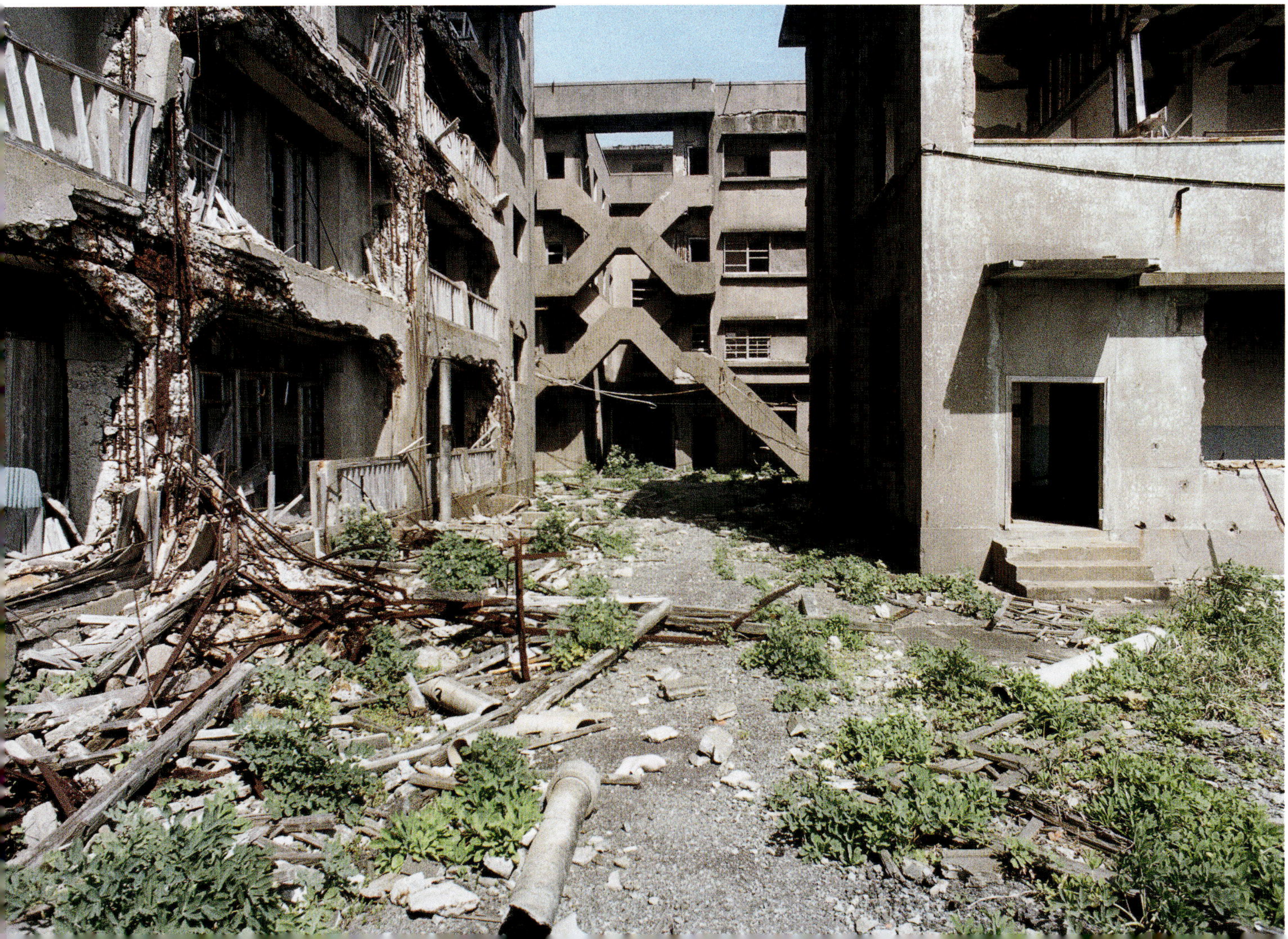

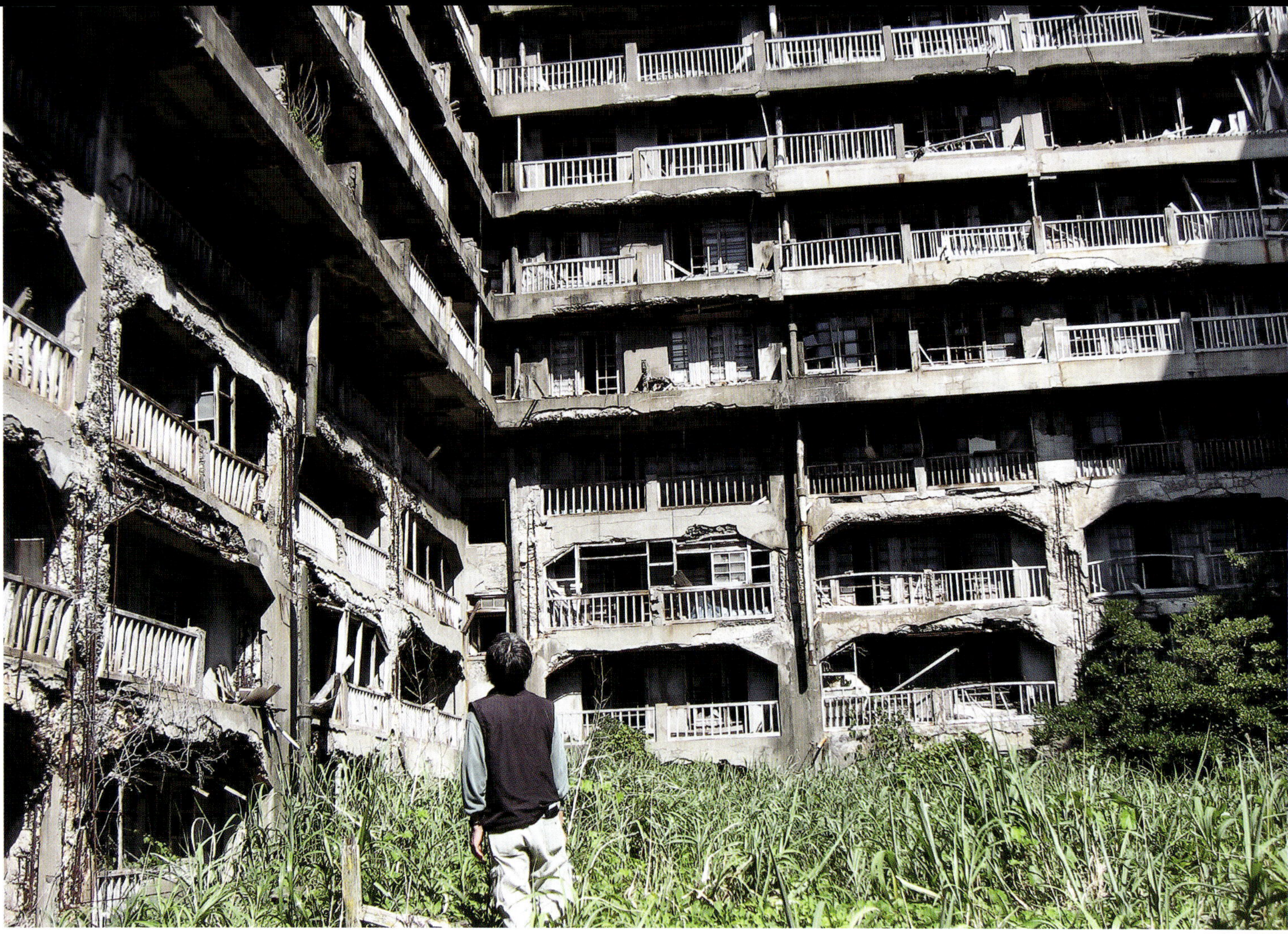

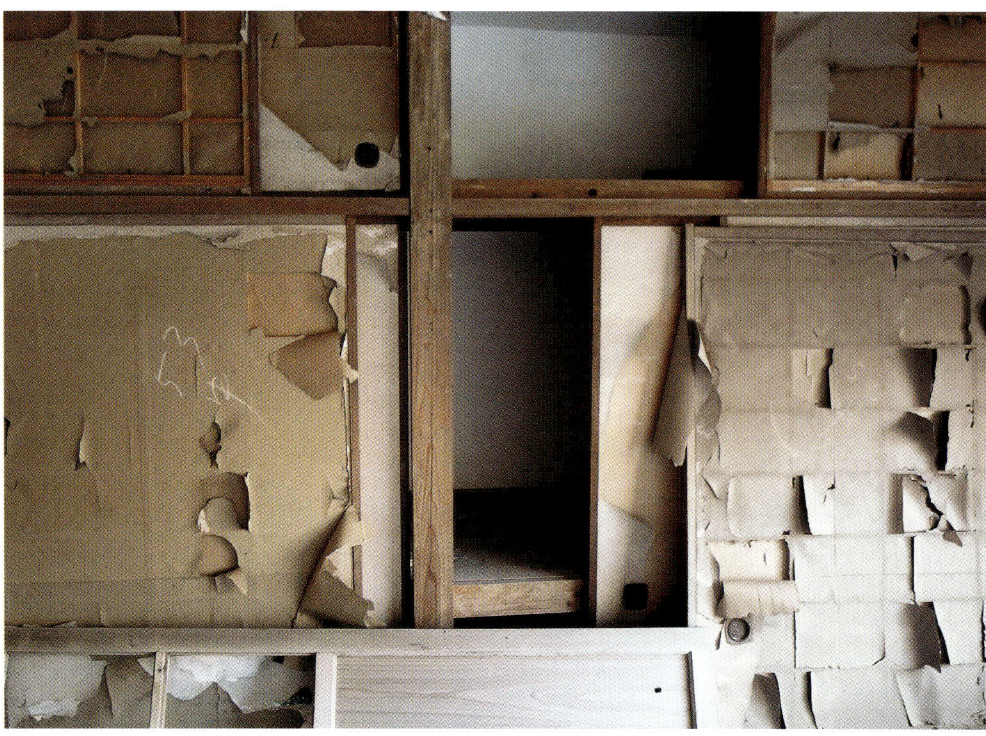

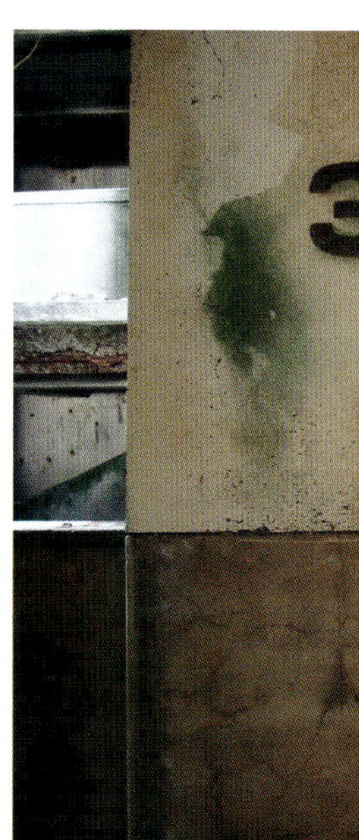

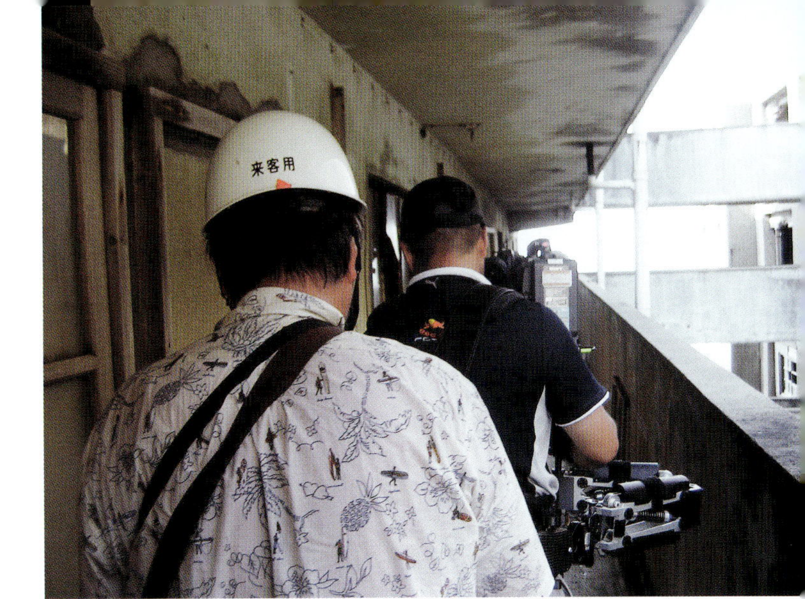
来客用

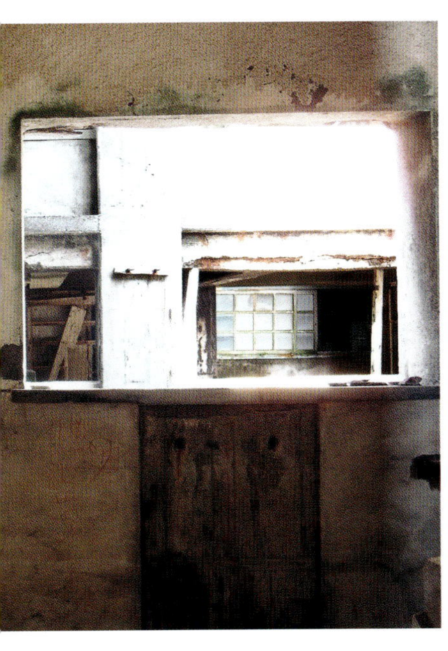

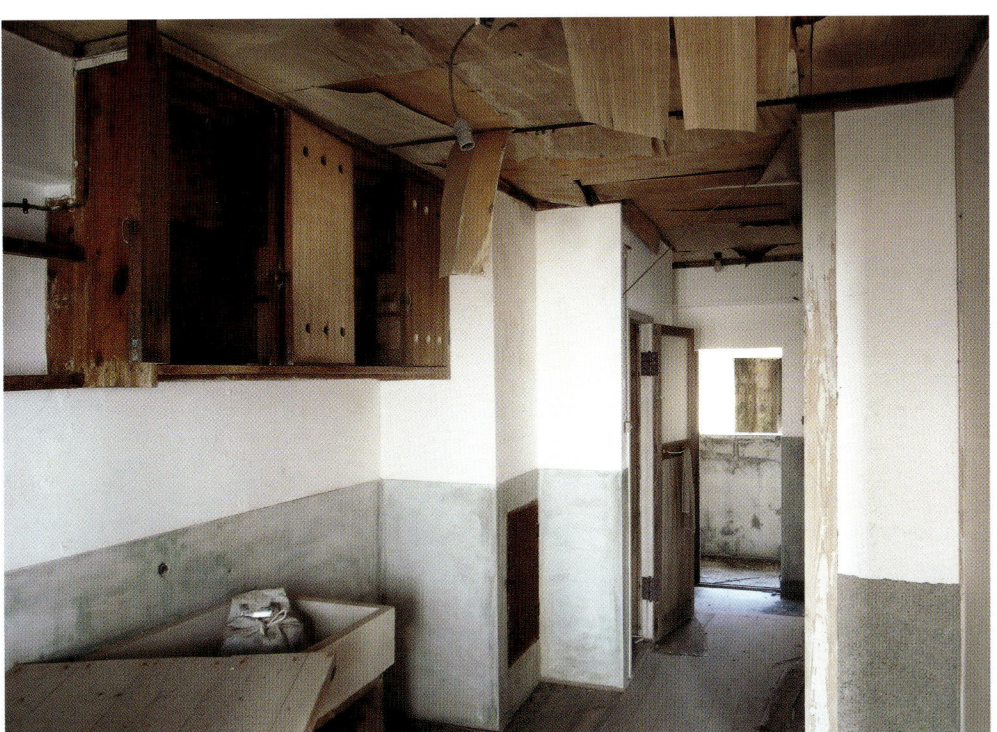

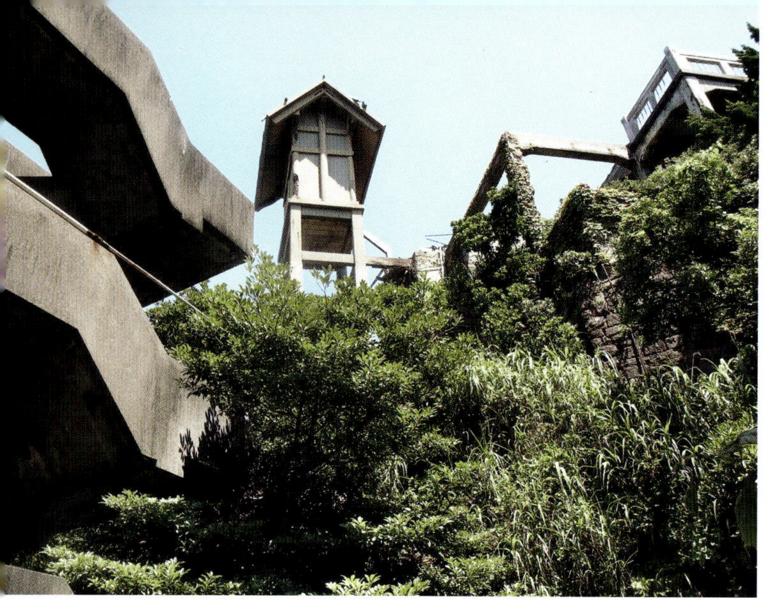

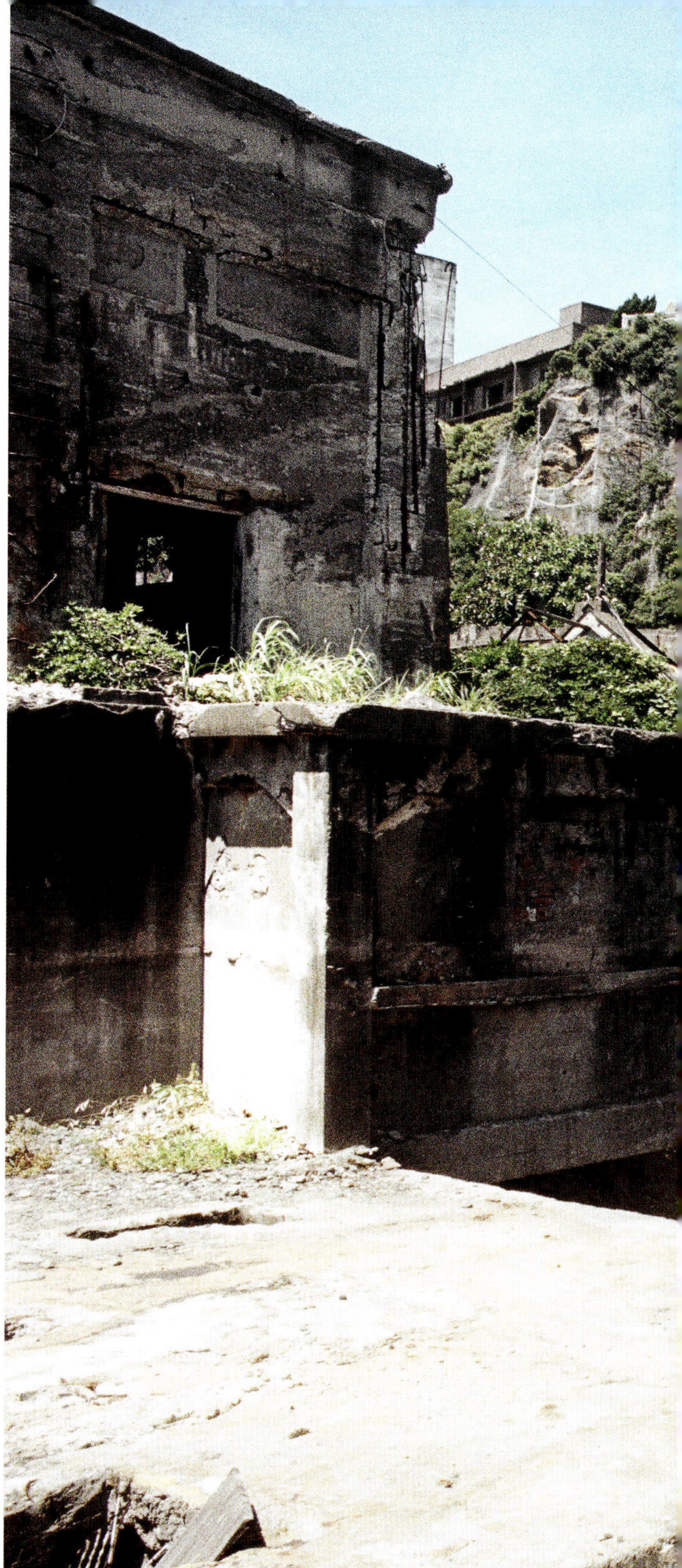

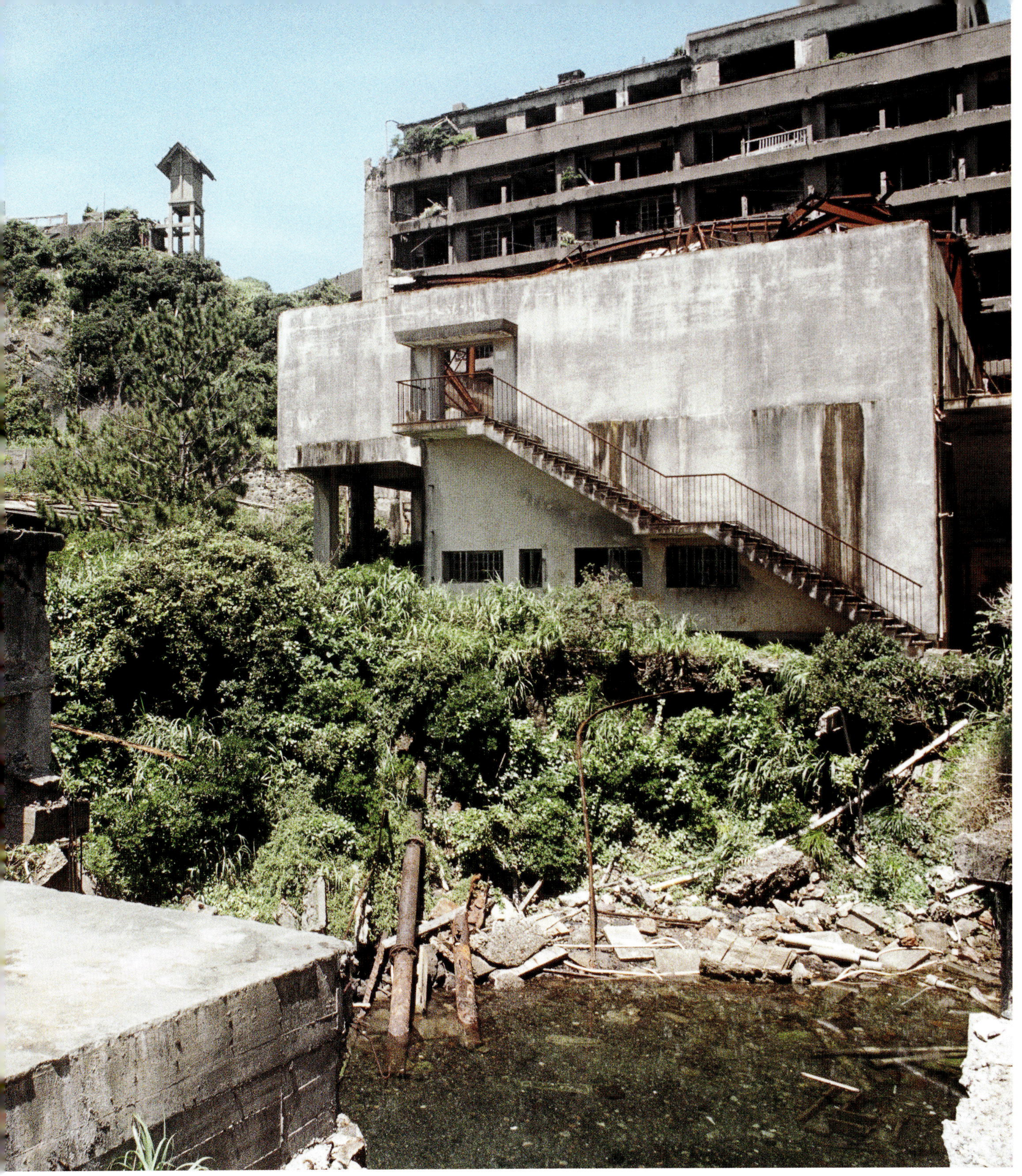

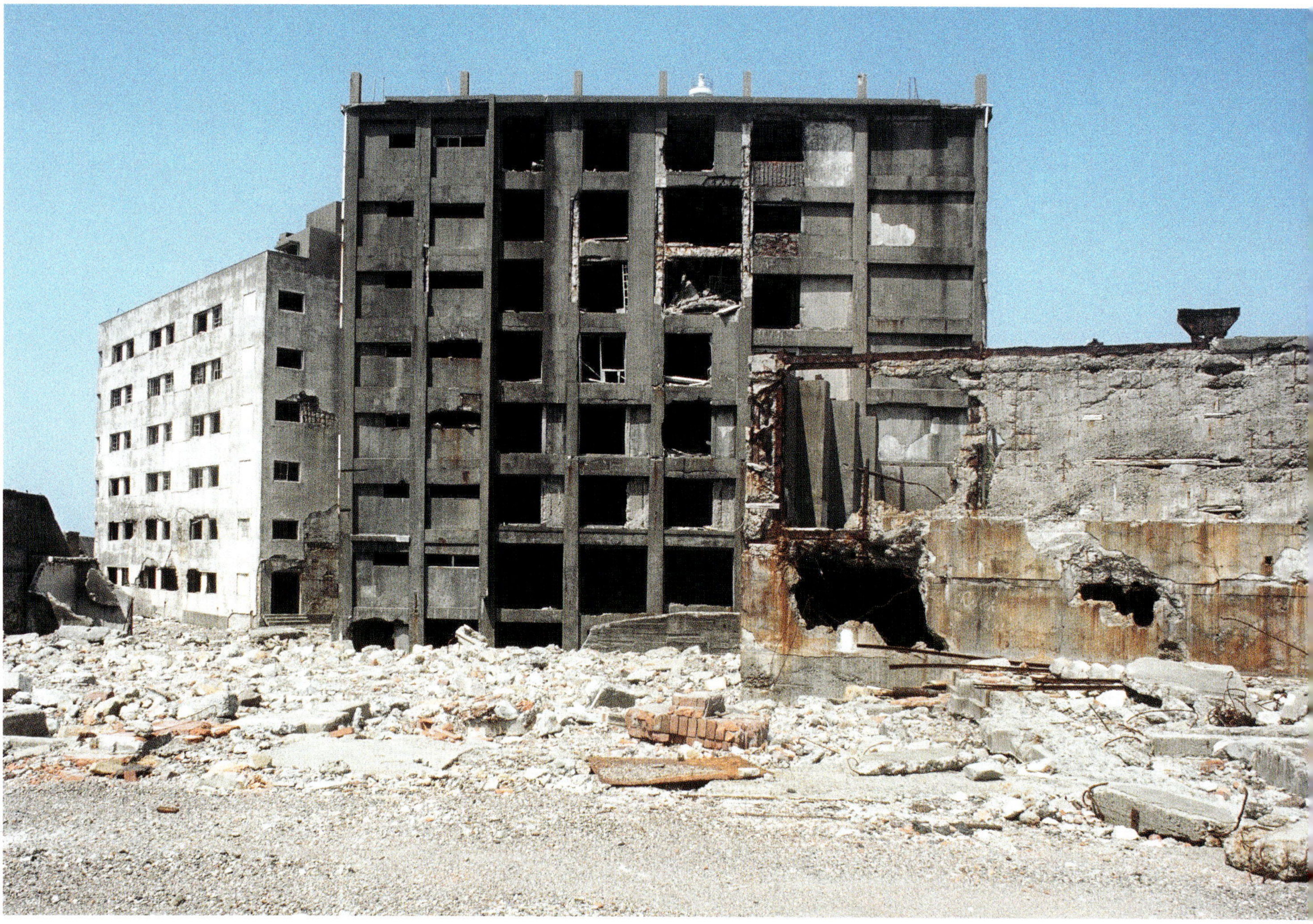

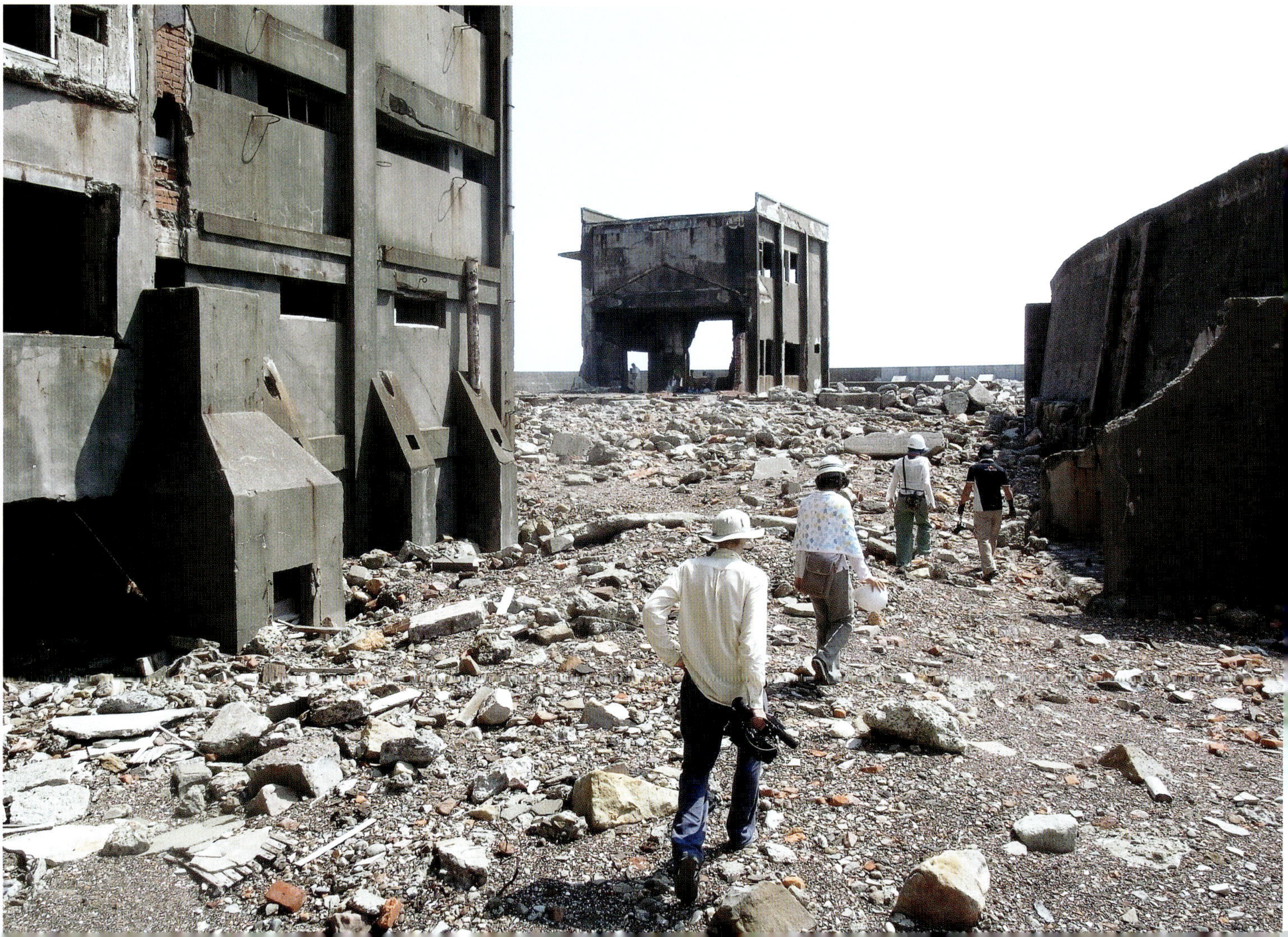

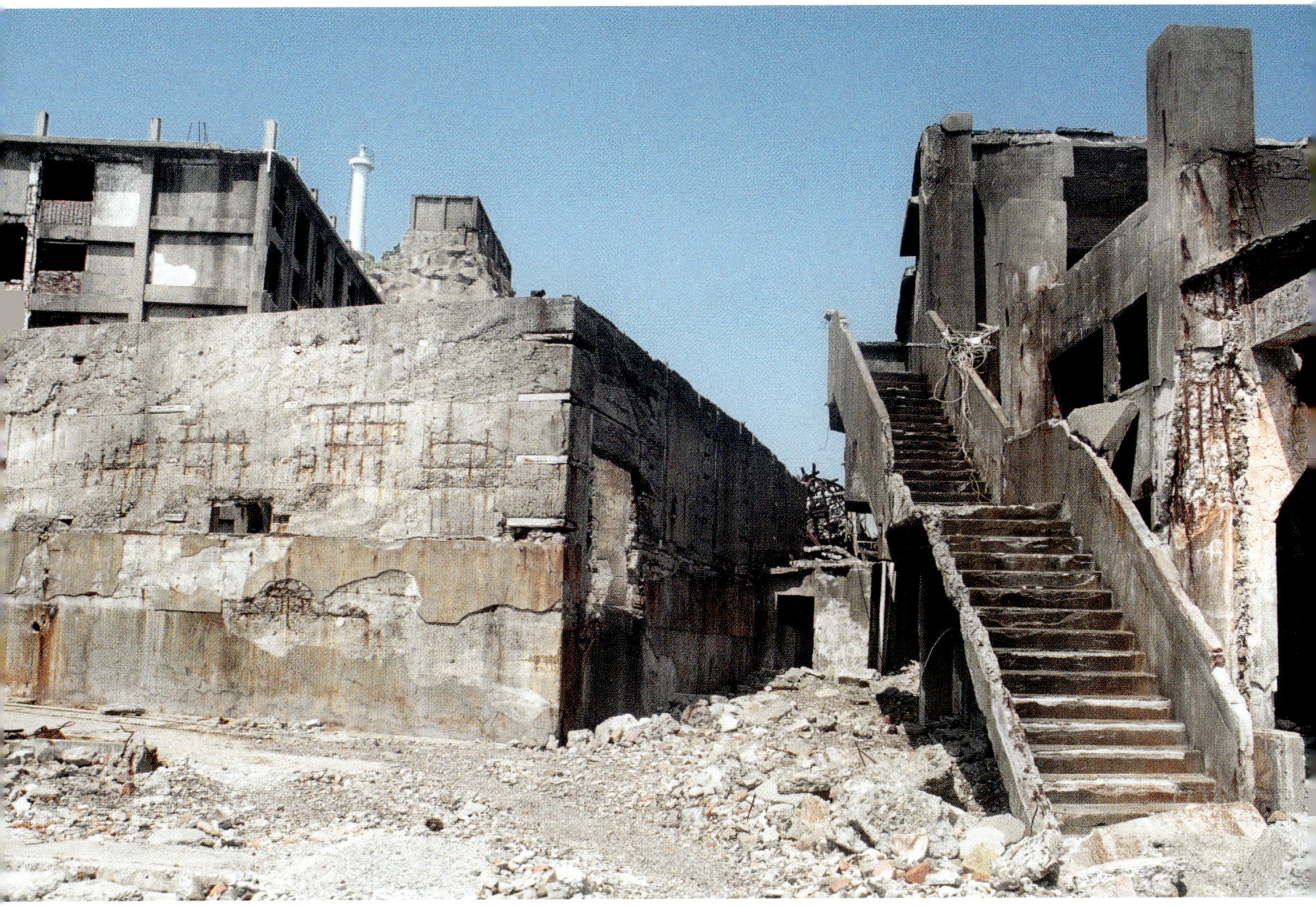

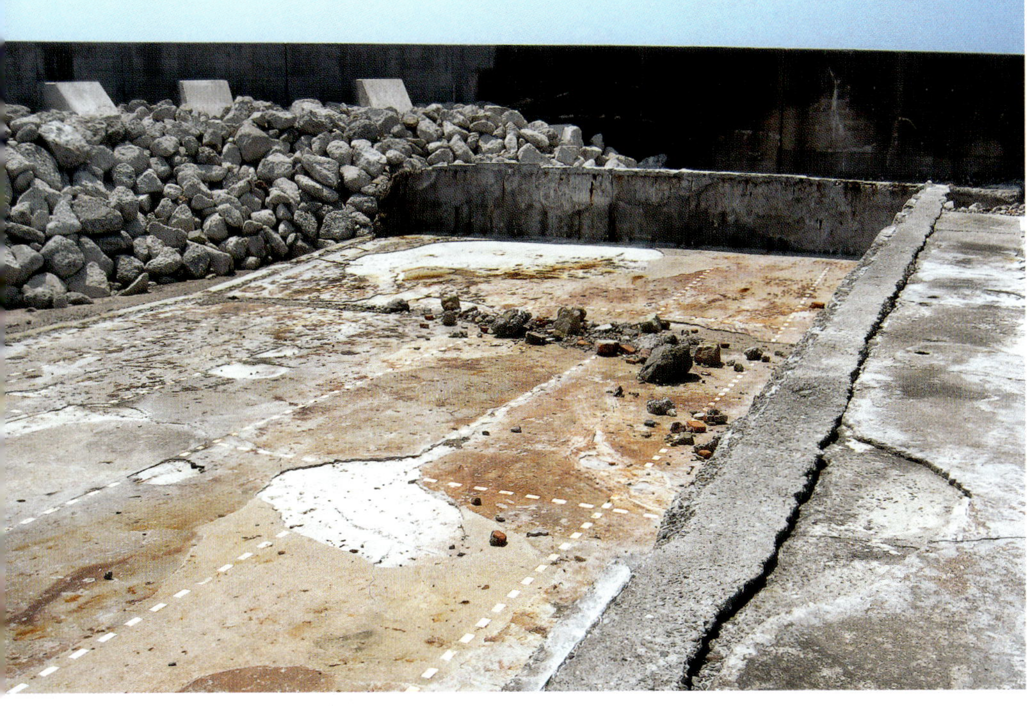

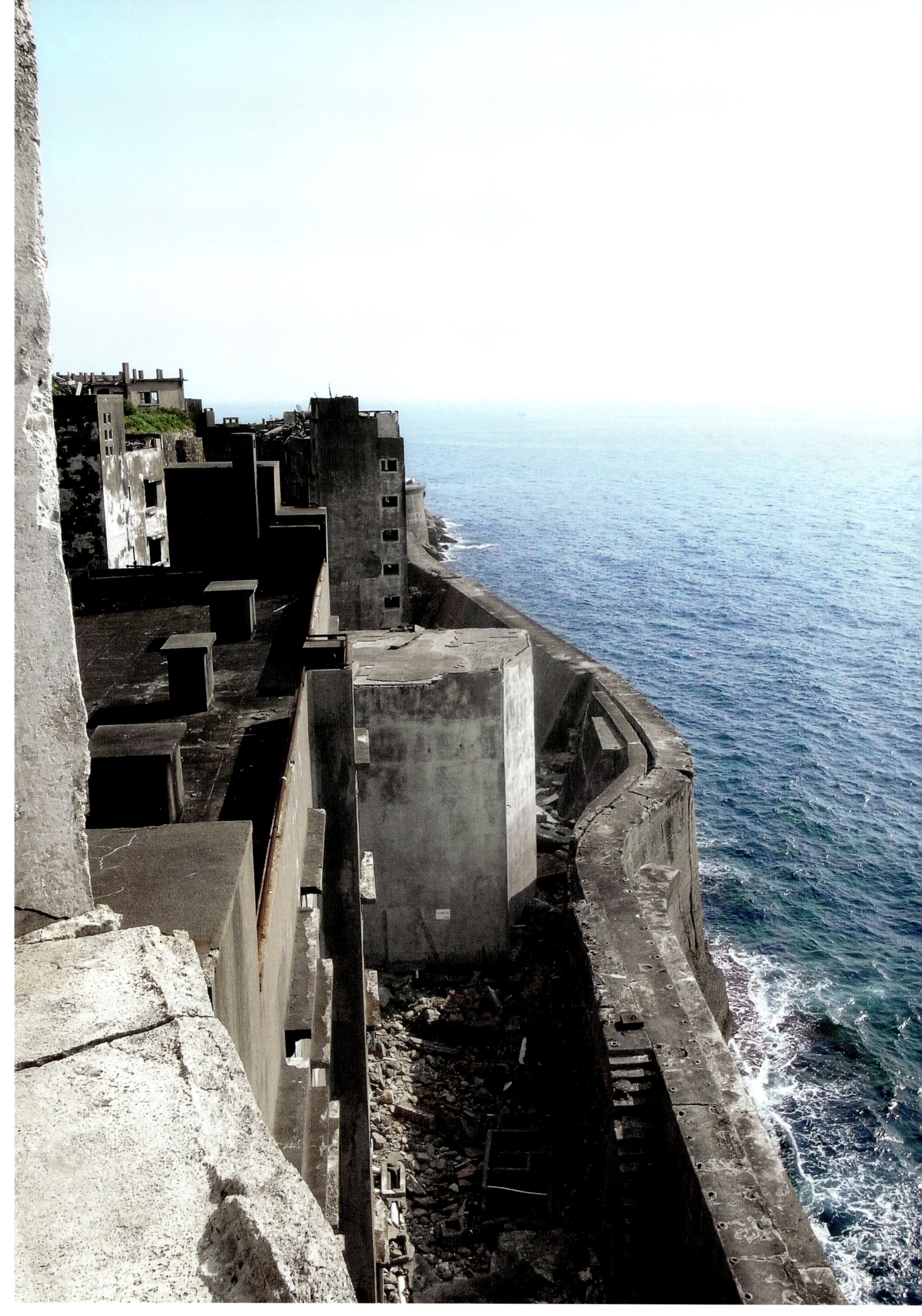

00:06:36 The sun will soon start to set, and on this island it was never dark even after the sun set. Earlier we saw the lighthouse, but at the time it wasn't there. There was no need for it. Because the mine was active 24 hours, so the light never went off. That's why the whole island also served as a lighthouse itself. When you got closer to the island, did you realise that you could hear the voices? As the light was coming closer, we used to be able to hear the voices and the sound from the island. Especially in the evening, you would hear the voices of children and families, also the sound of transporting coal, all of these sounds resonated all together, and when I heard the sounds in the evening, it really felt like I had come home. That was how it used to be, and later when the sun sets, there will be no light. There will only be a little bit of light from the lighthouse, you might not even recognise if there is the island. It makes me feel a bit sad.

もうしばらくしたら陽が落ちます。陽が落ちてもこの島は明るかったんですね。いま先ほど灯台が見えましたけど、灯台はなかったんですよ。無くて良かったんですよ。何故かというと、これが24時間操業してるから一晩中電気が付いていた。だから、この島自体が灯台の役割を持っていた。さっき軍艦島に近づくにつれて島が見えたときにね、声が聞こえるんですよ。明かりと共に声がわーっと広がっているのがわかるんですよ。夕方や夜になってくるとね。子供たちの声、家族の声、石炭を運ぶ音、そういったものが共鳴しあって、夜帰るときにそういうものが聞こえてくると、「ああ家に帰ってきたな」という思いがある。
そういう思いでいたから、あとしばらくして日が落ちて真っ暗になったら、もう明かりがないんですよ。灯台の明かりだけで真っ暗で、島がある事自体もわからないかもしれない。やっぱりそれを見ると寂しいなという思いがします。

00:07:29 Even now if I go there, there is still a name plate, my notebook from when I was a student as well as my desk. More than 30 years after we left home, it's nice that we are still able to see some traces of our lives on the island from those times, and this could never happen in this modern society. You would probably find your old house turning into a parking space, or a new mansion, but because the island has such history, it was left as it was, so it's almost a miracle to be able to see things from old times.
At the same time, the way this island served the coal mining industry is something significant for Japan, and I would like people to understand this. Also for people who used to live on the island and who had to leave for different places all over Japan and overseas, they can feel that their home has not gone and is still there when they see it on TV or read about it in the paper.

今でもあの部屋に行ったら表札が残ってるし、僕の学生時代のノートとか机が残ってるんですよ、今でも。今ふるさとを捨てて30数年経っても、この島には僕らが住んでいたという痕跡が残っているのは、とてもうれしい事だし、現代社会では多分考えられないと思うんですね。
捨てていった街とかそういったものが帰ってきたときには、そこが駐車場になったりマンションが建ったりするんだけど、たまたまこれはこういった島だったから、残されて僕らのふるさとが残っているというのはやっぱり奇跡だと思うんですね。奇跡であるし、またこの島が果たした石炭産業という部分の中で果たしたものは日本の産業にとってすごいものだと思うんです。
それをやっぱりみなさんにわかってほしいんだという思いと、この島に住んでた人たちにとってのふるさとだと。このふるさとがある限り、世界、日本中に散らばっている人たちがテレビや新聞とかで見たときに、「ああ自分のふるさとだった」と思い出せることが、ふるさとが無くなっていないというところとつながっているような気がします。

00:08:15 Just now, you can see building no.65, which is a three-walled structure in front of us, on top of it there is a beige coloured building, which was the kindergarten. From this point, you can see my house, left of the beige part, on the top floor, the balcony there was where I lived. The balcony was my room. I was allowed a space of one tatami mattress. It was my private room. Our family lived in an apartment with rooms the size of 6 tatami mattresses and 4 tatami mattresses, and there were 5 of us. When you reach the age of a junior high school or high school student, you start to need some privacy, so my dad put down one tatami mattress, and sealed up the room with a plywood panel to make a study room for me. It's still there.

コの字型の65号というのがちょうど正面に見えているんですが、あの一番上のベージュ色の建物が幼稚園です。ちょうど今、僕の家も見えてるんですね。あそこに、ベージュの左側のところの一番上の方の。あそこがベランダで僕が住んでたところ。
あのベランダに僕の部屋があった。一畳の畳の部屋を作ってもらって、あそこは部屋だった。僕の、なんていうかな、プライベートな部屋。6畳と4畳半で親子5人で住んでたわけだから、中学、高校になってくるとやっぱり自分のプライバシーが欲しくなるじゃない。親父がそこに畳一枚を敷いてくれて、ベニヤで目張りしてくれて、僕の勉強部屋を作ってくれた。今でも残っています。

00:08:39 You see the person in the empty space between buildings, there was a cinema. It was destroyed by a typhoon, but in the old days you could see a movie for just 50 or 80 yen, and they had Yujiro movies and such like.
The shrine you see on top of that hill was a meeting point especially for young couples at that time. I always visit it, to pray, when I come here.

今ちょうど、建物が、空白になってますよね。あそこに映画館があったんですね。今はもう台風で壊れてしまってますけど。あそこの映画館では、ちょうど僕らの時代だから50円か80円で観れたんですね。裕次郎とかああいうのが来てましたけどね。
あの岩の上に見えている神社は、当時若いカップルに特に人気の待ち合わせ場所だった。今でもこの島に来るたびに、あそこに行ってお参りするんです。

00:09:05 Later, you will see a rectangular-shaped building below the lighthouse. That's building no.30. It's the very first concrete residential mansion that was ever made in Japan. The rotating part that I explained earlier was also the first one in Japan. It was built in 1957. The upper part of the sea wall has been repaired. That was damaged by the typhoon last year.

今ちょうど灯台の下の方に四角っぽい建物があります。あれが三十号棟、日本で初めての鉄筋のマンション。人が住んだコンクリートの建物です。日本初です。先ほど説明した海底水道も二本あって、昭和32年にできてますから。今、岸壁が新しくなってますが、上のほうのね。あれは去年台風でやられたんです。

00:09:26 This side is the back of the island. The rock surface you see near the lighthouse, that's the original state of the island, just that. They reclaimed land from sea and made it into the shape it is now. It wasn't built to look like a war ship, but as they filled in the land, it started to look like a war ship from other directions such as the opposite shore.

ちょうどこれが島の後ろ側なんですよね。今灯台が見えているあたりの岩肌、あれがこの島の原形です。あれだけしかなかった。あれを埋め立てていって、今のような形にしたわけです。軍艦に似せて作ったのではなく、埋め立てていく間に、対岸から見たりすれば軍艦の形に見えたというだけです。

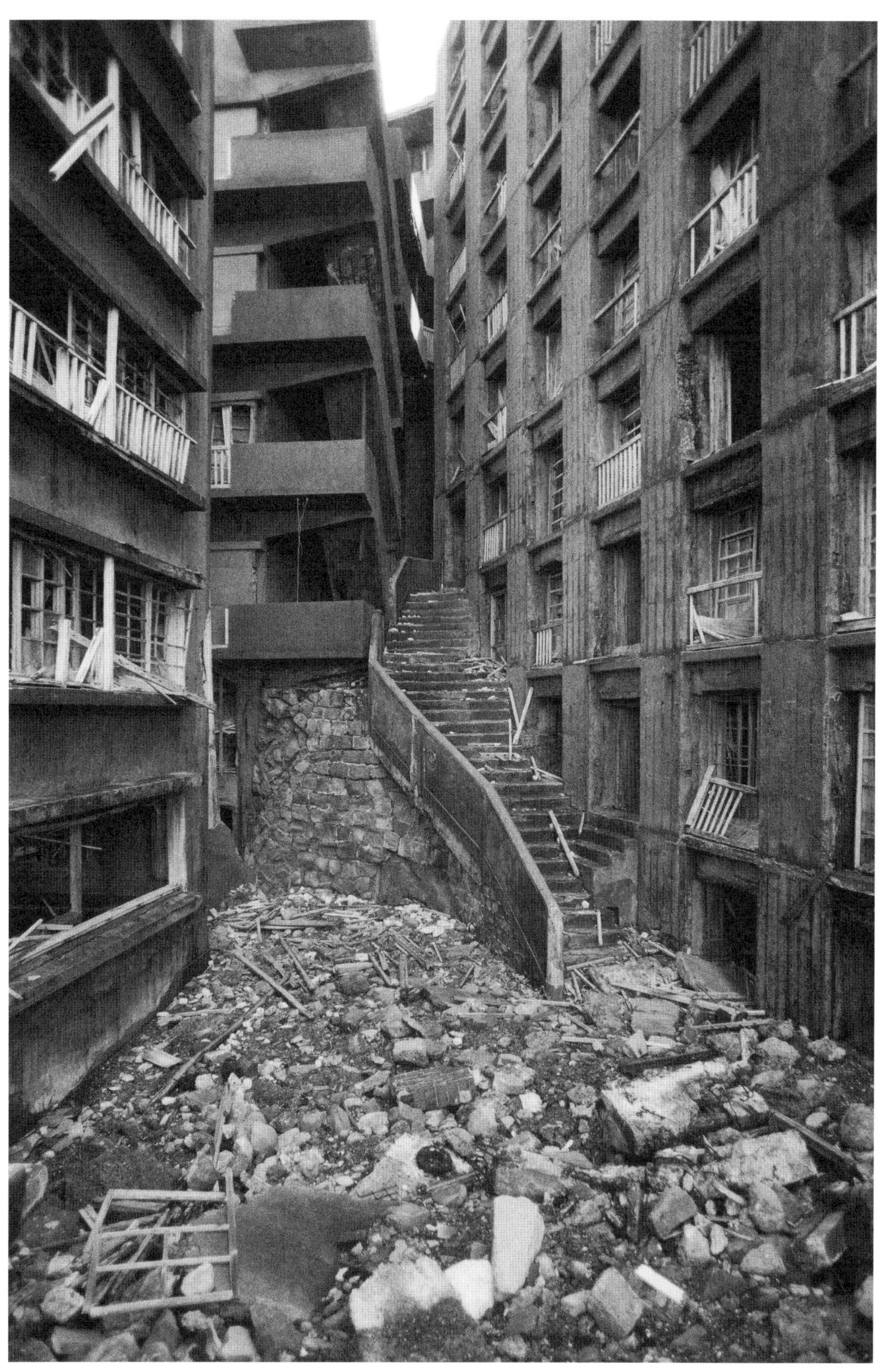

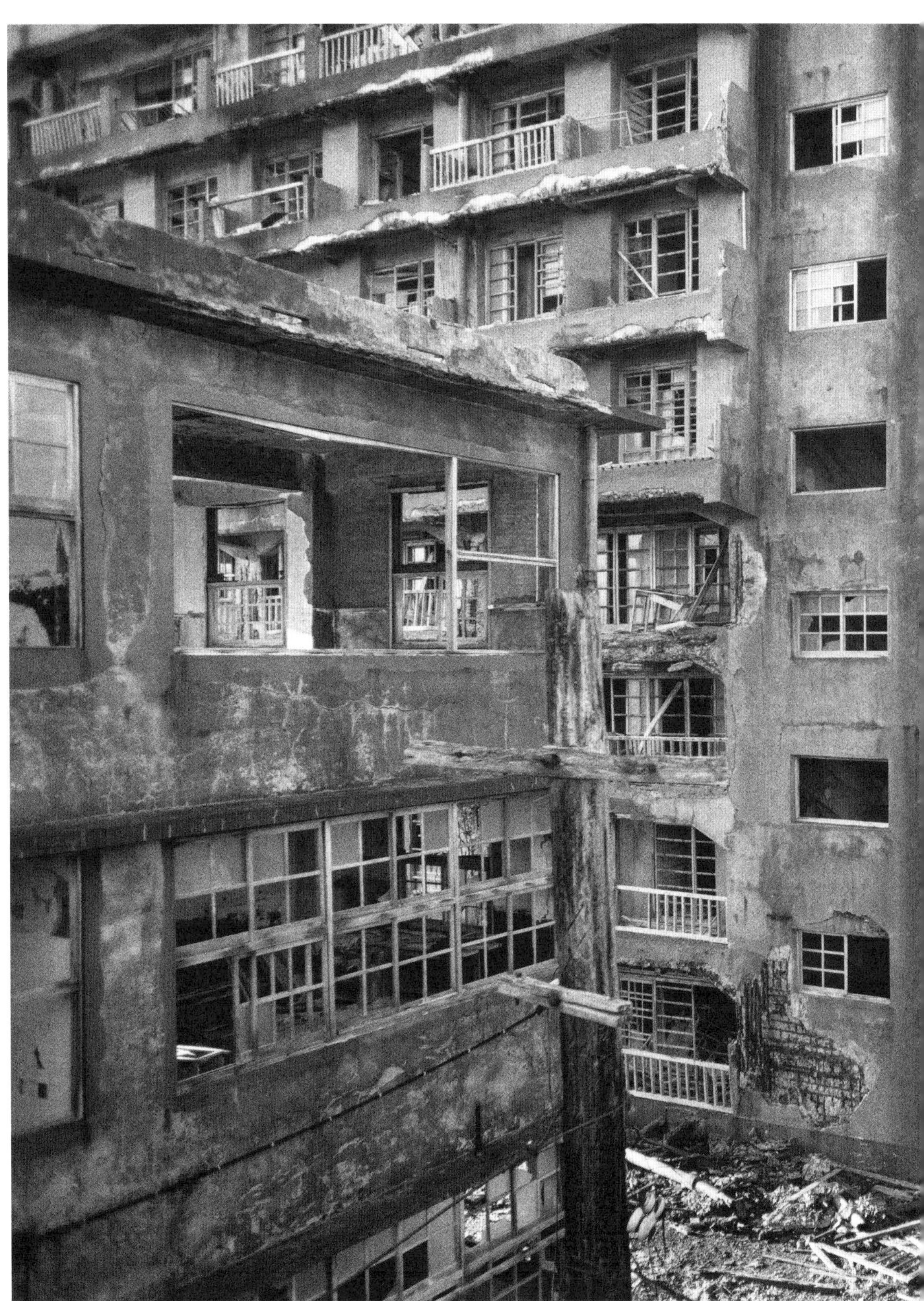

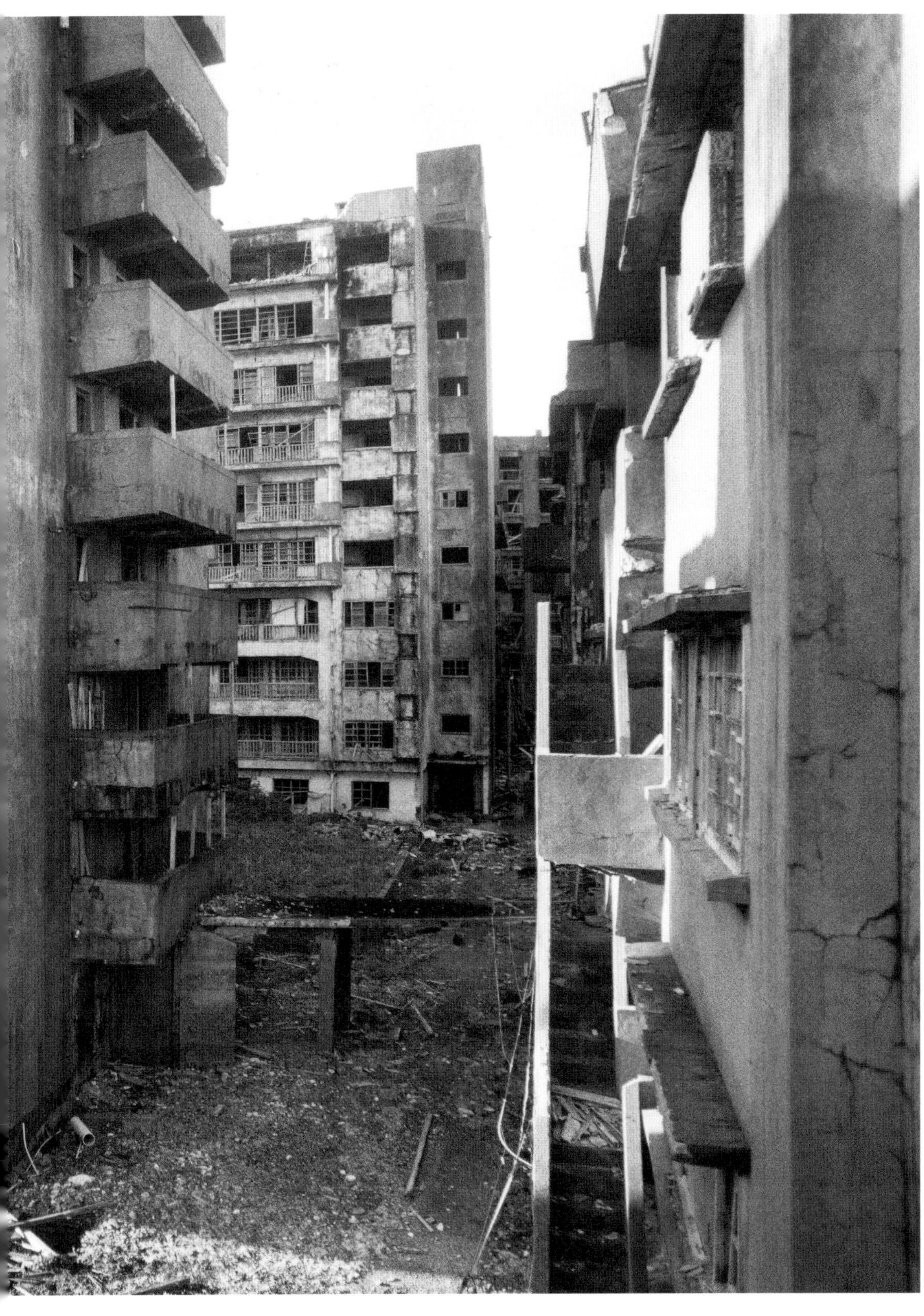

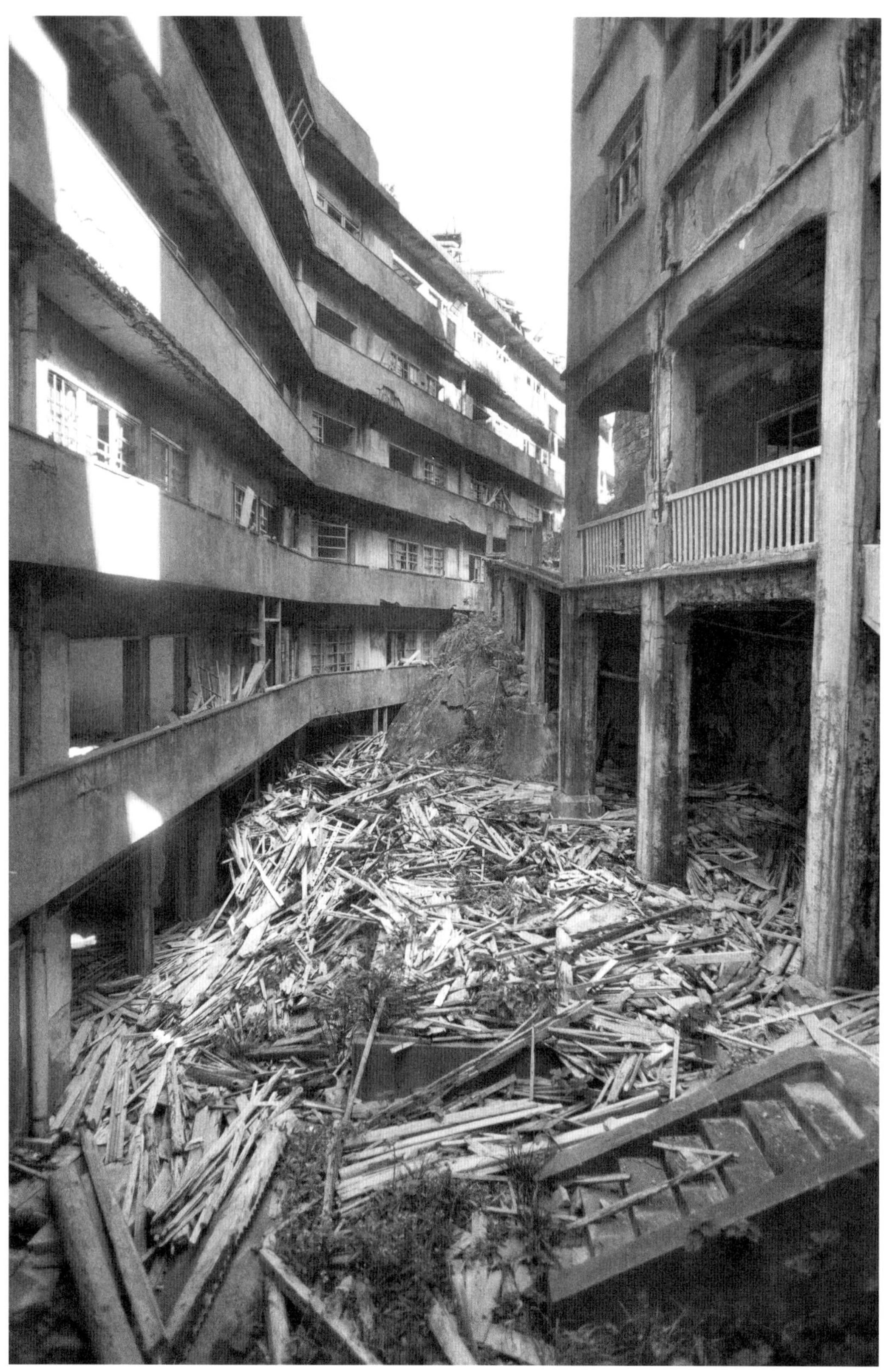

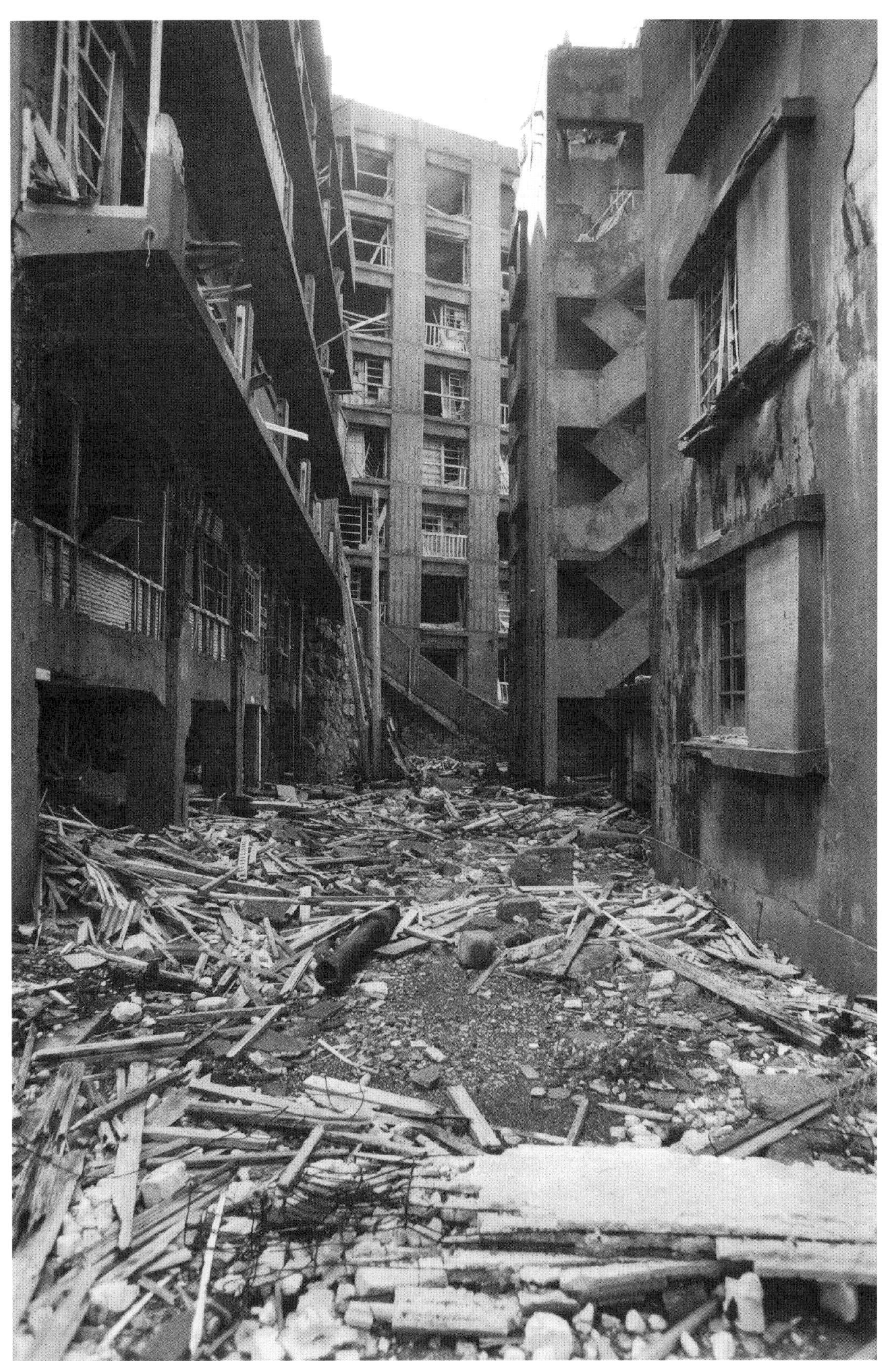

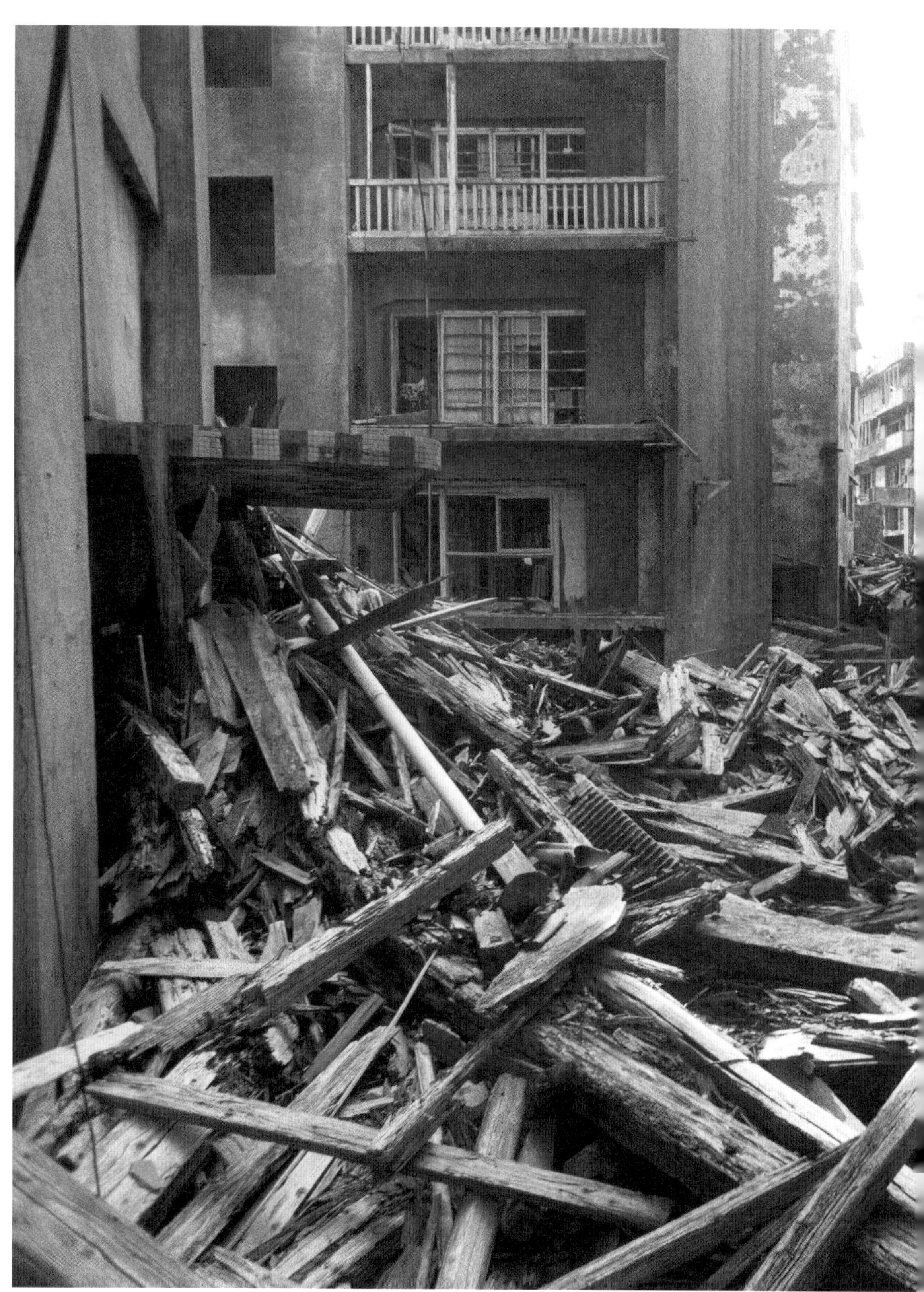

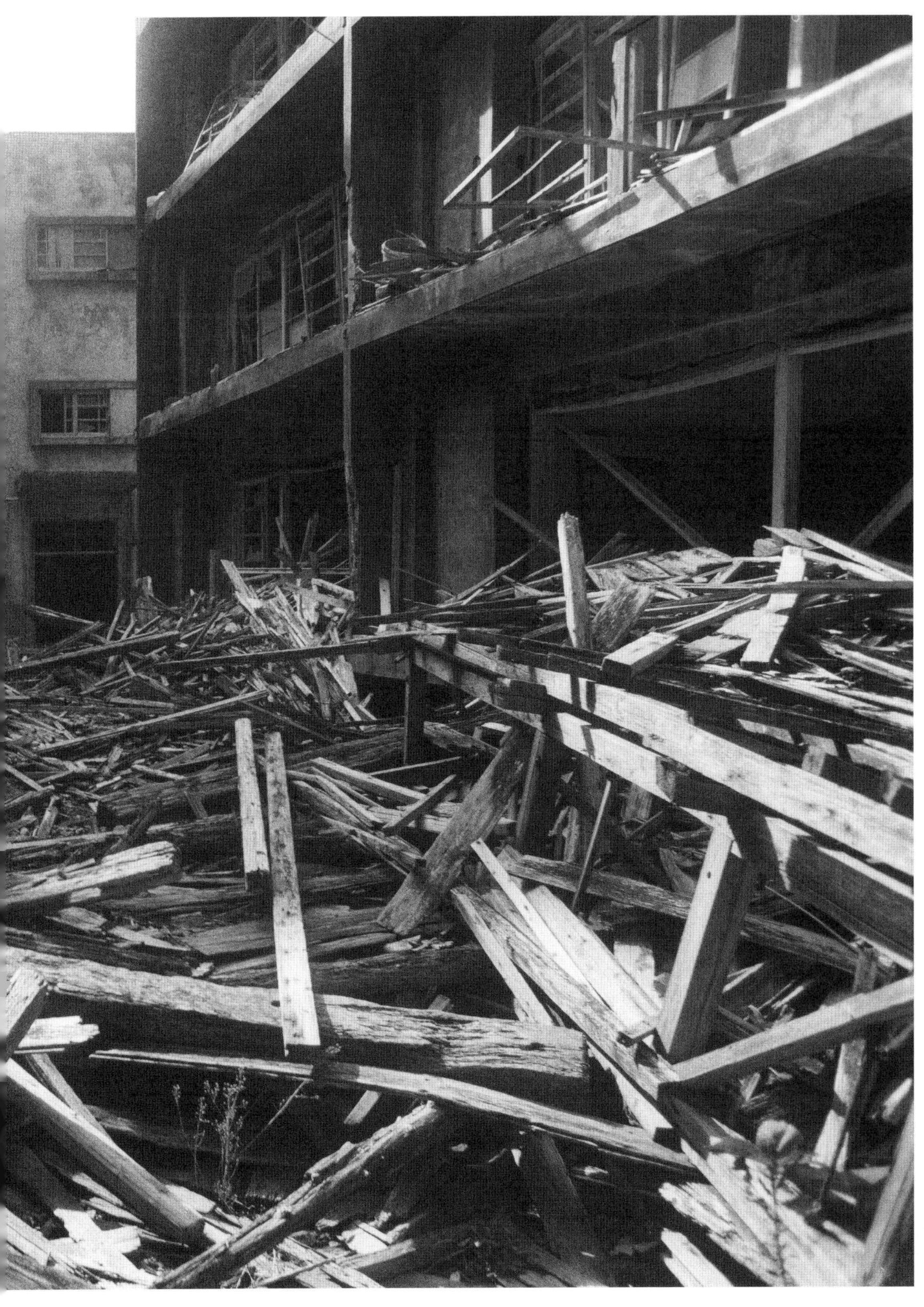

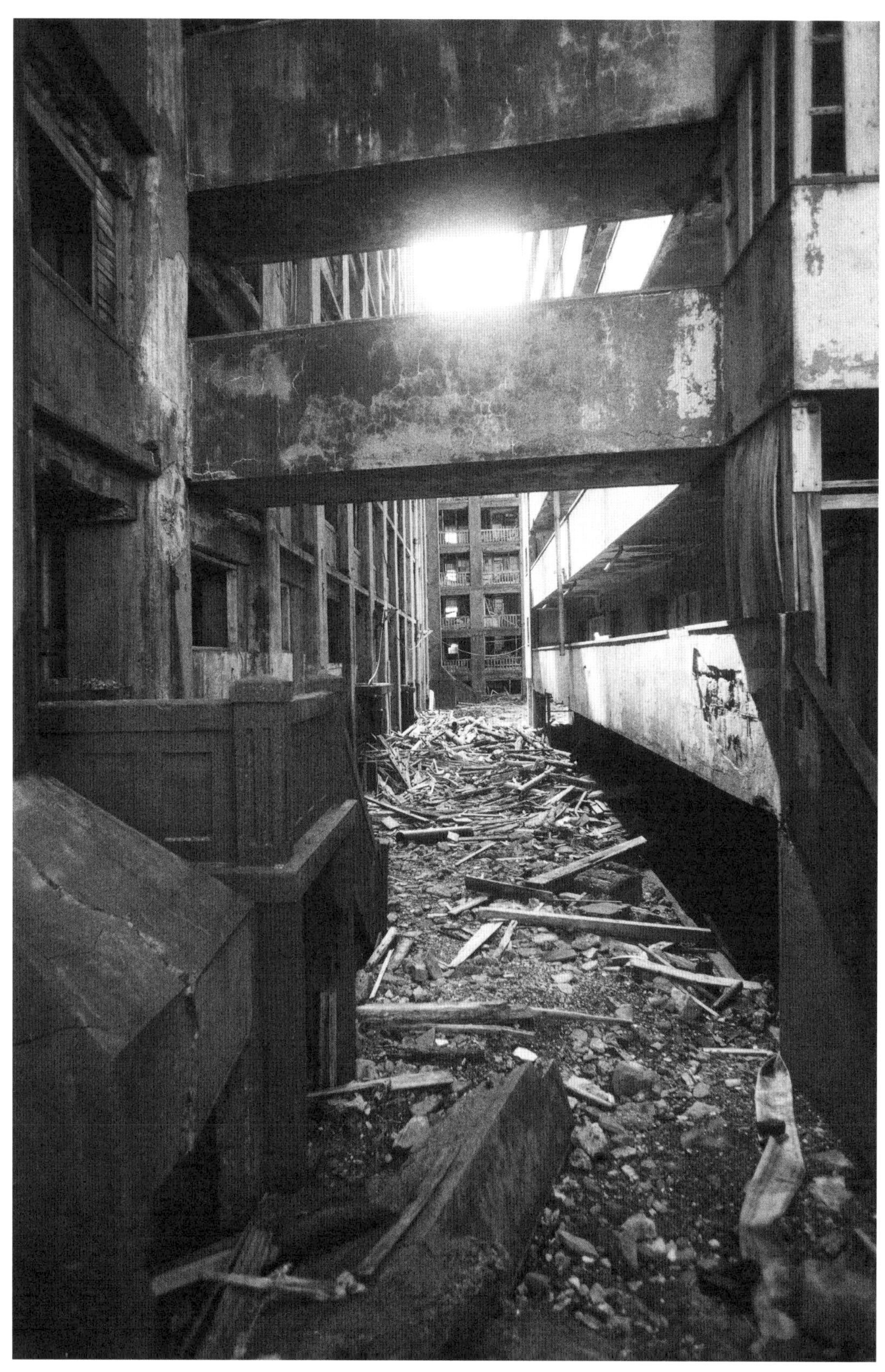

Hashima, 2009

端島 2009年

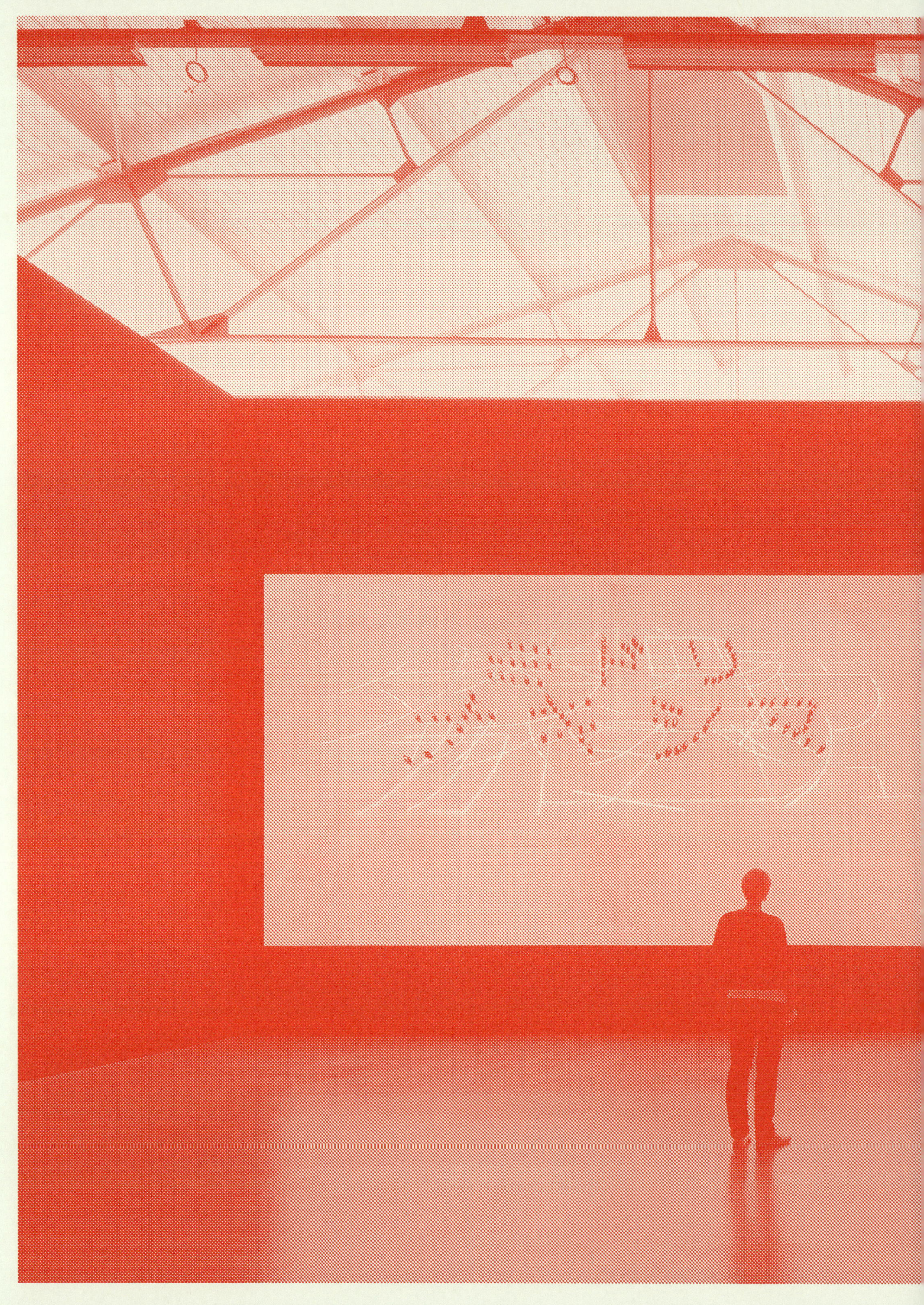

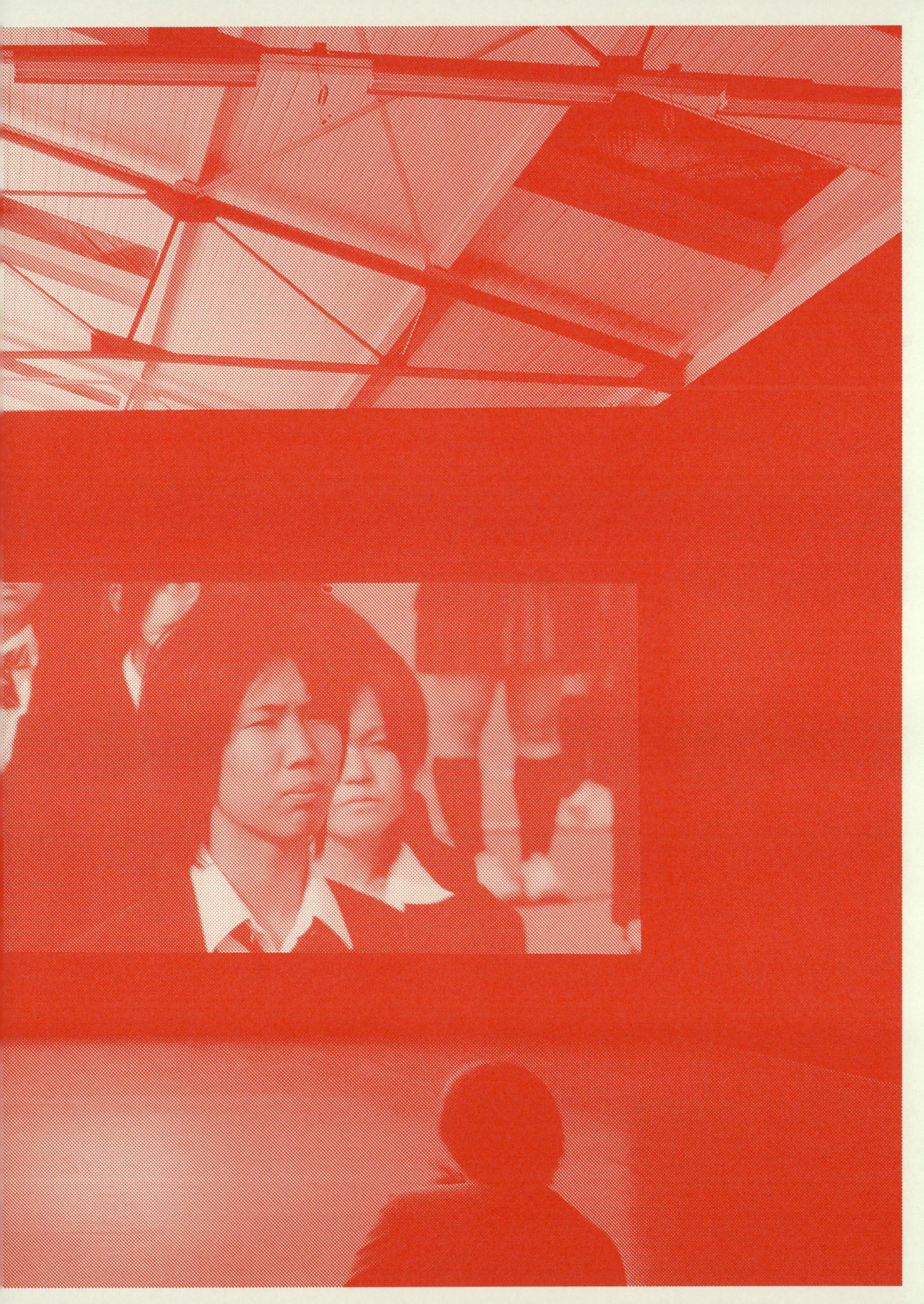

This book is part of the art-project: *Spelling Dystopia*, which consist of several parts: a 2-channel video installation *Spelling Dystopia*, a short film *Sayonara Hashima*, as well as series of photographs.

"Spelling Dystopia/Sayonara Hashima" HD, 16mm, colour, stereo, 17:25 min., 2009

Written, Directed and Edited by
Nina Fischer, Maroan el Sani
Camera Operator on Sony HD 790 and Arriflex 16mm
Takayuki Hashimoto
Steadycam Operator
Hiroki Izumi
Additional Camera Operator Bolex 16mm
Maroan el Sani
Sound Operator
Seiji Fujiwara
Production Assistants
Kyoko Tachibana, Motohiro Sunouchi
Translation
Kyoko Tachibana, Alida Speler
Animation After Effects
Bertold Stallmach
Post-Production Assistant
Florian Baron
Editing Advisor
Kathrin Hembus
Compositing
Koji Futatsugi, Miyanomori Studio Zero, Sapporo
Image Mastering
Seiji Fujiwara, New Peak Film, Sapporo
Colour Grading
Petra Gescher, Koppfilm, Berlin
Finishing
Tobias Schaarschmidt, Koppfilm, Berlin
Sound Editing/Mastering
Nico Berthold, Berlin
Voice-Over
Fubuki Asahina, Honami Ono, Doutoku Sakamoto
Film Music
Robert Lippok
Production
Fischer/el Sani, Berlin/Sapporo

Special thanks to Mami Odai, Takashi Homma, S-Air, Sapporo; Takashi Yoshioka, Akitoshi Hachiro, Kazuaki Satoh, Hiragishi High School Sapporo; Mitsuhiro Takemura, Sapporo City University; Toshio Inoue, Sapporo Film Comission; Doutoku Sakamoto, NPO The Way to World Heritage Gunkanjima; Prof. Keinosuke Gotoh, Nagasaki University; Ruriko Sekine, Nagasaki Film & Media Comission; Our students and colleagues of the Sapporo City University; Movielng Works Sapporo; Atsuko Ohno, Euro Space, Tokyo; Fujifilm Tokyo; Ryusuke Ito, Matthew Leonard Webb, Emiko Kato; Okwui Enwezor, Luz Gyalui, 7th Gwangju Biennale, Korea; Judy Lybke, Ingrid Buschmann, Inke Arns, Thomas Krüger, Gabriele Horn, Galerie Eigen+Art Leipzig/ Berlin; KW Berlin; Marlis Micha, Hauptstadtkulturfonds Berlin; medienboard Berlin Brandenburg GmbH, Teresa Hoefert de Turegano

Supported by
Hauptstadtkulturfonds, medienboard Berlin-Brandenburg

© Fischer/el Sani, Berlin 2009

Colophon

Nina Fischer & Maroan el Sani
Spelling Dystopia
スペリング・ディストピア

Edited by Christoph Keller, Nina Fischer, and Maroan el Sani

Graphic Design
Mathis Pfäffli, Markus Dreßen
Text
Mami Kataoka, Chief Curator Mori Art Museum, Tokyo
Interviews
Fubuki Asahina, Honami Ono, Hiragishi High School Sapporo; Doutoku Sakamoto, NPO The Way to World Heritage Gunkanjima
Manga
Story: Nina Fischer & Maroan el Sani; Illustrations: Kasuga Tsubaki
Translation
Pamela Miki, Kyoko Tachibana
Proofreading
Clare Manchester, Kyoko Tachibana
Photography
Nina Fischer & Maroan el Sani, except p. 116 Uwe Walter
Image Editing
Carsten Humme
Printing
Messedruck Leipzig
Binding
Buchbinderei Mönch OHG, Leipzig
Font
BauLF, Kozuka Mincho Pro
Paper
Munken Lynx Rough, MaxiGloss

All works courtesy the artists and Galerie EIGEN+ART, Leipzig/Berlin Galleria Marie-Laure Fleisch, Rome

www.fischerelsani.net
www.eigen-art.com
www.galleriamlf.com

© for the reproduced works: VG Bild-Kunst Bonn, the artists

The editor has made every reasonable effort within his limited means to trace, clear, and acknowledge the copyrights of the pictures used in this book. It is nonetheless possible that some attributions or ownerships have been omitted or are incorrect, in which case credits will be added if required in any subsequent editions.

The realisation of this artist's book has been made possible by the financial support of Hauptstadtkulturfonds

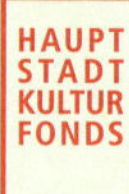

Produced in Germany

This publication is part of the artists' books series Christoph Keller Editions published by JRP|Ringier Kunstverlag AG, Zurich

© 2012 Nina Fischer & Maroan el Sani, Christoph Keller Editions and JRP|Ringier Kunstverlag AG, Zurich

All rights reserved. No part of this publication may be reproduced in any manner whatsoever without permission in writing by the publisher.

ISBN 978-3-03764-275-7

Christoph Keller Editions
Published in a limited print run, this series of artists' books and conceptual art publications, edited and selected by Christoph Keller, aims to explore the bandwidth of artistic book-making and the mediation of contemporary art in the printed format of the book.

Other titles in this series
Emmanuelle Antille, Helen Mirra Jonathan Meese & Slavoj Žižek, Peter Piller, Mungo Thomson, Stuart Bailey & Ryan Gander, Matias Faldbakken, Johannes Wohnseifer, Mai-Thu Perret, Julien Berthier, Michael Stevenson, Jonathan Monk, Zilla Leutenegger, Aglaia Konrad, Jeanne Faust, Loris Gréaud, Claudia & Julia Müller, Boris Groys & Andro Wekua, Korpys/Löffler, Anna Lea Hucht, Yann Sérandour, Falke Pisano, Heidi Specker & Theo Deutinger, Philip Lachenmann, Hinrich Sachs, Stefan Marx, Rita McBride, Mischa Kuball/Harald Welzer, Gitte Villesen, Jakob Kolding, Slavs and Tatars

Published by:
JRP|Ringier
Letzigraben 134, CH-8047 Zurich
+41 (0) 43 311 27 50
+41 (0) 43 311 27 51
info@jrp-ringier.com
www.jrp-ringier.com

JRP|Ringier books are available internationally at selected bookstores and the following distribution partners:

Switzerland: AVA Verlagsauslieferung AG, www.ava.ch
France: Les presses du réel, www.lespressesdureel.com
Germany and Austria: Vice Versa Vertrieb, www.vice-versa-vertrieb.de
UK and other European countries: Cornerhouse Publications, www.cornerhouse.org/books
USA, Canada, Asia, and Australia: Art Book/D.A.P., www.artbook.com

For a list of our partner bookshops or for any general questions, please contact JRP|Ringier directly at info@jrp-ringier.com, or visit our homepage www.jrp-ringier.com for further information about our program.

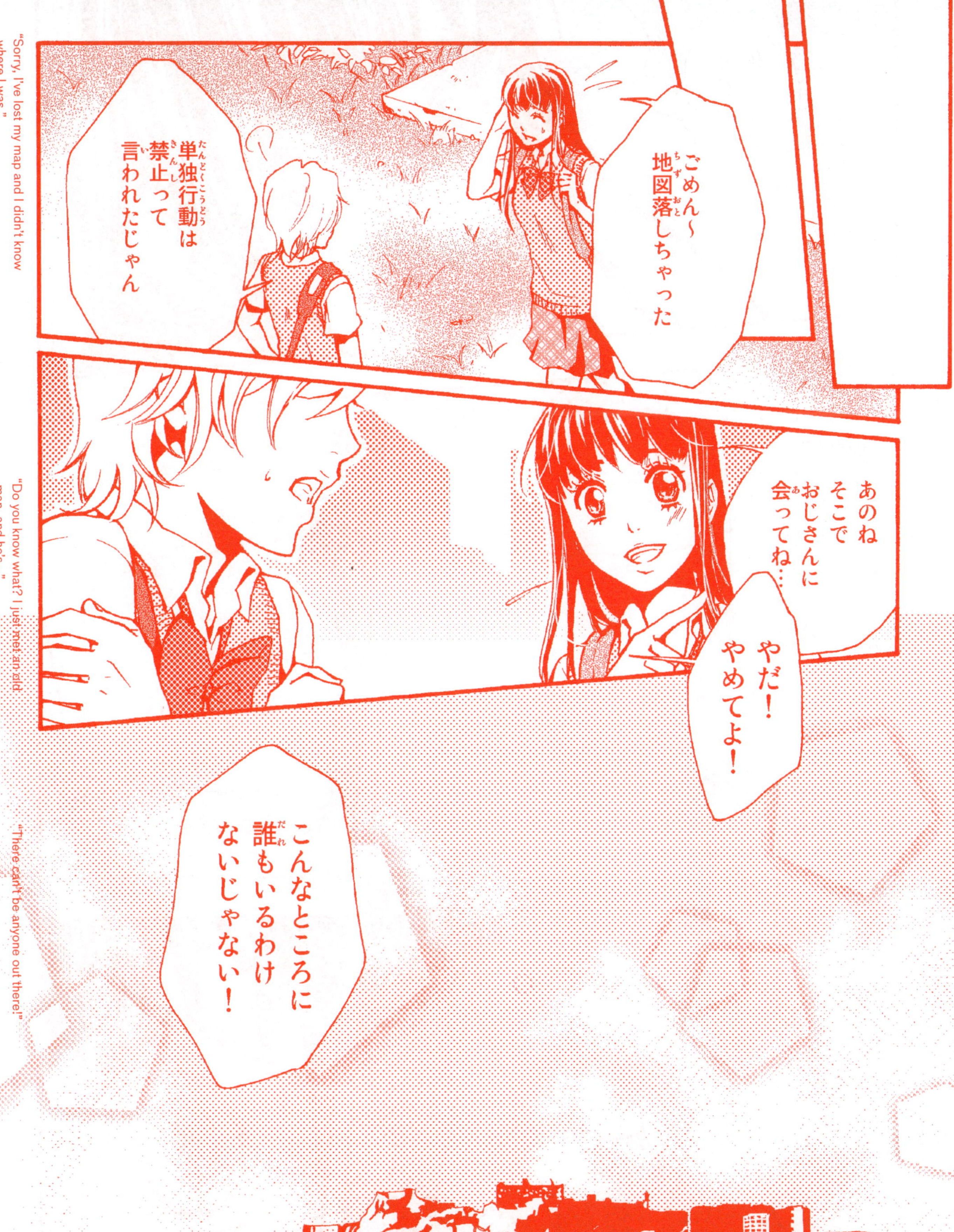

"Sorry, I've lost my map and I didn't know where I was."

"They told us we shouldn't go on our own, didn't they?"

"Do you know what? I just met an old man, and he's..."

"Stop scaring me!"

"There can't be anyone out there!"

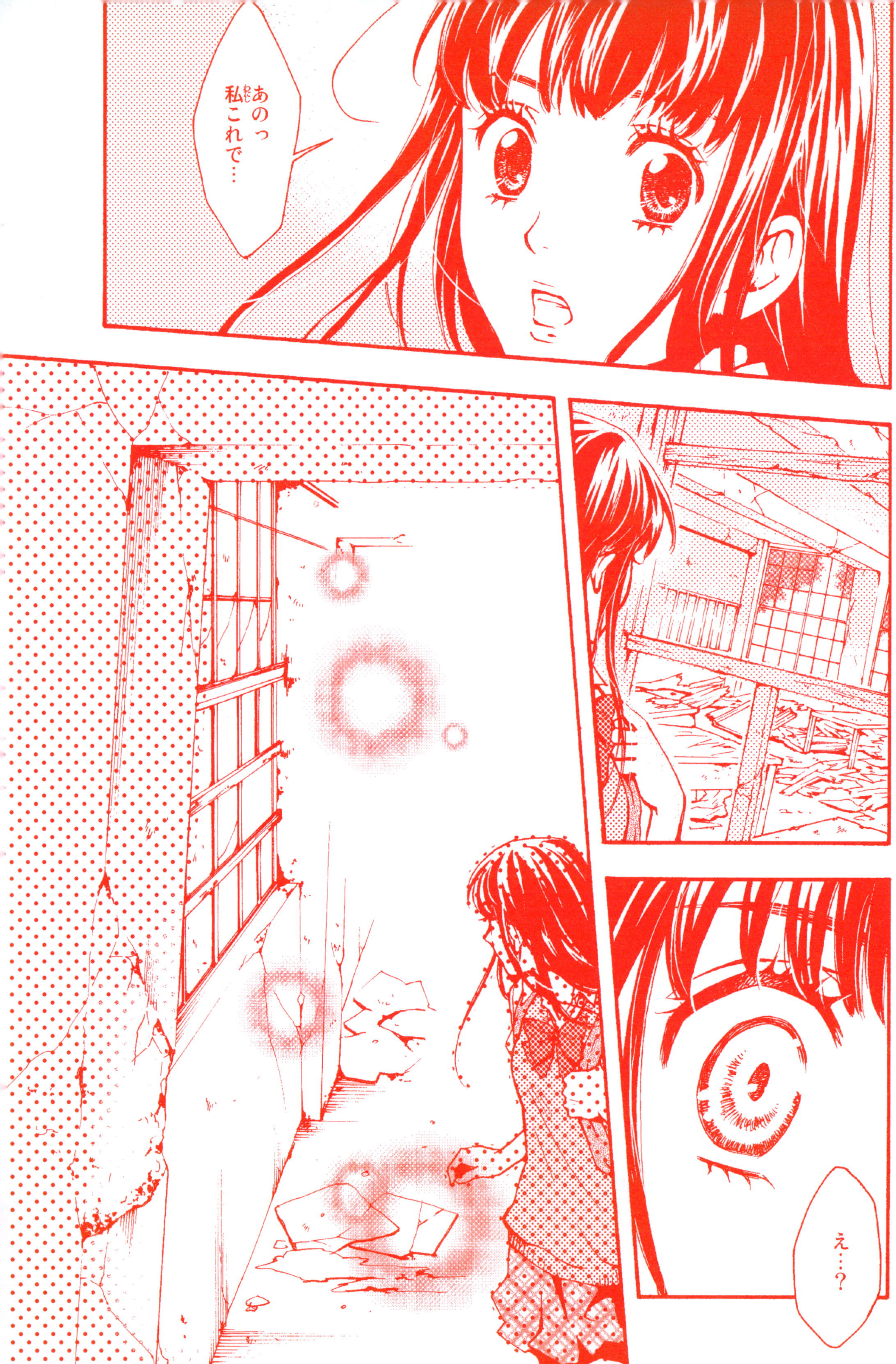

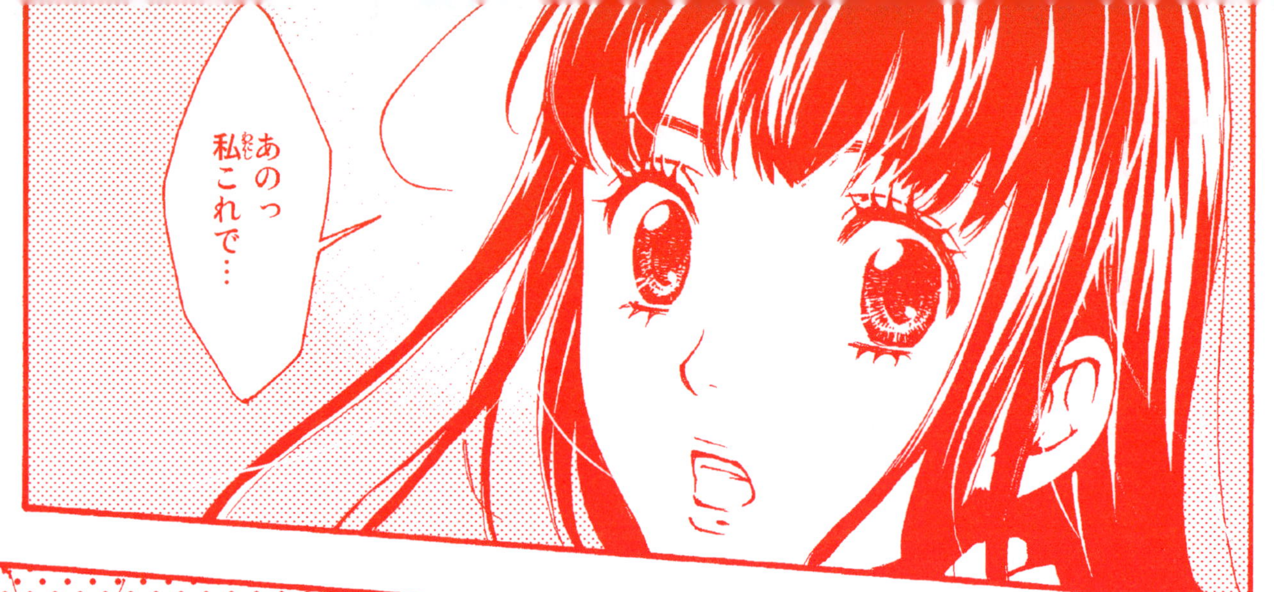

"Excuse me, I..."

え…？

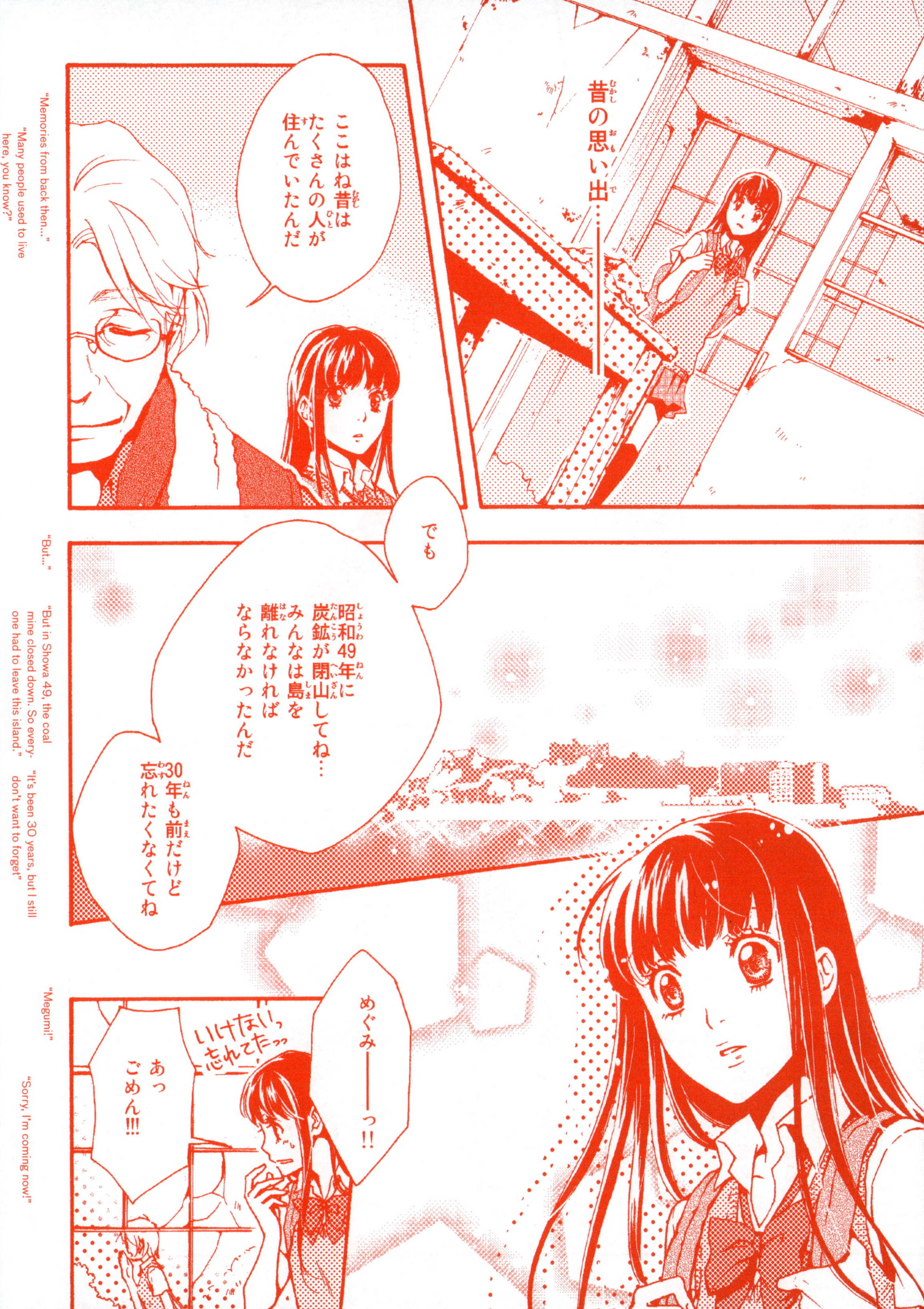

昔の思い出…──
ここはね昔はたくさんの人が住んでいたんだ
でも
昭和49年に炭鉱が閉山してね…みんなは島を離れなければならなかったんだ
30年も前だけど忘れたくなくてね
めぐみ──っ!!
いけないっ忘れてたっ
あっごめん!!!
"Memories from back then..."
"Many people used to live here, you know?"
"But..."
"But in Showa 49, the coal mine closed down. So every-one had to leave this island."
"It's been 30 years, but I still don't want to forget"
"Megumi!"
"Sorry, I'm coming now!"

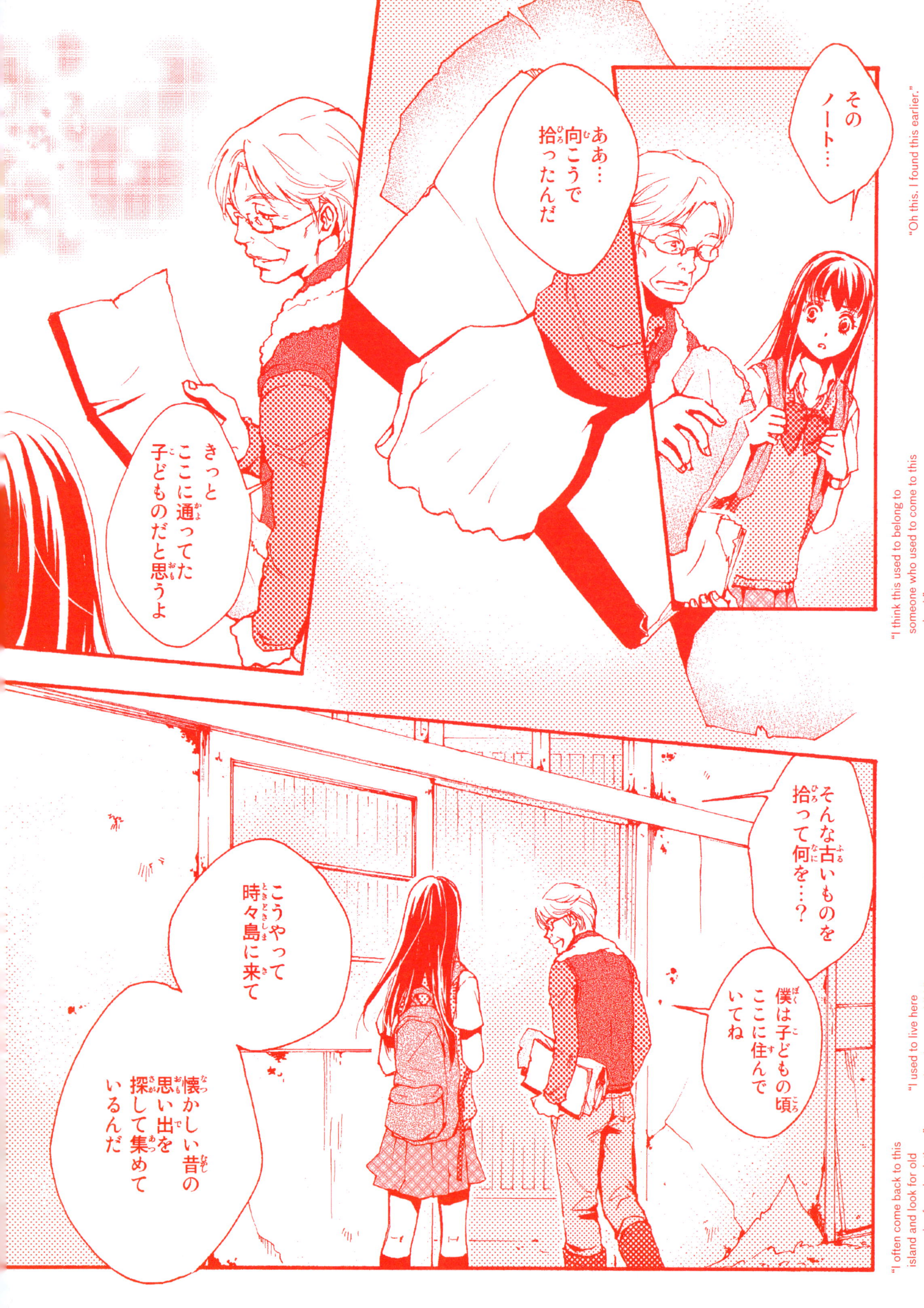
そのノート…
ああ…向こうで拾ったんだ
きっとここに通ってた子どものだと思うよ
そんな古いものを拾って何を…？
僕は子どもの頃ここに住んでいてね
こうやって時々島に来て
懐かしい昔の思い出を探して集めているんだ
"The notebook..."
"Oh this. I found this earlier."
"I think this used to belong to someone who used to come to this school."
"Why did you pick that up? It's old."
"I used to live here when I was a child."
"I often come back to this island and look for old memories from back then."

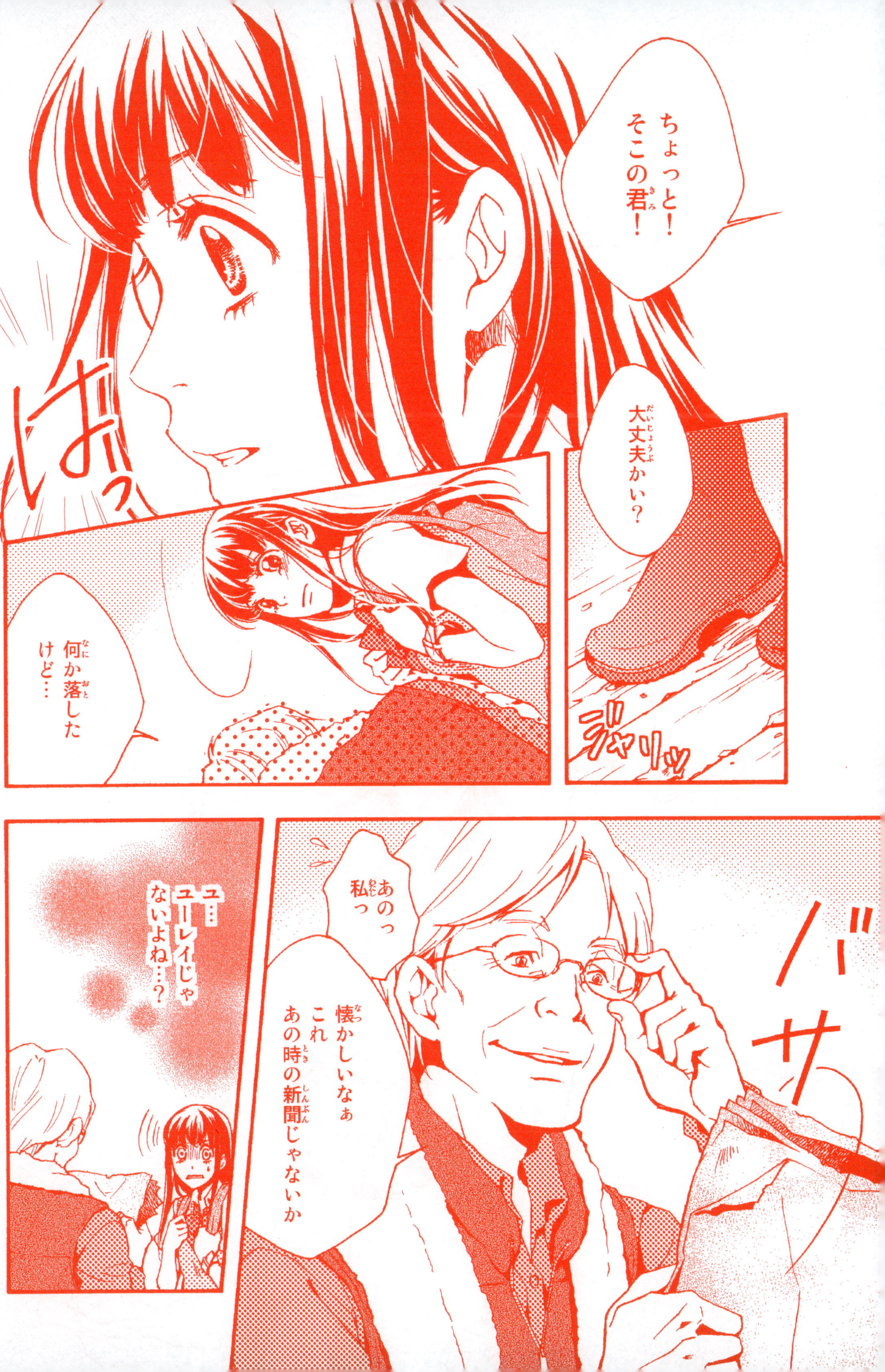

ちょっと！
そこの君！

はっ

大丈夫かい？

ジャリッ

何か落した
けど…

バサッ

あのっ
私っ

懐かしいなぁ
これ
あの時の新聞じゃないか

ユ…
ユーレイじゃ
ないよね…？

"Hi there!"

"Are you allright?"

"You dropped something..."

"That's..."

"He's not a ghost, is he?"

"Oh, I haven't seen this for a long time..."

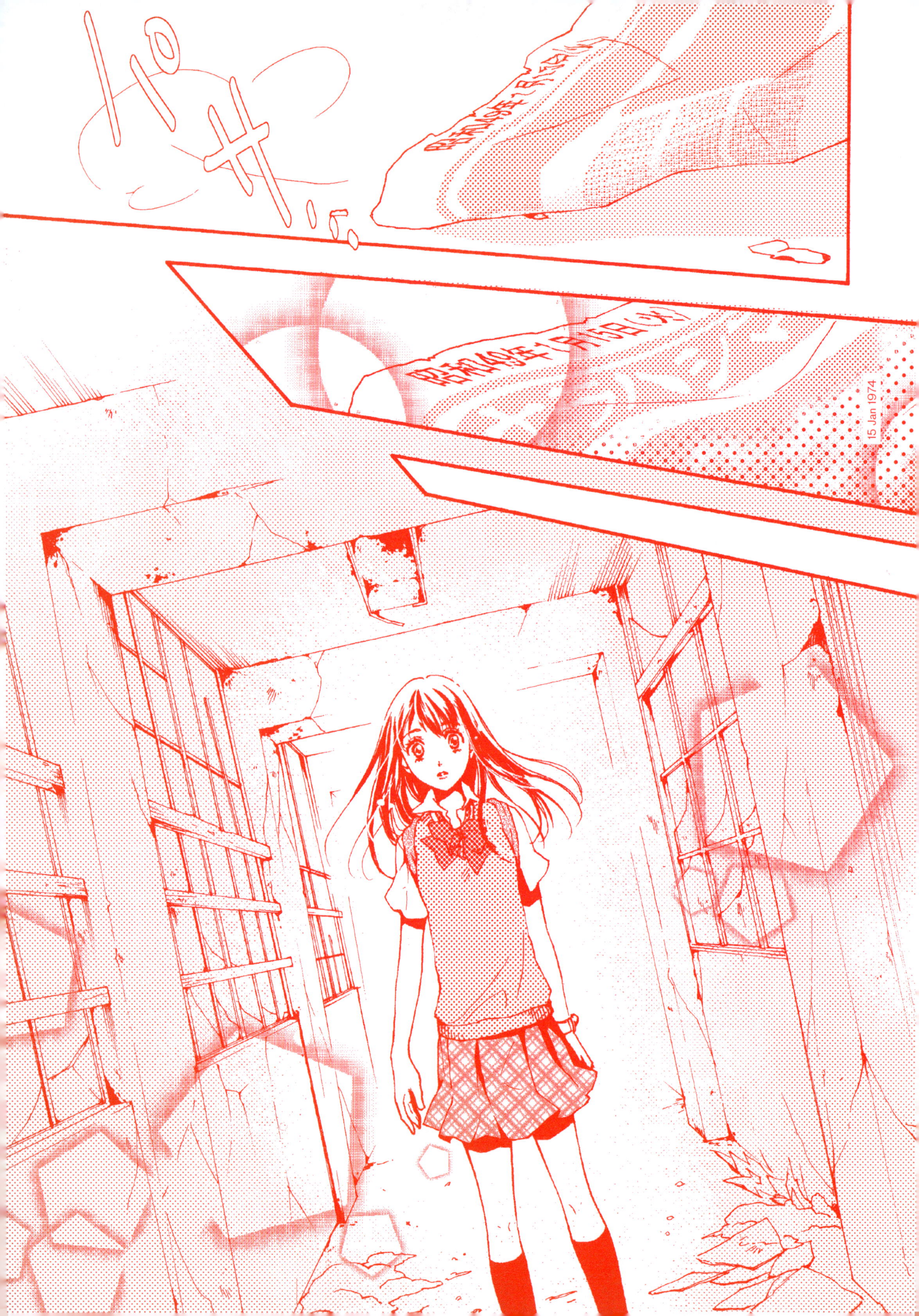
パサ…
15 Jan 1974

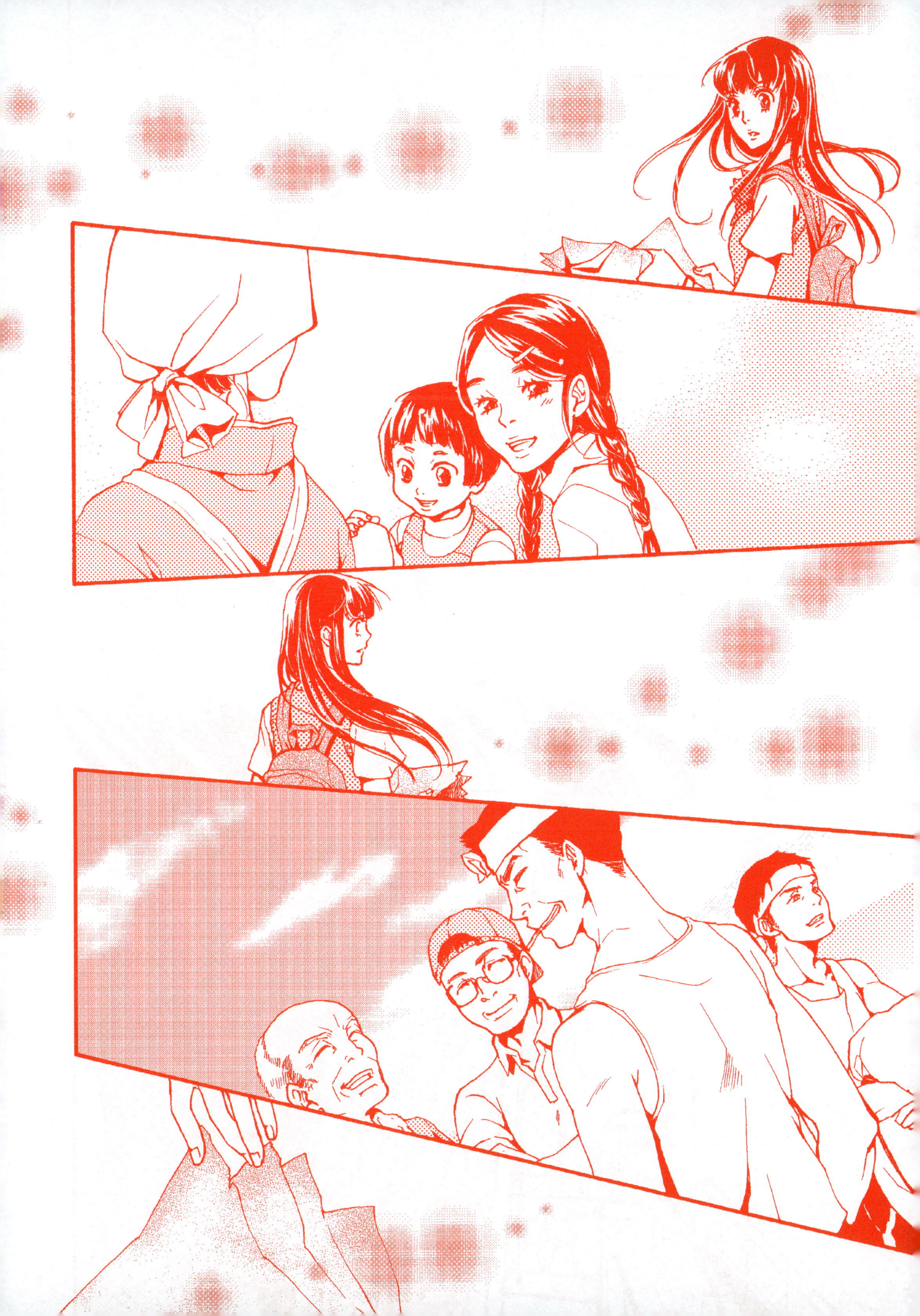

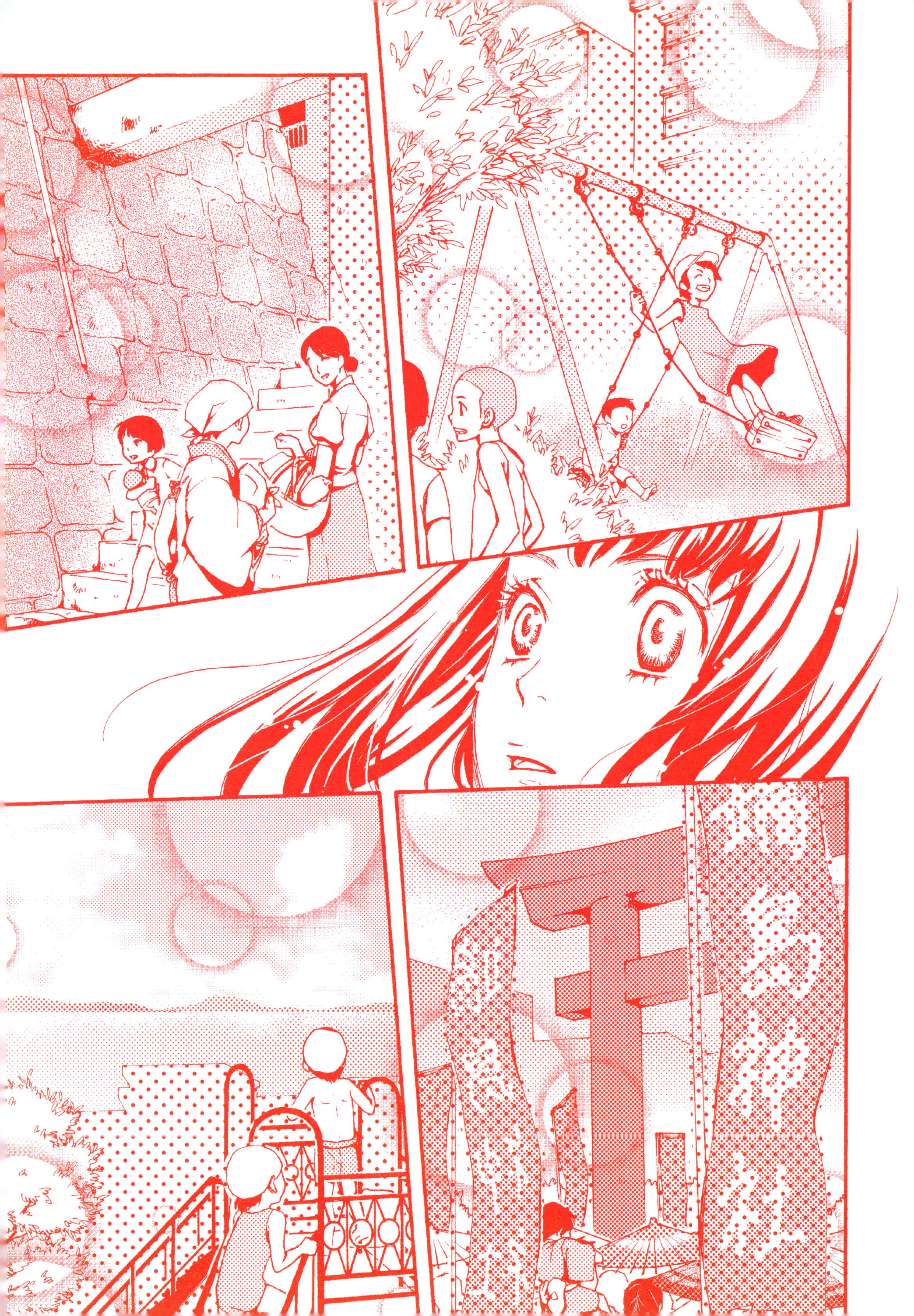

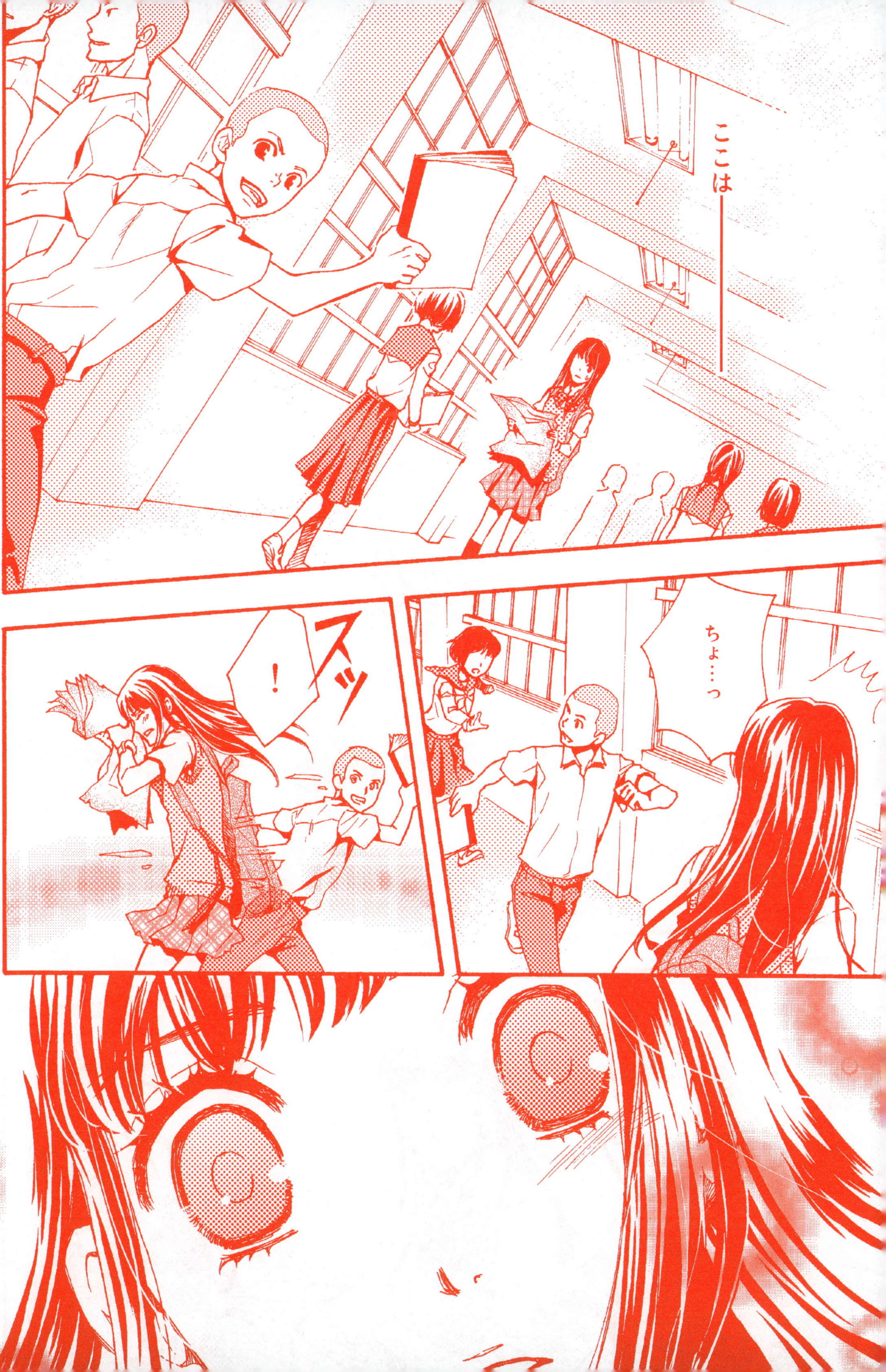

ここは——

ちょ…っ

!

スッ

"This is..."

"Hey!"

Swish!

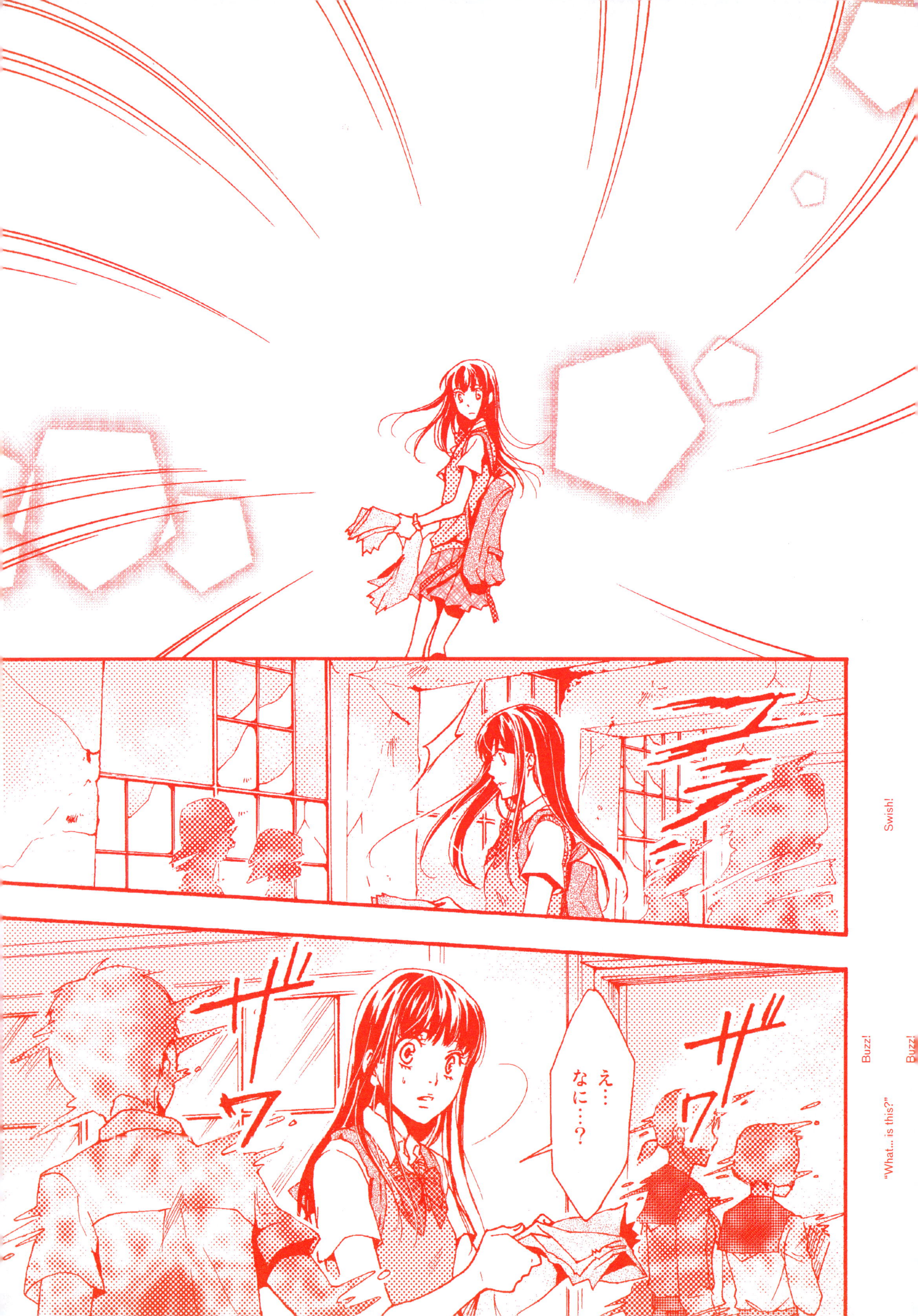

Swish!
ザワ
Buzz!
え…
なに…？
"What... is this?"
ザワ
Buzz!

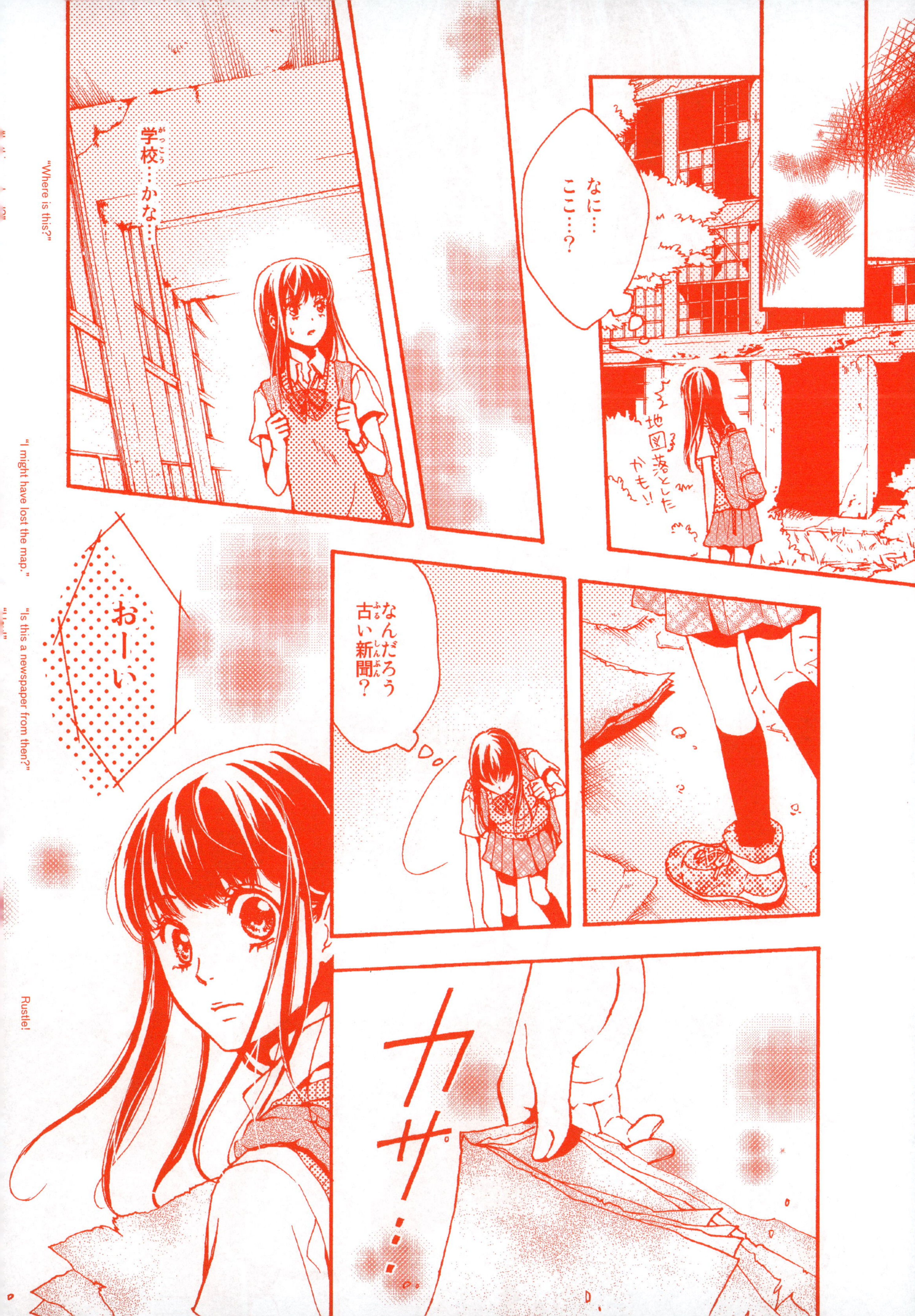

なに…ここ…？
地図落としたかも!!
学校…かな…
なんだろう古い新聞？
おーい
カサ…
"Where is this?"
"I might have lost the map."
"Is this a newspaper from then?"
Rustle!

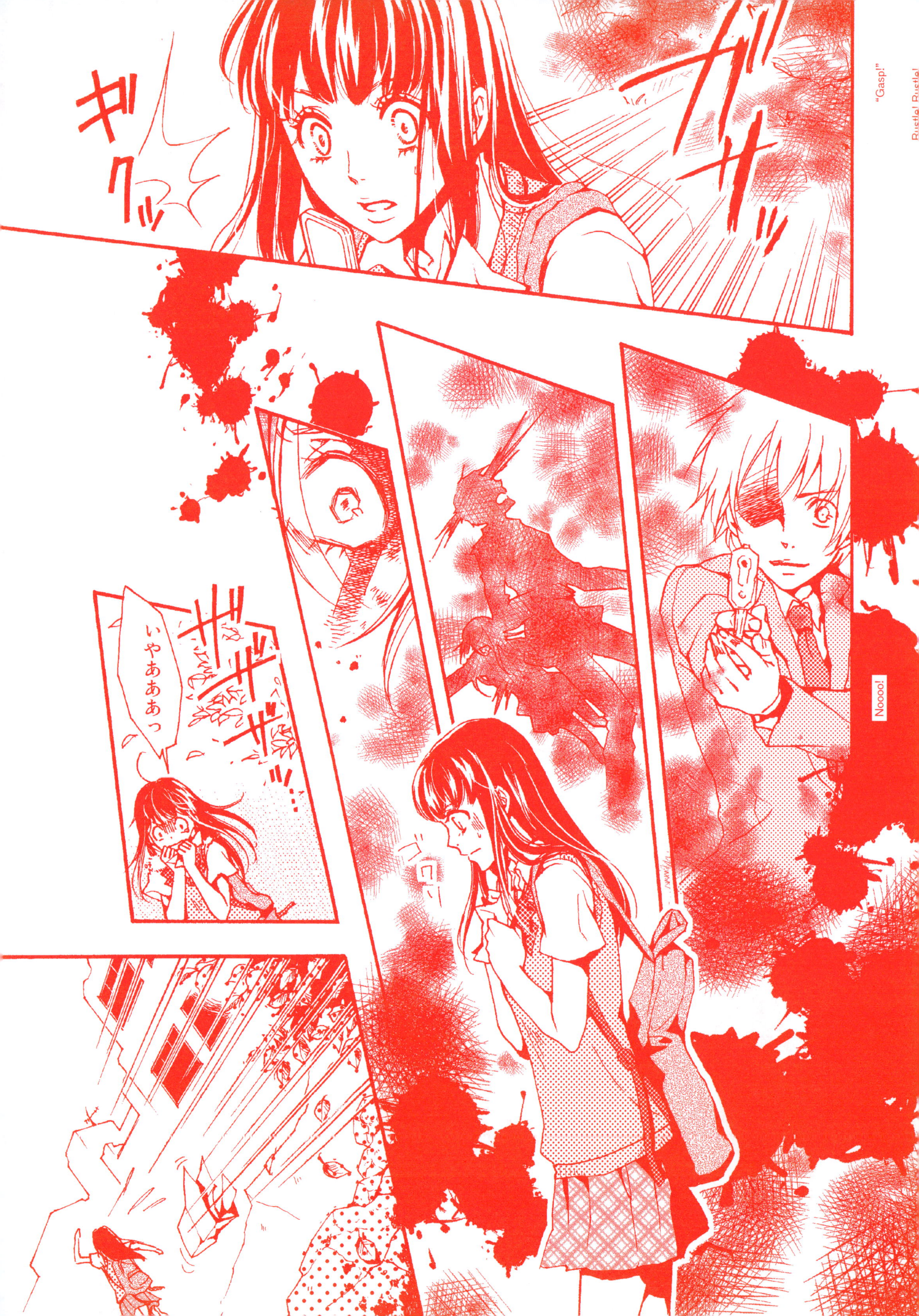
"Gasp!"
Rustle! Rustle!
ギクッ
ガサッ
Noooo!
いやあああっ
ゴクッ

きゃあああああっっ！

ばっ
わっ
わっ

み…
見間違い!?

きっと映画の観すぎだよね…

"Aa Aaaaah!"
"Oh!"
"Oh!"
"Maybe I watch too many movies"
"It was just my imagination then..."

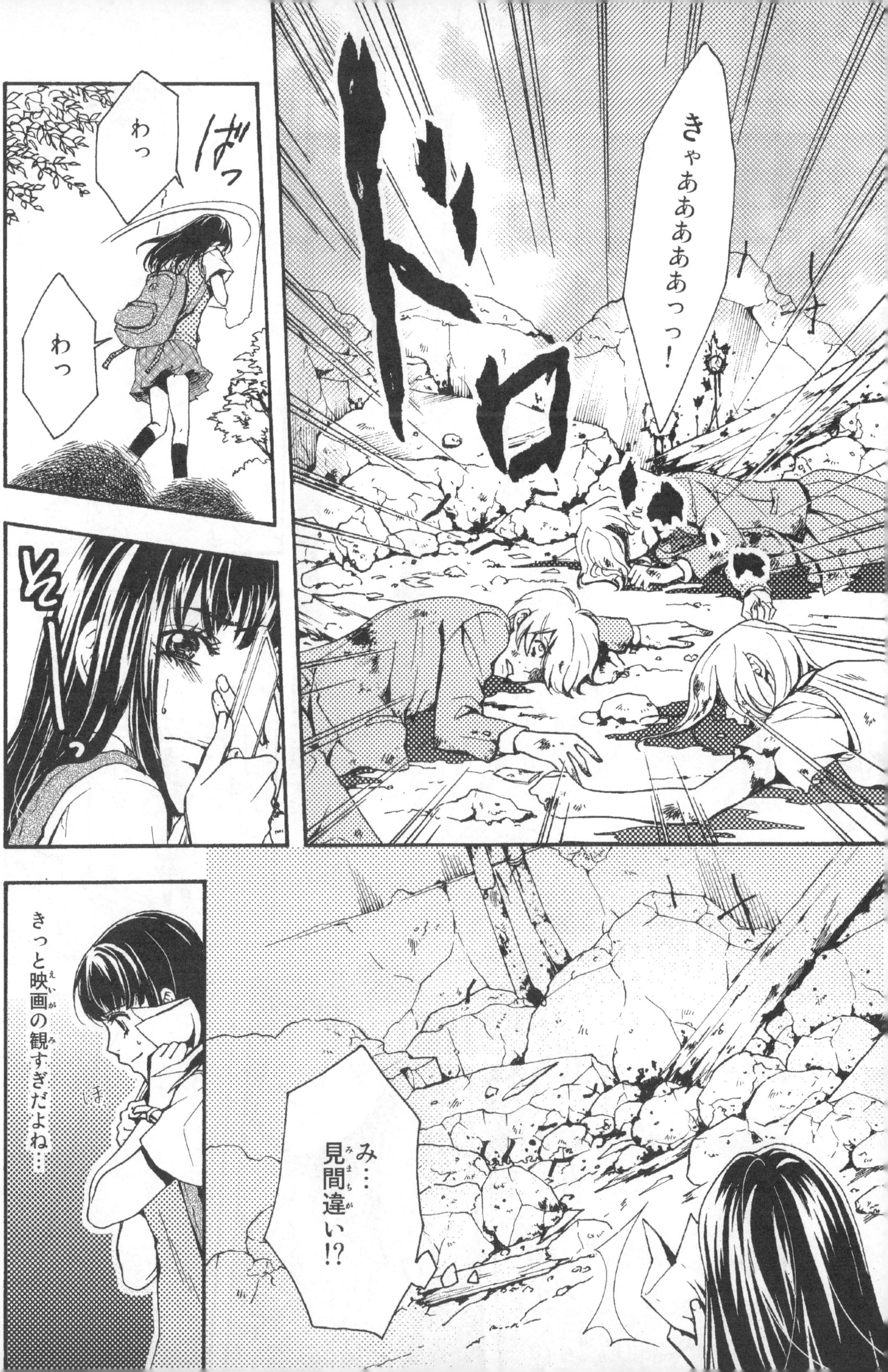

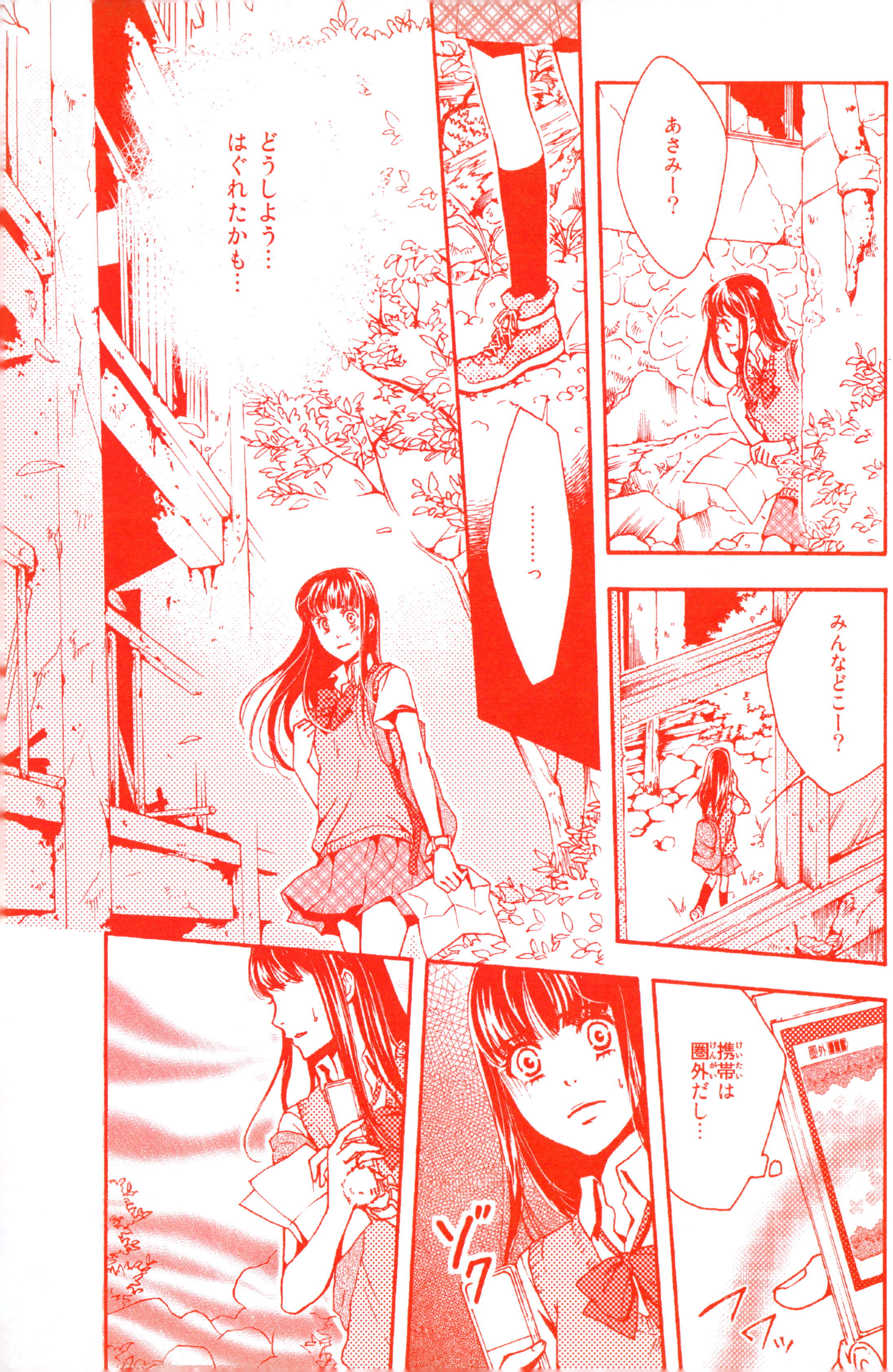

あさみー？

……っ

どうしよう…
はぐれたかも…

みんなどこー？

携帯は圏外だし…

圏外

ゾク

"Asami?"

"What should I do?
I lost everyone...?"

"Where is erveryone?"

"It's out of reception."

Shiver

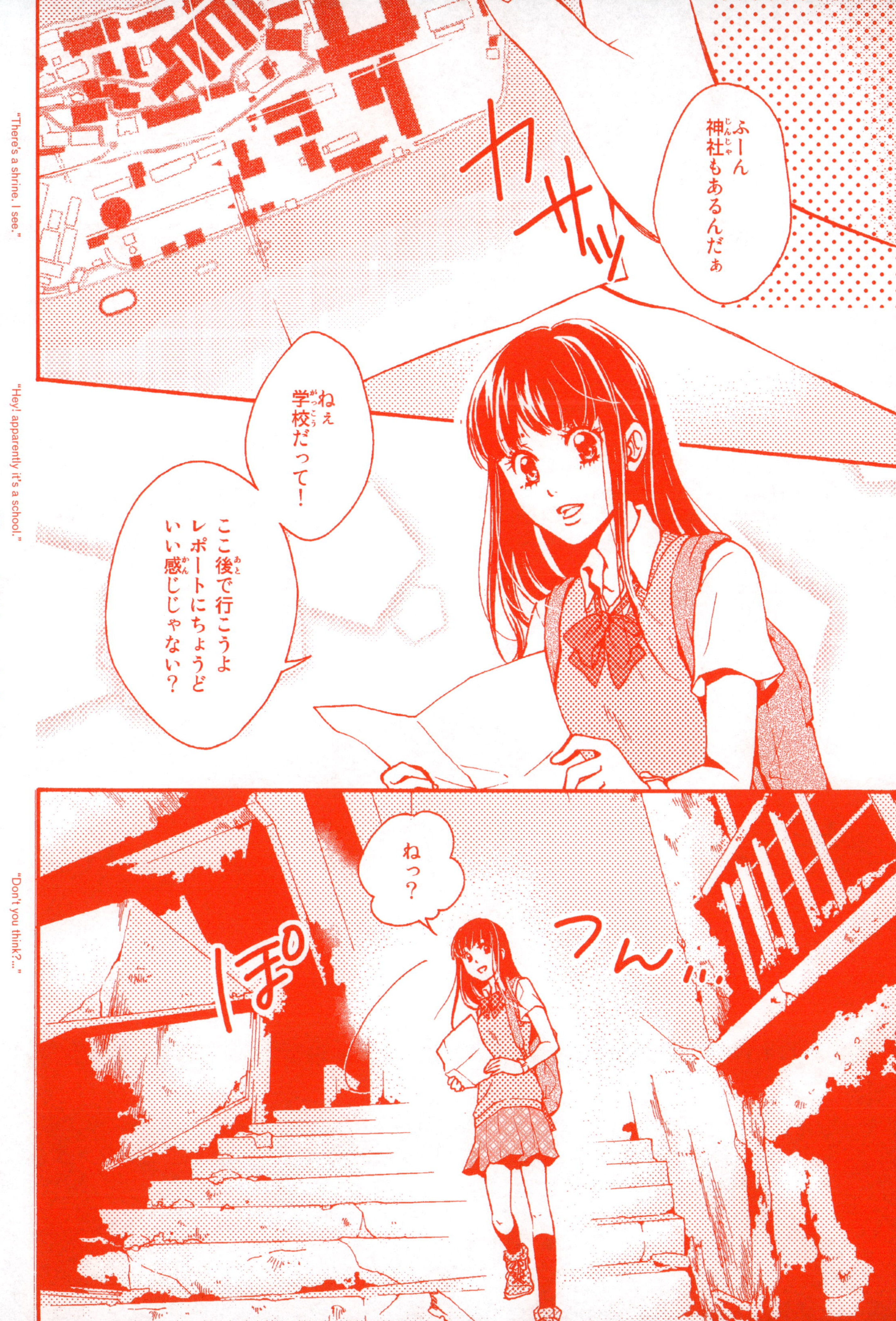

"There's a shrine. I see."

Rustle!

"Hey! apparently it's a school."

"We can go there later on, can't we?
It sounds like a good subject to write a report on."

"Don't you think?..."

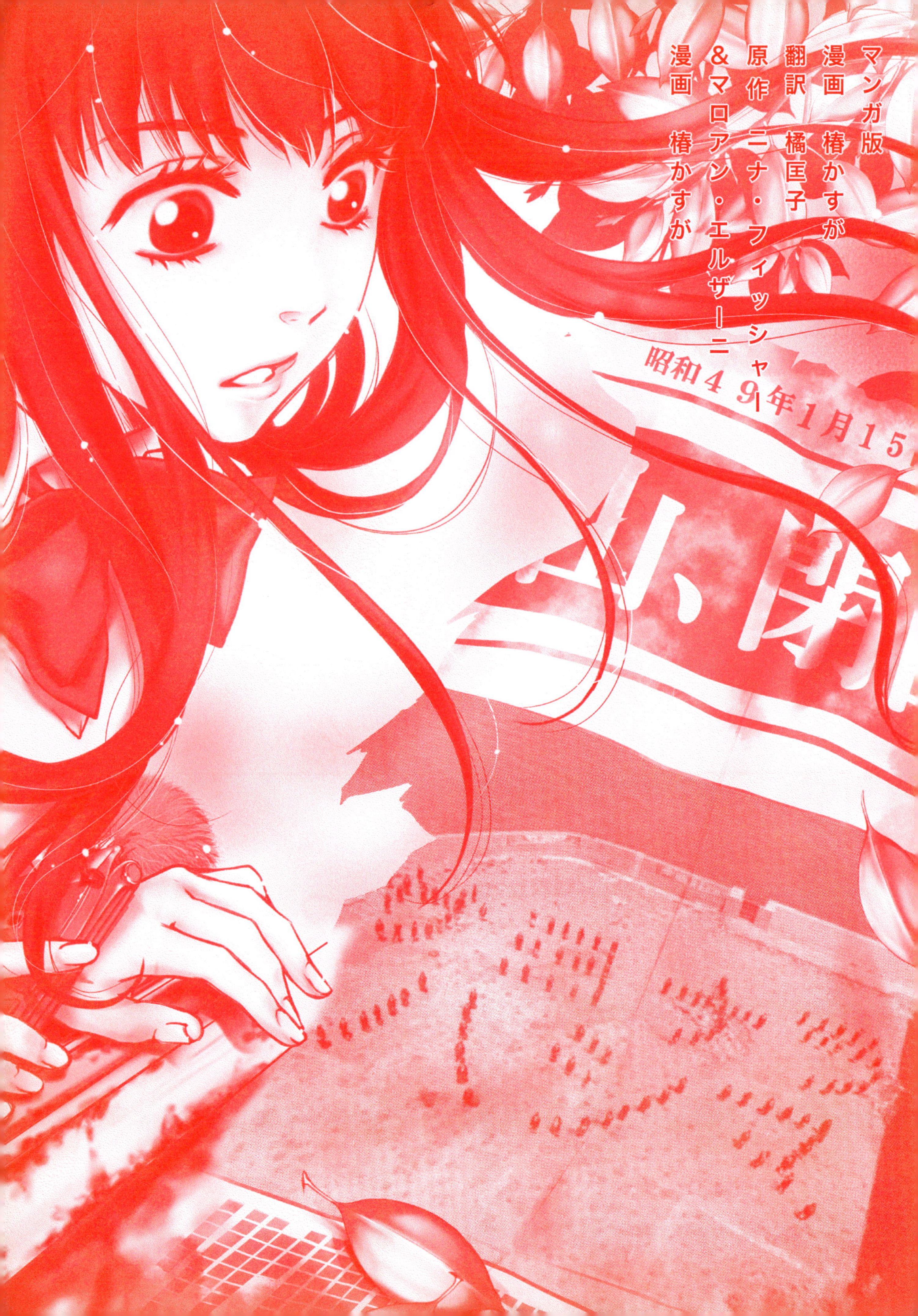
マンガ版
漫画 椿かすが
翻訳 橘国子
原作 ニナ・フィッシャー
&マロアン・エルザーニ
漫画 椿かすが
昭和49年1月15